# The *Best* of COUNTRY COOKING
## 1999

**Editor:** Jean Steiner
**Art Director:** Claudia Wardius
**Food Editor:** Coleen Martin
**Assistant Editor:** Julie Schnittka
**Food Photography Artist:** Stephanie Marchese
**Photography:** Scott Anderson, Glenn Thiesenhusen
**Photo Studio Manager:** Anne Schimmel
**Publisher:** Roy Reiman

©1999 Reiman Publications, LLC
5400 S. 60th St., Greendale WI 53129
International Standard Book Number: 0-89821-256-1
International Standard Serial Number: 1097-8321
All rights reserved.
Printed in U.S.A.

For additional copies of this book or information on other books, write:
*Taste of Home* Books, P.O. Box 990, Greendale WI 53129.
**Credit card orders call toll-free: 1-800/558-1013.**

**PICTURED ON COVER**. Clockwise from the top: Whole Wheat Biscuits (p. 92), Frosty Lemon Pie (p. 121), Barbecued Spareribs (p. 19) and Pimiento Potato Salad (p. 69).

**PICTURED ABOVE**. Clockwise from the top: Angel Food Dream, Fried Garlic Toast, Zesty Steak Salad and Summertime Green Beans (all recipes on p. 137).

# A Year's Worth of Down-Home Country Cooking...and More!

WELCOME to another mouth-watering array of the most-satisfying home-style recipes you will find anywhere—*The Best of Country Cooking 1999*.

This giant collection's 385 down-home recipes—one for every day of the year and then some—include the very best ones from recent issues of *Country Woman*, *Country*, *Country EXTRA*, *Reminisce* and *Reminisce EXTRA* magazines plus other proven favorites. All are hearty, wholesome and family-pleasing—guaranteed.

You see, these recipes weren't "developed" in some high-tech industrial "kitchen". Instead, they're from the personal recipe files of hundreds of home cooks across North America. Each has been sampled and approved by the toughest critic around—a hungry family just like yours!

But that's not all. Before being selected, *every* recipe in this book was thoroughly tested—many of them twice—by us as well. So you can be doubly confident it's a "keeper" that doesn't require a tryout first.

Go ahead *today* and take your pick of this beautiful book's 73 Main Dishes—Creamy Pork Tenderloin (a weekly dish on Janice Christofferson's Eagle River, Wisconsin table), Baked Almond Chicken (family-favorite fare from Diana Frankford of Sarasota, Florida) and 71 others.

There's also a Breakfast & Brunch chapter full of rise-and-shine recipes like Ham 'n' Cheese Strata from Marilyn Kroeker of Steinbach, Manitoba. And turn to Snacks & Beverages for lip-smacking treats such as Jalapeno Pepper Appetizers shared by Peggy Roberts of Lockney, Texas.

Apple Snack Squares—in the Cakes & Cookies chapter—has always been a real crowd-pleaser at Julia Quintrell's family gatherings in Sumerco, West Virginia. And a fresh batch of Jumbo Chocolate Chip Cookies can usually be found in Lori Sporer's Oakley, Kansas cookie jar.

As you page through *The Best of Country Cooking 1999*, watch for the special symbol at right. It signifies a "best of the best" recipe—a winner of a coast-to-coast cooking contest one of our magazines sponsored.

That's just a *small* sample of what's inside this tried-and-true taste treasury that in addition contains a mouth-watering medley of hearty salads, show-stealing side dishes and oven-fresh breads besides.

You'll enjoy some extra-special features, too, most other cookbooks overlook:

**Thirty-Minute Meals**—Six complete meals (19 recipes in all) that go from start to finish in *half an hour or less!*

**Memorable Meals**—Seven complete meals featuring family favorites from home cooks.

**Cooking for Two**—A separate chapter with 45 recipes all properly proportioned to serve two people.

Want more? *The Best of Country Cooking 1999* offers individual sections on cooking quick-and-easy fare that you can whip up for your hungry family with little effort.

Finally, throughout this colorful compendium are lots of ingenious kitchen tips from everyday cooks plus dozens of "restricted diet" recipes marked with this check ✓ that use less fat, sugar or salt.

See why we call this book "The Best"? Now, wait 'til you and your family *taste* why!

# CONTENTS

**IT'S EASY** *to satisfy any craving with this chapter's appealing assortment of hearty appetizers, refreshing beverages and lip-smacking snacks.*

**SNACK ATTACK.** Clockwise from top left: Strawberry Nectar (p. 7), Crunchy Vegetable Dip (p. 8), Cold Vegetable Pizza (p. 7) and Jalapeno Pepper Appetizers (p. 7).

# Snacks & Beverages

## JALAPENO PEPPER APPETIZERS

*Peggy Roberts, Lockney, Texas*

**(Pictured at left)**

*These appetizers are so easy to make and they taste so good. I have to warn you that eating them can be habit-forming!*

- 10 medium fresh jalapeno peppers
- 4 ounces cream cheese, softened
- 10 bacon strips, halved

Cut peppers in half lengthwise; remove seeds and center membrane. Stuff each half with about 2 teaspoons of cream cheese. Wrap with bacon and secure with a toothpick. Place on a broiler rack that has been coated with nonstick cooking spray. Bake at 350° for 20-25 minutes or until bacon is crisp. Remove toothpicks. Serve immediately. **Yield:** 20 appetizers.

## COLD VEGETABLE PIZZA

*Marlene Reichart, Leesport, Pennsylvania*

**(Pictured at left)**

*This is one of my favorite vegetable recipes. Even youngsters love it. I've made it for a light lunch and served it as an hors d'oeuvre at a get-together.*

- 2 tubes (8 ounces *each*) refrigerated crescent rolls
- 1 cup mayonnaise
- 1 package (8 ounces) cream cheese, softened
- 1 tablespoon dill weed
- 2-1/2 cups mixed chopped fresh vegetables (green pepper, radishes, broccoli, onion, carrots, celery, cucumber, mushrooms)
- 1/2 cup sliced ripe olives
- 3/4 cup shredded cheddar cheese
- 3/4 cup shredded mozzarella cheese

Unroll the crescent rolls and place in an ungreased 15-in. x 10-in. x 1-in. baking pan. Flatten dough to fit the pan, sealing seams and perforations. Bake at 375° for 12-14 minutes or until golden brown. Cool. In a small mixing bowl, beat the mayonnaise, cream cheese and dill until smooth; spread over crust. Top with the vegetables of your choice. Sprinkle with olives and cheeses; press lightly. Cover and chill for at least 1 hour. Cut into squares. **Yield:** 12-15 servings.

## STRAWBERRY NECTAR

*Rose Ann Goodman, Richville, Minnesota*

**(Pictured at left)**

*I developed this delectably different beverage after over-picking strawberries one year. I had so many that I decided to do more than make plain jam.*

- 4 quarts fresh strawberries
- 5 to 6 medium pink grapefruit
- 1 quart water
- 1-1/2 cups sugar

In a blender or food processor, puree strawberries. Squeeze grapefruit to make 1 qt. juice; strain. In a large kettle, combine pureed strawberries, grapefruit juice, water and sugar. Cook, uncovered, over medium heat until temperature reaches 190°. Remove from the heat; skim off foam. Strain. Ladle hot liquid into hot jars, leaving 1/4-in. headspace. Cover with lids. Process for 15 minutes in a boiling-water bath. Serve chilled and undiluted. **Yield:** 4 quarts.

## NUTTY CHEESE CROCK

*Linda Skiles, Lyons, Wisconsin*

*I got this cracker spread from Carol Huebner, whose appetizing recipe appears in a family cookbook.*

- 1 cup (4 ounces) shredded cheddar cheese
- 3/4 cup butter *or* margarine, softened
- 3/4 cup grated Parmesan cheese
- 1/4 cup chopped salted peanuts
- 1/4 cup Dijon mustard
- 1 to 2 garlic cloves, minced

Assorted crackers

In a mixing bowl, combine all ingredients; beat on medium until blended. Serve on crackers. Store in the refrigerator. **Yield:** 1-3/4 cups.

## MULLED CRANBERRY CIDER

*Lois Fetting, Nelson, Wisconsin*

*Whipping up this tasty beverage for a gathering is simple. I served it at a group function, and everyone loved it! Its flavor is different from ordinary cider.*

> 1 quart apple juice
> 2 cups cranberry juice
> 1 cup orange juice
> 3/4 cup lemon juice
> 1/2 cup sugar
> 1 teaspoon whole allspice
> 1 teaspoon whole cloves
> 3 cinnamon sticks (2 inches)

Pour juices into a large saucepan; stir in sugar. Tie spices in a cheesecloth bag; add to juice mixture. (Or place loose spices in saucepan and strain before serving.) Cover and simmer for 1 hour; remove spice bag. **Yield:** 15 (1/2-cup) servings.

## SPICY CHICKEN WINGS

*Varina Caton, Appleton, New York*

**(Pictured below)**

*This area is known for its chicken wings, and these are the best I've ever tasted. They make great appetizers.*

> 16 to 18 chicken wings (about 4 pounds)
> Vegetable oil
> 1/2 cup butter *or* margarine, melted
> 1/2 cup hot pepper sauce
> 2 tablespoons cider vinegar
> Carrots and celery sticks
> Blue cheese dressing

Cut wings into three pieces; discard the wing tips. Fry chicken in hot oil until crisp and juices run clear (5-7 minutes for the small part, 6-8 minutes for drumettes). Combine butter, hot pepper sauce and vinegar in a bowl; add chicken and toss to coat. Drain. Serve with carrots, celery and dressing. **Yield:** about 3 dozen.

## ... DIP

*... ...nessee*

*...was a big hit ...tizer or for a*

*...eese,*

> 1/2 cup diced celery
> 1/2 cup diced cucumber
> 1/2 cup diced green pepper
> 1/3 cup diced green onions
> **Assorted crackers *or* bread**

In a mixing bowl, beat cream cheese, mayonnaise, lemon juice, salt and pepper until smooth. Stir in vegetables. Cover and refrigerate for 2-3 hours. Serve with crackers or use as a sandwich spread. **Yield:** about 2 cups.

## DIABETIC MILK SHAKE

*Evelyn Archer, Elkville, Illinois*

*My husband could drink this refreshing beverage every day and never get tired of it!*

☑ This tasty dish uses less fat, sugar or salt. Recipe includes Nutritional Analysis and Diabetic Exchanges.

> 3/4 cup sugar-free vanilla ice cream
> 3/4 cup skim milk
> 1 large ripe banana, quartered
> Artificial sweetener equivalent to 4 teaspoons sugar
> 1/8 teaspoon vanilla extract

Combine all ingredients in a blender container; cover and process on low until smooth. Serve immediately. **Yield:** 2 servings. **Nutritional Analysis:** One 1-cup serving equals 162 calories, 99 mg sodium, 9 mg cholesterol, 29 gm carbohydrate, 6 gm protein, 3 gm fat. **Diabetic Exchanges:** 1 starch, 1 fruit, 1 fat.

# Festive Appetizers Round Up Fans!

EVERY TIME Maryeileen Jahnke of South Milwaukee, Wisconsin serves these hearty, finger-lickin' appetizers at parties, people go absolutely *nuts* over them.

"Our oldest daughter found the basic recipe in a magazine," pens Maryeileen. "We adapted it to suit our tastes, then I added my own homemade barbecue sauce. The result was delicious!"

With so many birthday parties, showers and holiday get-togethers to host, you may be looking for a little different party starter to serve. If so, keep Maryeileen's Barbecued Nutballs in mind …and see if your circle of friends doesn't agree that these nutty creations are not to be missed.

### BARBECUED NUTBALLS

2 cups crushed butter-flavored crackers
1 cup (4 ounces) finely shredded cheddar cheese
1 cup ground pecans
1/2 cup finely chopped onion
2 tablespoons wheat germ
6 eggs
1 tablespoon Worcestershire sauce
1-1/2 teaspoons dark brown sugar
SAUCE:
1 cup ketchup
1/4 cup water
2 tablespoons dark brown sugar
2 tablespoons molasses
2 tablespoons Worcestershire sauce
1 tablespoon finely chopped onion
1 teaspoon salt
1/4 teaspoon pepper

In a large bowl, combine the crackers, cheddar cheese, pecans, onion and wheat germ. In another bowl, whisk the eggs, Worcestershire sauce and sugar; add to cracker mixture. Shape into 1-in. balls. Place in a greased 13-in. x 9-in. x 2-in. baking dish. Combine the sauce ingredients; pour over nutballs. Cover and bake at 350° for 1 hour (do not stir). Serve warm. **Yield:** about 5-1/2 dozen.

### HOT CRABMEAT SPREAD

*Sally Kerns, Virginia Beach, Virginia*

*I've enjoyed seafood all my life and my family does, too. I first made this delicious crab recipe for a party, and I've made it many times since. There are never any leftovers when I serve it.*

1 cup half-and-half cream
2 packages (3 ounces *each*) cream cheese, softened
1 small onion, chopped
1 tablespoon mayonnaise
2 teaspoons prepared horseradish
1/2 teaspoon lemon juice
1/2 teaspoon Worcestershire sauce
1/2 teaspoon minced fresh parsley
1/2 teaspoon garlic salt
1/2 teaspoon onion salt
1/4 teaspoon pepper
8 to 10 drops hot pepper sauce
2 cans (6 ounces *each*) crabmeat, drained and cartilage removed
Assorted crackers

In a saucepan, combine the first 12 ingredients. Cook and stir over low heat until the mixture is smooth. Add the crab and heat through. Serve with crackers. **Yield:** 2-1/2 cups.

### LEMON-LIME PUNCH

*Karen Engstrand, Alma, Wisconsin*

*This festive-looking green punch has starred at many holiday parties and other events. The recipe comes from a cookbook I won in a drawing when I was a child. The cover is lost now, and the pages are yellowing…but the recipes are as wonderful as ever.*

1 envelope (.13 ounce) unsweetened lemon-lime drink mix
1 quart pineapple juice, chilled
1 quart lime sherbet
2 quarts ginger ale, chilled

Pour drink mix into a punch bowl. Stir in pineapple juice. Spoon sherbet into bowl; add ginger ale and stir gently. Serve immediately. **Yield:** about 3-1/2 quarts.

1 can (14-3/4 ounces) pink salmon,
   drained, flaked and bones removed
2/3 cup mayonnaise
8 drops liquid smoke, optional
**Assorted crackers**

Place olives and onions in a blender or food processor; process for about 15 seconds. Add salmon, mayonnaise and liquid smoke if desired; process until dip reaches desired consistency. Chill. Serve with crackers. **Yield:** about 3 cups.

## CHEESE CUTOUT SANDWICHES

*Gloria Porter, Grandin, North Dakota*

*These sandwiches are a cut above the rest. They're simple to make and tasty, too!*

2 slices process American cheese
2 slices process Swiss cheese
1/4 cup butter or margarine, softened
4 slices white bread
4 slices fully cooked ham

Cut cheese slices with a 2-in. apple cookie cutter. Place American cheese apples into Swiss cheese cutouts and Swiss cheese apples into American cheese cutouts; set aside. Spread butter on both sides of bread; brown both sides in a large skillet. Remove. Heat ham in the same skillet; place on bread. Top with cheese slices. Serve immediately. **Yield:** 4 servings. **Editor's Note:** If cookie cutter is sticking to the cheese, dip the cutter in hot water first.

## MORNING ORANGE DRINK

*Joyce Mummau, Mt. Airy, Maryland*

**(Pictured above)**

*Although it requires only a few basic ingredients and little preparation, this drink always draws raves from overnight guests about its "wake-up" taste.*

1 can (6 ounces) frozen orange juice
   concentrate
1 cup cold water
1 cup milk
1/3 cup sugar
1 teaspoon vanilla extract
10 ice cubes

Combine the first five ingredients in a blender; process at high speed. Add ice cubes, a few at a time, blending until smooth. Serve immediately. **Yield:** 4-6 servings.

## PARTY SAUSAGES

*Jo Ann Renner, Xenia, Ohio*

*Don't want any leftovers the day after your party? Serve your guests these sausages! I have never had even one end up uneaten.*

2 pounds fully cooked smoked sausage
   links
1 bottle (8 ounces) Catalina salad dressing
1 bottle (8 ounces) Russian salad dressing
1/2 cup packed brown sugar
1/2 cup pineapple juice

Cut sausages diagonally into 1/2-in. slices; cook in a skillet over medium heat until lightly browned. Transfer sausages to a slow cooker; discard drippings. Add dressings, sugar and juice to skillet; cook and stir over medium-low heat until sugar is dissolved. Pour over sausages. Heat on low for 1-2 hours or until heated through. **Yield:** 16 servings. **Editor's Note:** French salad dressing may be substituted for one or both dressings.

## SMOKED SALMON DIP

*Doreen McDaniels, Seattle, Washington*

*Salmon is practically a way of life here in the Pacific Northwest. My husband can make a meal of this dip. It's great for holiday parties.*

1 can (16 ounces) pitted ripe olives,
   drained
8 green onions, cut into 2-inch pieces

## POPCORN NUT CRUNCH

*Midge Stolte, Blackfalds, Alberta*

*I usually double this recipe so I can put some in tins or baskets for hostess gifts when we're invited out. As long as it's kept in a dry place, this crunchy treat will last up to 3 weeks if you seal it in a tin.*

  2 quarts popped popcorn
  1 cup blanched whole almonds, toasted
  1 cup *each* pecan halves, cashews, Brazil
      nuts and hazelnuts, toasted
1-1/2 cups sugar
  1 cup dark corn syrup
1/2 cup butter *or* margarine
  1 teaspoon vanilla extract
1/2 teaspoon ground cinnamon

Place the popcorn and nuts in a lightly greased 5-qt. Dutch oven. Bake at 250° for 20 minutes. Meanwhile, in a medium saucepan, combine the sugar, corn syrup and butter; bring to a boil over medium heat, stirring constantly. Cook, without stirring, until a candy thermometer reads 290° (soft-crack stage). Remove from the heat; stir in vanilla and cinnamon. Pour a small amount at a time over the popcorn mixture, stirring constantly until the mixture is well coated. Immediately spread on greased baking sheets. Cool; break into pieces. Store in airtight containers. **Yield:** about 4 quarts.

## SPINACH BALLS

*Faye Buffenmeyer, Lebanon, Pennsylvania*

*Either as an appetizer or side dish, this is delicious! And, since it can be made ahead, you might think about doubling the recipe and freezing some for unexpected guests.*

  1 package (10 ounces) frozen chopped
      spinach
2-1/2 cups herb-seasoned stuffing mix
  1 medium onion, finely chopped
  3 eggs, beaten
1/4 cup grated Parmesan cheese
  6 tablespoons butter *or* margarine, melted
1/2 teaspoon garlic salt
1/4 teaspoon pepper

Cook spinach according to package directions; drain well, squeezing out excess liquid. Combine spinach with remaining ingredients in a large bowl. Shape into 1-in. balls; place on an ungreased baking sheet. Bake at 350° for 10 minutes or until very lightly browned. **Yield:** about 4 dozen. **Editor's Note:** Balls can be made ahead and refrigerated overnight before baking.

## CHEDDAR-BACON DIP

*Carol Werkman, Neerlandia, Alberta*

**(Pictured below)**

*Both children and adults enjoy this dip. I like it, too—it's so quick and easy to prepare. I make it for special occasions like birthdays or holiday parties.*

  1 package (8 ounces) cream cheese,
      softened
  1 cup (8 ounces) sour cream
  5 green onions, thinly sliced
  4 medium tomatoes, chopped
  1 large green pepper, chopped
  1 jar (16 ounces) taco sauce
  2 cups (8 ounces) shredded cheddar
      cheese
  1 pound sliced bacon, cooked and
      crumbled
**Tortilla *or* taco chips**

In a mixing bowl, beat cream cheese and sour cream. Spread in an ungreased 13-in. x 9-in. x 2-in. dish or on a 12-in. plate. Combine onions, tomatoes and green pepper; sprinkle over the cream cheese layer. Pour taco sauce over the vegetables. Sprinkle with cheddar cheese. Refrigerate. Just before serving, sprinkle with bacon. Serve with tortilla or taco chips. **Yield:** 10-12 servings.

# Top Nut Tips

• For variety on our Christmas cookie plate, I cut nut bars into different shapes. Small rectangles and diamonds are a nice change from square bars.
—*Mary Snelling, Columbus, Ohio*

• I find that toasting nuts (any kind) before using them in a recipe intensifies their flavor. Spread the nuts on a baking sheet and toast at 350° for 10 minutes or 'til they're lightly browned.
—*Catherine Davison*
*Winnipeg, Manitoba*

• Keeping different kinds of nuts in the freezer allows me to quickly make a variety of treats for my family. Sometimes, I just remove the nuts and sprinkle them with salt for a snack.
—*Ruth Cook, Lake Point, Utah*

• An easy way to remove most of the papery skins from hazelnuts is to put warm toasted nuts in a clean kitchen towel, fold the towel over the nuts and rub vigorously.
—*Elaine Walter*
*Portland, Oregon*

• My family enjoys an easy candy during the holidays that has only two ingredients—1-1/2 pounds of melted white, dark or milk chocolate confectionery coating and 1 can of mixed nuts. Drop by teaspoonfuls onto waxed paper to harden, then store in an airtight container.
—*Glenda Bush*
*Alvin, Texas*

• I love the taste of black walnuts but rarely have any on hand. So I substitute English walnuts and add black walnut extract. I've discovered it provides nearly the same flavor.
—*Lucile Hall*
*Libby, Montana*

• Toasted almonds warm from the oven are much easier to chop than untoasted ones.
—*Cathy Medley*
*Pennville, Indiana*

• To keep chopped nuts from sinking to the bottom of cakes and quick breads, shake them in flour before adding to the batter.
—*Dorothy Vanis*
*Ulysses, Nebraska*

• For added nutty flavor in cakes, try sprinkling finely chopped pecans on greased and floured cake pans before pouring in the batter.
—*Cairol Ostrander*
*Marianna, Florida*

• To make quick work of coarsely chopping almonds, I use a blender.
—*Judy Ewen, San Diego, California*

• Nut breads make welcome holiday gifts—and are so versatile! They can be served as a dessert with a dollop of whipped cream…as a fancy sandwich when spread with cream cheese and cut into finger shapes…as a breakfast dish when covered with applesauce…and as an evening snack with fresh fruit slices.
—*Esther Bane, Glidden, Iowa*

• To prevent black walnut husks from leaving stubborn dark brown stains on your hands, wear rubber gloves.
—*Marny Malloy*
*Ocean Shores, Washington*

• I buy nuts in bulk around the holidays when the price is low, then put them in 1-cup portions in small bags and store in the freezer.
—*Esther Emmerick*
*Murrysville, Pennsylvania*

## MARINATED SHRIMP

*Margaret McGehee, Knoxville, Tennessee*

*It figures that this colorful and carefree dish is a favorite with my family. The recipe evolved from adding and subtracting ingredients until everyone liked the results.*

    2 quarts water
    3 small onions, sliced, *divided*
    1 garlic clove, minced
    1 bay leaf
    3 teaspoons salt, *divided*
2-1/2 pounds uncooked shrimp, peeled and
        deveined
  3/4 to 1 cup ketchup
  1/2 cup vinegar
    6 tablespoons vegetable oil
    1 tablespoon chopped chives
1-1/2 teaspoons Worcestershire sauce
  1/4 teaspoon pepper
  1/8 teaspoon curry powder

In a large kettle, combine water, 1 onion, garlic, bay leaf and 1 teaspoon salt; bring to a boil. Reduce heat; simmer, uncovered, for 5 minutes. Add shrimp; simmer for 5-7 minutes or until shrimp turn pink. Drain immediately; rinse in cold water. Place in a large glass or plastic bowl with remaining onions. In a small bowl, combine ketchup, vinegar, oil, chives, Worcestershire sauce, pepper, curry powder and remaining salt. Pour over shrimp. Cover and chill for 6 hours or overnight. Drain before serving. **Yield:** 10-12 servings.

## NUTS AND BOLTS

*Penny Peterson, Grand Centre, Alberta*

*Since I was a child, we've made buckets of this mix each Christmas for everyone. These days, though, I fix it for just about any occasion.*

    2 cups Cheerios
    2 cups bite-size Shredded Wheat
    2 cups pretzel sticks
1-1/2 cups salted peanuts
  1/4 cup butter *or* margarine
    1 tablespoon Worcestershire sauce
  1/2 teaspoon *each* celery, onion and garlic
        salt
  1/2 teaspoon paprika

In a large bowl, combine cereals, pretzels and nuts. In a saucepan, melt butter; stir in seasonings. Pour over cereal mixture; toss to coat. Spread on an ungreased 15-in. x 10-in. x 1-in. baking pan. Bake at 250° for 1 hour, stirring every 15 minutes. Store in an airtight container. **Yield:** 8 cups.

## CLAM FRITTERS

*Cecelia Wilson, Rockville, Connecticut*

**(Pictured above)**

*We had clam fritters every time we went to Rhode Island. I looked for a recipe and finally found this one. Now we have them whenever we want.*

  2/3 cup all-purpose flour
    1 teaspoon baking powder
  1/4 teaspoon salt
  1/8 teaspoon pepper
    1 can (6-1/2 ounces) minced clams
    1 egg
    3 tablespoons milk
  1/3 cup diced onion
Oil for deep-fat frying
Tartar sauce *and/or* lemon wedges, optional

In a bowl, combine flour, baking powder, salt and pepper; set aside. Drain clams, reserving 2 tablespoons juice; set clams aside. In a small bowl, beat egg, milk and reserved clam juice; stir into dry ingredients just until moistened. Add the clams and onion. In an electric skillet or deep-fat fryer, heat oil to 350°. Drop batter by tablespoonfuls into oil. Fry for 2-3 minutes, turning occasionally, until golden brown. Drain on paper towels. Serve with tartar sauce and/or lemon if desired. **Yield:** 14-16 fritters.

# Quick & Easy Nut Recipes

THERE'S no need to let the busy preparations for a party or other get-together drive you "nuts". All of the recipes on this page can be made in about 30 minutes…none of them have more than nine ingredients…and almost all would be ideal as quick homemade gifts.

## CURRIED PEANUTS

*Debbie Lewis, Longview, Washington*

*I make a big batch of these nuts at least once or twice a week to satisfy our six children. They never last long around our house, but I don't mind because I can whip up another batch in a matter of minutes.*

1-1/2 teaspoons butter *or* margarine
4-1/2 teaspoons brown sugar
 1/4 to 1/2 teaspoon curry powder
 3/4 cup salted dry roasted peanuts

In a heavy skillet, melt butter; stir in sugar and curry powder. Add peanuts. Cook and stir over medium heat for 3-4 minutes. Spread on a sheet of foil; separate nuts. Cool. Store in an airtight container. **Yield:** 1 cup.

## CINNAMON-GLAZED ALMONDS

*Crescent Dragonwagon*
*Eureka Springs, Arkansas*

*The nutty goodness and versatility of almonds make them a favorite ingredient in many of my recipes. They add crunchy texture and a delicious twist to traditional down-home recipes. Plus they taste great on their own as a snack, like in this much-requested recipe.*

 1/3 cup butter *or* margarine
 2 egg whites
Pinch salt

1 cup sugar
4 teaspoons ground cinnamon
3 cups whole almonds

Place butter in a 15-in. x 10-in. x 1-in. baking pan. Bake at 325° until melted, about 5-7 minutes. Meanwhile, in a mixing bowl, beat egg whites with salt until soft peaks form. Gradually add sugar, beating until stiff peaks form. Fold in cinnamon and almonds; pour over butter and toss to coat. Bake at 325° for 40 minutes, turning every 10 minutes, or until almonds are crisp. **Yield:** 3 cups.

## ITALIAN NUT MEDLEY

*Karen Riordan, Fern Creek, Kentucky*

*This is just great to nibble on and makes a satisfying salty snack. Italian salad dressing mix is the easy secret ingredient—it adds just the right zip to plain mixed nuts! Whenever I set out a bowl of these nuts, they disappear quickly.*

 2 tablespoons butter *or* margarine
 4 cups mixed nuts
 1 tablespoon soy sauce
 1 envelope Italian salad dressing mix

In a skillet, melt the butter over medium heat. Add nuts; cook and stir constantly for 2 minutes. Stir in soy sauce. Sprinkle with salad dressing mix; stir to coat. Immediately transfer to a greased baking pan and spread in a single layer. Cool. Store in an airtight container. **Yield:** 4 cups.

## SPICED NUTS

*Becky Cleveland, Waterville, Nova Scotia*
*Each Christmas, I fill jars with these special nuts, tie*

the top with a piece of colored ribbon and give them away as gifts. Everyone is always pleasantly surprised by their zesty taste.

> 3 tablespoons butter *or* margarine, melted
> 1 tablespoon brown sugar
> 1 tablespoon soy sauce
> 1/2 teaspoon salt
> 1/8 teaspoon cayenne pepper
> 1/8 teaspoon chili powder
> 1 cup whole unblanched almonds
> 1 cup pecan halves
> 1 cup pistachios *or* macadamia nuts

In a large bowl, combine the first six ingredients; mix well. Add nuts and stir until coated. Spread evenly in an ungreased 15-in. x 10-in. x 1-in. baking pan. Bake at 325° for 15-20 minutes, stirring two or three times. Spread on a waxed paper-lined baking sheet. Cool. Store in an airtight container. **Yield:** 3 cups.

## MIXED NUT BARS

*Bobbi Brown, Waupaca, Wisconsin*

**(Pictured at right)**

*Here's a tasty treat that is a wonderful time-saver. No matter where I take these bars, no one can eat just one and I always get asked for the recipe. They look great piled high on a pretty platter and taste even better!*

> 1-1/2 cups all-purpose flour
> 3/4 cup packed brown sugar
> 1/4 teaspoon salt
> 1/2 cup plus 2 tablespoons cold butter *or* margarine, *divided*
> 1 can (11-1/2 ounces) mixed nuts
> 1 cup butterscotch chips
> 1/2 cup light corn syrup

In a bowl, combine flour, sugar and salt. Cut in 1/2 cup of butter until mixture resembles coarse crumbs. Press into a greased 13-in. x 9-in. x 2-in. baking pan. Bake at 350° for 10 minutes. Sprinkle with nuts. Melt butterscotch chips. Add corn

syrup and remaining butter; mix well. Pour over nuts. Bake for 10 minutes. Cool. **Yield:** about 3-1/2 dozen.

## ICED ALMONDS

*Susan Marie Taccone, Erie, Pennsylvania*

**(Pictured below)**

*My mother-in-law gave me this recipe some 15 years ago. I've made well over 100 batches since then!*

> 1/4 cup butter *or* margarine
> 2-1/2 cups whole unblanched almonds
> 1 cup sugar
> 1 teaspoon vanilla extract

In a heavy saucepan, melt butter over medium-high heat. Add almonds and sugar. Cook and stir constantly for 7-8 minutes or until syrup is golden brown. Remove from the heat; stir in vanilla. Immediately drop by clusters or separate almonds on a greased baking pan. Cool. Store in an airtight container. **Yield:** 4 cups.

## HAM AND CHEESE ROLL-UPS

*Sara Hooks, Springfield, California*

*There are only three ingredients in this tasty recipe—and one is a surprise. It's the ranch dressing that makes it so delicious.*

> 1 container (8 ounces) soft cream cheese
> 2 tablespoons ranch dressing mix
> 1 package (12 ounces) sliced fully cooked deli ham

Combine cream cheese and dressing mix; spread on each slice of ham. Roll up tightly. Wrap in plastic wrap; chill several hours or overnight. Slice into 1-in. pieces. **Yield:** about 5 dozen.

## STRAWBERRY PUNCH

*Carol Schwartz, Hegins, Pennsylvania*

*I was looking for a very special beverage to serve at my daughter's wedding when I found the recipe for this pretty pink punch with a little zing to it. It got lots of compliments from our guests.*

> 1 can (46 ounces) pineapple juice, chilled
> 2-1/4 cups water
> 1 can (6 ounces) frozen pink lemonade, thawed
> 3/4 cup sugar
> 1 quart strawberry ice cream
> 2-1/2 quarts ginger ale, chilled

In a punch bowl, combine the first four ingredients. Add ice cream; stir gently. Add ginger ale; stir gently. Serve immediately. **Yield:** 6 quarts.

## PARTY BEAN DIP

*Kelly Hardgrave, Hartman, Arkansas*

*This easy-to-fix dip is bursting with heartiness, making it ideal for all sorts of occasions. I like to make it during fall when friends come over to watch football games.*

> 1 can (16 ounces) pinto beans, undrained
> 1/2 cup shredded cheddar cheese
> 2 teaspoons vinegar
> 2 teaspoons Worcestershire sauce
> 1 teaspoon chili powder
> 1/2 to 1 teaspoon garlic salt
> 1/8 to 1/4 teaspoon liquid smoke, optional
> Dash cayenne pepper
> 2 bacon strips, cooked and crumbled
> Tortilla chips

Puree beans in a food processor; pour into a heavy saucepan. Add the next seven ingredients; cook

## APPLE SALSA WITH CINNAMON CHIPS

*Carolyn Brinkmeyer, Aurora, Colorado*

**(Pictured above)**

*I've served this unique salsa as an appetizer and a snack. Plus it's so easy to transport.*

SALSA:
> 2 medium tart apples, chopped
> 1 cup chopped strawberries
> 2 medium kiwifruit, peeled and chopped
> 1 small orange
> 2 tablespoons brown sugar
> 2 tablespoons apple jelly, melted

CHIPS:
> 8 flour tortillas (7 *or* 8 inches)
> 1 tablespoon water
> 1/4 cup sugar
> 2 teaspoons ground cinnamon

In a bowl, combine apples, strawberries and kiwi. Grate orange peel to measure 1-1/2 teaspoons; squeeze juice from orange. Add peel and juice to apple mixture. Stir in brown sugar and jelly. For chips, brush tortillas lightly with water. Combine sugar and cinnamon; sprinkle over tortillas. Cut each tortilla into 8 wedges. Place in a single layer on ungreased baking sheets. Bake at 400° for 6-8 minutes or until lightly browned. Cool. Serve with salsa. **Yield:** 4 cups salsa.

over low heat until the cheese is melted, stirring occasionally. Transfer to a serving dish; top with bacon. Serve hot with chips. **Yield:** 1-1/2 cups.

## CHILI-CHEESE SPREAD

*Lynette Clement, Grand Junction, Colorado*

*This full-of-zip spread's sure to be the star of any New Year's gathering! It can also easily be formed into alternate shapes for serving at other festive times, like an egg for Easter or a leaf for fall.*

- 12 ounces cream cheese, softened
- 1 cup (4 ounces) shredded sharp cheddar cheese
- 1 teaspoon prepared horseradish
- 1 can (4 ounces) chopped green chilies, drained
- 1 jar (2 ounces) diced pimientos, drained, *divided*
- 1/2 cup chopped pecans

Assorted crackers

In a medium bowl, beat cheeses and horseradish until smooth. Add chilies. Reserve 1 tablespoon pimientos for garnish; add remainder to cheese mixture and mix well. Chill for 1 hour. Form into a star shape on a serving platter; press pecans onto sides of star. Outline star with pimientos. Cover and chill until ready to serve. Serve with crackers. **Yield:** about 3-1/2 cups.

## ALMOND CHEDDAR APPETIZERS

*Linda Thompson, Southampton, Ontario*

**(Pictured below)**

*I always try to have a supply of these on hand in the freezer. If guests drop in, I just pull out and reheat some. You can serve them as a snack or alongside a light lunch entree.*

- 1 cup mayonnaise
- 2 teaspoons Worcestershire sauce
- 1 cup (4 ounces) shredded sharp cheddar cheese
- 1 medium onion, chopped
- 3/4 cup slivered almonds, chopped
- 6 bacon strips, cooked and crumbled
- 1 loaf (1 pound) French bread

In a bowl, combine mayonnaise and Worcestershire sauce; stir in cheese, onion, almonds and bacon. Cut bread into 1/2-in. slices; spread with cheese mixture. Cut slices in half; place on a greased baking sheet. Bake at 400° for 8-10 minutes or until bubbly. **Yield:** about 4 dozen. **Editor's Note:** Unbaked appetizers may be frozen. Place in a single layer on a baking sheet; freeze for 1 hour. Remove from baking sheet and store in an airtight container up to 2 months. When ready to use, place unthawed appetizers on a greased baking sheet. Bake at 400° for 10 minutes or until bubbly.

*SERVING new and interesting main dishes doesn't have to be a challenge. These great grilling ideas, hearty oven entrees and satisfying skillet suppers are guaranteed to put an end to menu monotony.*

**BARBECUE'S BEST.** Clockwise from top left: Barbecued Spareribs (p. 19), Grilled Cheese Loaf (p. 19), Marinated Catfish Fillets (p. 20) and Pork with Tangy Mustard Sauce (p. 20).

# Main Dishes

## BARBECUED SPARERIBS

*Jane Uphoff, Idalia, Colorado*

**(Pictured at left and on cover)**

*My whole family loves to eat these zesty barbecued spareribs.*

1 tablespoon ground mustard
1 tablespoon chili powder
1/2 teaspoon cayenne pepper
1/4 teaspoon garlic powder
3 pounds pork spareribs *or* baby back ribs
2/3 cup ketchup
1/2 cup water
1/2 cup chopped onion
1/4 cup lemon juice
2 tablespoons vegetable oil
1 teaspoon dried oregano
1/2 teaspoon salt
1/4 teaspoon pepper

Combine the first four ingredients; rub over ribs. For sauce, combine the remaining ingredients; mix well and set aside. Grill ribs, covered, over medium-low coals for 1 hour, turning occasionally. Add 10 briquettes to coals. Grill 30 minutes longer, basting both sides several times with sauce, or until meat is tender. **Yield:** 4 servings.

## PORK CHOW MEIN

*Jo Groth, Plainfield, Iowa*

*I've found stir-frying to be a good way of disguising vegetables that kids don't normally eat.*

☑ This tasty dish uses less fat, sugar or salt. Recipe includes Nutritional Analysis and Diabetic Exchanges.

1 pound pork tenderloin, trimmed
1 cup low-sodium chicken broth
1/4 cup low-sodium soy sauce
1 tablespoon cornstarch
1/2 to 1 teaspoon ground ginger
1 garlic clove, minced
1 cup thinly sliced carrots
1 cup thinly sliced celery
1 cup chopped onion
1 cup coarsely chopped cabbage
1 cup coarsely chopped fresh spinach

Partially freeze pork. Slice across the grain into 1/4-in.-thick strips; set aside. Combine broth, soy sauce, cornstarch and ginger; set aside. In a large skillet that has been coated with nonstick cooking spray, stir-fry pork and garlic for 5 minutes or until lightly browned. Add carrots, celery, onion, cabbage and spinach; stir-fry for 3 minutes. Add broth mixture; cover and simmer for 3 minutes. **Yield:** 5 servings. **Nutritional Analysis:** One 1-cup serving equals 167 calories, 506 mg sodium, 55 mg cholesterol, 11 gm carbohydrate, 22 gm protein, 4 gm fat. **Diabetic Exchanges:** 2 lean meat, 2 vegetable.

THIS BREAD, shared by Debbi Baker of Green Springs, Ohio, is the perfect accompaniment to any grilled main dish.

## GRILLED CHEESE LOAF

**(Pictured at left)**

1 package (3 ounces) cream cheese, softened
2 tablespoons butter *or* margarine, softened
1 cup (4 ounces) shredded mozzarella cheese
1/4 cup chopped green onions
1/2 teaspoon garlic salt
1 loaf (1 pound) French bread, sliced

In a mixing bowl, beat cream cheese and butter. Add cheese, onions and garlic salt; mix well. Spread on both sides of each slice of bread. Wrap loaf in a large piece of heavy-duty foil (about 28 in. x 18 in.); seal tightly. Grill, covered, over medium coals for 8-10 minutes, turning once. Unwrap foil; grill 5 minutes longer. **Yield:** 10-12 servings.

# Pork Perfected with Zesty Sauce

"IF YOU can't stand the heat, get out of the kitchen." When the weather is too warm, many cooks —like Ginger Johnson of Farmington, Illinois—heed that sage advice by heading outdoors to the grill.

Ginger makes Pork with Tangy Mustard Sauce for special-occasion meals. "Everyone who's tried it loves the 'bite' of the mustard horseradish sauce mixed with the sweet/sour taste of the preserves," she says.

Even before tasting it, guests can't help savoring her pretty pork dish. "As it's cooking," Ginger assures, "the aroma is mouth-watering…and the sauce forms a colorful, crusty glaze.

"I usually slice the meat and serve it on a big platter with extra sauce drizzled across the top."

### PORK WITH TANGY MUSTARD SAUCE

(Pictured on page 18)

1 boneless pork loin roast (2-1/2 to 3 pounds)
2 teaspoons olive *or* vegetable oil
1-1/4 teaspoons ground mustard
3/4 teaspoon garlic powder
1/4 teaspoon ground ginger
1/2 cup horseradish mustard*
1/2 cup apricot *or* pineapple preserves

Rub roast with oil. Combine mustard, garlic powder and ginger; rub over roast. Place in a large resealable plastic bag or shallow glass container; seal bag or cover container. Refrigerate overnight. Grill roast, covered, over indirect heat for 60 minutes. Combine the horseradish mustard and preserves. Continue grilling for 15-30 minutes, basting twice with sauce, or until a meat thermometer reads 160°-170°. Let stand for 10 minutes before slicing. Heat remaining sauce to serve with roast. **Yield:** 10-12 servings. **\*Editor's Note:** As a substitute for horseradish mustard, combine 1/4 cup spicy brown mustard and 1/4 cup prepared horseradish.

### MARINATED CATFISH FILLETS

*Pauletta Boese, Macon, Mississippi*

(Pictured on page 18)

*Recently, we hosted a group of young people from Canada. Since we wanted to give them a true taste of the South, this was served. They raved about it.*

6 catfish fillets (about 8 ounces *each*)
1 bottle (16 ounces) Italian salad dressing
1 can (10-3/4 ounces) condensed tomato soup, undiluted
3/4 cup vegetable oil
3/4 cup sugar
1/3 cup vinegar
3/4 teaspoon celery seed
3/4 teaspoon salt
3/4 teaspoon pepper
3/4 teaspoon ground mustard
1/2 teaspoon garlic powder

Place fillets in a large resealable plastic bag or shallow glass container; cover with salad dressing.

Seal bag or cover container; refrigerate for 1 hour, turning occasionally. Drain and discard marinade. Combine remaining ingredients; mix well. Remove 1 cup for basting. (Refrigerate remaining sauce for another use.) Grill fillets, covered, over medium-hot coals for 3 minutes on each side. Brush with the basting sauce. Continue grilling for 6-8 minutes or until fish flakes easily with a fork, turning once and basting several times. **Yield:** 6 servings. **Editor's Note:** Reserved sauce may be used to brush on grilled or broiled fish, chicken, turkey or pork.

### LAZY HAM BAKE

*Elaine Green, Mechanicsville, Maryland*

*One day when I had leftover ham I did some experimenting and came up with this recipe.*

1-1/2 pounds fully cooked ham, cubed
1 package (16 ounces) frozen cut broccoli, thawed and drained
2-1/2 cups milk, *divided*

1 can (10-3/4 ounces) condensed cream of
  mushroom soup, undiluted
1 can (10-3/4 ounces) condensed cheddar
  cheese soup, undiluted
1/2 teaspoon onion powder
1/4 teaspoon garlic powder
2 cups biscuit/baking mix
Minced fresh parsley, optional

In a bowl, combine the ham, broccoli, 1 cup milk,
soups, onion powder and garlic powder; mix
well. Spoon into an ungreased 13-in. x 9-in. x 2-
in. baking dish. Combine biscuit mix and remaining milk; mix well. Pour over ham mixture.
Bake, uncovered, at 450° for 30 minutes or until
hot and bubbly. Garnish with parsley if desired.
**Yield:** 8-10 servings.

## HERBED ORANGE ROUGHY

*Sue Kroening, Mattoon, Illinois*

*The simple seasonings in this recipe enhance the pleas-
ant, mild flavor of orange roughy. It's a quick and easy
way to prepare fish.*

    2 tablespoons lemon juice
    1 tablespoon butter *or* margarine, melted
1/2 teaspoon dried thyme
1/2 teaspoon grated lemon peel
1/4 teaspoon salt
1/4 teaspoon paprika
1/8 teaspoon garlic powder
    4 orange roughy, red snapper, catfish *or*
      trout fillets (6 ounces *each*)

In a small bowl, combine the first seven ingredients; dip fillets. Grill, covered, over hot coals for
10 minutes or until fish flakes easily with a fork.
**Yield:** 4 servings.

## SOUTHERN FRIED CHICKEN

*Jo Ruh, Covington, Kentucky*

**(Pictured at right)**

*Here's a traditional recipe from our area of the coun-
try. My husband is a ham radio operator, and we've
shared this recipe with folks from all over the world.*

    2 eggs
    2 tablespoons milk
1-1/4 cups all-purpose flour
1-1/2 teaspoons salt
1/2 teaspoon pepper
1/4 teaspoon ground cumin
1/4 teaspoon dried oregano
1/4 teaspoon paprika

    2 broiler-fryer chickens (3 to 3-1/2
      pounds *each*), cut up
    1 cup shortening
MILK GRAVY:
1/4 cup all-purpose flour
1/2 teaspoon salt
1/8 teaspoon pepper
    1 cup milk
    1 cup water
1/8 teaspoon browning sauce, optional
Fresh oregano, optional

In a medium bowl, beat eggs and milk. In another bowl, combine flour and seasonings. Dip chick-
en pieces in egg mixture, then in flour mixture.
Heat shortening in a large skillet; brown chicken
on both sides. Cover and cook over low heat for
45 minutes or until juices run clear. Remove
chicken from skillet; keep warm. Reserve 1/4 cup
drippings in skillet. For gravy, stir in flour, salt and
pepper. Cook and stir over medium heat for 5
minutes or until browned. Combine milk and water; add to skillet. Bring to a boil; boil and stir for
2 minutes. Add browning sauce if desired. Serve
with chicken. Garnish with oregano if desired.
**Yield:** 8 servings.

## CHICKEN FAJITAS

*Betty Foss, San Marcos, California*

**(Pictured below)**

*I was born and raised on a farm in Iowa but have been a California resident for many years. Southwestern-style recipes like these chicken fajitas soon became family favorites. I like to serve them with salsa and guacamole.*

✓ This tasty dish uses less fat, sugar or salt. Recipe includes Nutritional Analysis and Diabetic Exchanges.

```
3/4 cup lime juice
1/2 cup olive or vegetable oil
  3 garlic cloves, minced
  2 teaspoons dried oregano
  1 teaspoon ground cumin
1/2 teaspoon pepper
1-1/2 pounds boneless skinless chicken
        breasts, cut into thin strips
  3 small zucchini, julienned
  2 small yellow summer squash, julienned
  2 medium green peppers, julienned
  2 medium sweet red peppers, julienned
 12 flour tortillas (10 inches), warmed
```

Combine the first six ingredients; divide the mixture between two large resealable plastic bags. Add chicken to one and vegetables to the other; seal bags and turn to coat. Refrigerate for 2-4 hours, turning bags occasionally. Drain chicken and vegetables, discarding marinade. In a large skillet over medium heat, saute chicken for 6-7 minutes or until juices run clear. Remove chicken and keep warm. Drain skillet. Saute vegetables for 3-4 minutes or until crisp-tender; drain. Spoon chicken and vegetables onto tortillas; fold in sides. Serve immediately. **Yield:** 12 servings. **Nutritional Analysis:** One serving equals 299 calories, 301 mg sodium, 31 mg cholesterol, 35 gm carbohydrate, 17 gm protein, 10 gm fat. **Diabetic Exchanges:** 2 starch, 1 meat, 1 vegetable, 1 fat.

## ZUCCHINI PORK DINNER

*Helen Vail, Glenside, Pennsylvania*

*I work full-time, but I love to cook—so I need to rely on meals that are wholesome and fast. This dish deliciously combines both traits! Plus, I like the fact that it doesn't dirty a pile of pots and pans.*

```
3/4 pound pork cutlets, cubed
  2 tablespoons vegetable oil
  1 large onion, chopped
  2 garlic cloves, minced
  1 can (12 ounces) tomato juice
1/2 teaspoon dried rosemary, crushed
1/2 teaspoon dried oregano
1/2 teaspoon salt
Pinch cayenne pepper
  3 medium zucchini, halved and cut into
      1/2-inch slices
Hot cooked noodles
```

In a skillet over medium heat, cook pork in oil until browned, about 5 minutes. Add onion and garlic; cook for 5 minutes or until onion is tender. Add tomato juice and seasonings; simmer, uncovered, for 5 minutes. Add the zucchini; cook and stir until crisp-tender, about 5 minutes. Serve over noodles. **Yield:** 4-6 servings.

## PESTO MEAT LOAF

*Margaret Pache, Mesa, Arizona*

*This is one of my favorite meat loaf recipes. The salsa gives it just the right amount of tang, and if you grow basil, the pesto is a tasty way to use it.*

**PESTO:**
```
  2 garlic cloves
```

1/3 cup olive *or* vegetable oil
1 cup fresh basil leaves
3/4 cup cooked long grain rice
1/4 cup chopped walnuts
1/4 cup shredded sharp cheddar cheese
1/4 teaspoon salt
MEAT LOAF:
1/2 cup quick-cooking oats
1/2 cup finely chopped green onions
1 egg, beaten
1/4 cup salsa
2 garlic cloves, minced
1/2 teaspoon salt
2 pounds lean ground beef

Place pesto ingredients in the order listed in a food processor or blender; cover and process on low speed until a paste forms. In a bowl, combine the first six meat loaf ingredients; add pesto. Add beef and mix well. Press into a greased 9-in. x 5-in. x 3-in. loaf pan. Bake at 350° for 50-60 minutes or until no longer pink, draining off fat when necessary. Let stand in pan for 10 minutes before slicing. **Yield:** 8 servings.

▰▰▰▰▰▰▰▰▰▰▰

## WALLEYE DELIGHT

*Connie Reilly, Stanchfield, Minnesota*

*I love fish, and I think grilling is one of the best ways to prepare it. This fish recipe is nutritious as well as flavorful. The combination of lemon juice, basil and lemon-pepper seasoning is fantastic.*

☑ This tasty dish uses less fat, sugar or salt. Recipe includes Nutritional Analysis and Diabetic Exchanges.

1 pound walleye, pike, perch *or* trout fillets
2 teaspoons margarine, softened
1 tablespoon lemon juice
1 tablespoon snipped fresh basil *or* 1/2 to 1 teaspoon dried basil
1 teaspoon lemon-pepper seasoning
1/2 teaspoon garlic salt
4 ounces fresh mushrooms, sliced

Coat an 18-in. x 18-in. piece of heavy-duty foil with nonstick cooking spray. Place fillets on foil. Spread with margarine. Sprinkle with lemon juice, basil, lemon pepper and garlic salt. Top with mushrooms. Bring opposite edges of foil together; fold down several times. Fold remaining edges toward fish and seal tightly. Grill, covered, over hot coals for 10-14 minutes, turning once, or until fish flakes easily with a fork. **Yield:** 4 servings.
**Nutritional Analysis:** One serving equals 183 calories, 199 mg sodium, 70 mg cholesterol, 2 gm carbohydrate, 23 gm protein, 9 gm fat. **Diabetic Exchanges:** 3 lean meat.

▰▰▰▰▰▰▰▰▰▰▰

 ## BAVARIAN BEEF DINNER

*Dot Christiansen, Bettendorf, Iowa*

**(Pictured above)**

*I've had this recipe for quite a number of years. I won second place with it in a cooking contest sponsored by our local newspaper.*

2 pounds boneless chuck roast, cut into 1-inch cubes
2 tablespoons vegetable oil
1-1/2 cups beef broth
2 medium onions, sliced
1 garlic clove, minced
1 teaspoon *each* dill seed, caraway seed, paprika and salt
1/4 teaspoon pepper
1/4 cup cold water
3 tablespoons all-purpose flour
1 cup (8 ounces) sour cream
Hot cooked rice
1 can (14 ounces) sauerkraut, warmed

In a Dutch oven, brown beef in oil. Add broth, onions, garlic and seasonings. Cover and simmer for 2-1/2 hours or until beef is tender; reduce heat. Combine water and flour until smooth; gradually stir into the beef mixture. Cook and stir for 2 minutes. Add sour cream and heat through (do not boil). Serve over rice with sauerkraut on the side. **Yield:** 6-8 servings.

1 cup cubed process American cheese
1 tube (12 ounces) refrigerated biscuits
2 to 3 tablespoons butter *or* margarine, melted
1/3 cup yellow cornmeal

In a saucepan over medium heat, brown the beef; drain. Add the beans, corn, soup, milk, onion, chili powder and salt; bring to a boil. Remove from the heat; stir in cheese until melted. Spoon into a greased 2-1/2-qt. baking dish. Bake, uncovered, at 375° for 10 minutes. Meanwhile, brush all sides of biscuits with butter; roll in cornmeal. Place on top of bubbling meat mixture. Return to the oven for 10-12 minutes or until biscuits are lightly browned and cooked through. **Yield:** 6-8 servings.

## PORK CHOPS WITH MUSHROOM GRAVY

*Nancy Schilling, Berkeley Springs, West Virginia*

*Based on the "moist meat" method of preparation my grandmother used, this gets passed around the table a second time. Even people who think that pork is dry like it. I serve it with mashed potatoes, peas and cranberry sauce.*

1/2 cup all-purpose flour, *divided*
1/2 cup seasoned bread crumbs, *divided*
4 pork chops (1/2 inch thick)
2 tablespoons vegetable oil
1 medium onion, sliced
2 garlic cloves, minced
1/4 teaspoon pepper
3 cups water
2 tablespoons instant beef bouillon granules
1 teaspoon browning sauce
2 bay leaves
1 jar (4-1/2 ounces) sliced mushrooms, drained
1/2 cup cold water

In a shallow bowl, combine half of the flour and half of the bread crumbs; coat the pork chops. In a large skillet over medium heat, brown pork chops on both sides in oil. Add onion, garlic, pepper and water. Stir in bouillon, browning sauce and bay leaves; bring to a boil. Reduce heat; cover and simmer for 1-1/2 hours or until pork is tender. Remove bay leaves. Remove pork to serving platter and keep warm. Add mushrooms to skillet. Combine cold water and remaining flour until smooth; stir into pan juices. Bring to a boil, stirring constantly until thickened and bubbly. Stir in the remaining bread crumbs. Serve over pork chops. **Yield:** 4 servings.

## BEEF 'N' BISCUIT BAKE

*Erin Schneider, St. Peters, Missouri*

**(Pictured above)**

*This recipe is not only quick and easy, it's very satisfying and has the best flavor. I think it's a great example of Midwest cuisine, because it just tastes good!*

1 pound ground beef
1 can (16 ounces) kidney beans, rinsed and drained
1 can (15-1/4 ounces) whole kernel corn, drained
1 can (10-3/4 ounces) condensed tomato soup, undiluted
1/4 cup milk
2 tablespoons minced onion
1/2 teaspoon chili powder
1/4 teaspoon salt

Main Dishes

# Hot Hints for Best Barbecues

● For tender, flavorful spareribs, begin by parboiling them in pineapple juice. Then add a homemade barbecue sauce while grilling. —*Alice Loen Starbuck, Minnesota*

● If you coat the rack with nonstick cooking spray first, there isn't much scrubbing to do after grilling.
—*Anne McKay Oliver, British Columbia*

● When you're making hamburger patties, place them on waxed paper on a tray. Once you start grilling, you can just lift the corner of the waxed paper to easily remove them.
—*Ruth Ann Miller Sugarcreek, Ohio*

● It's really simple to grill acorn squash. Pierce the skin with a fork a couple of times, then wrap the whole squash in aluminum foil. Grill over direct heat for 1 hour, turning once. Remove from grill. Cut in half; remove and discard seeds. Season with butter, salt and pepper. —*Bonnie Isaacs Kalkaska, Michigan*

● Old baking pans clean up easily after grilling if they are completely covered with aluminum foil first. When done cooking, just remove the foil and discard. —*Sharon Gentzle Homewood, Illinois*

● To roast corn, pull back husks and remove silk. Replace husks; tie at top with heavy twine or string. Soak in salted water for 1 hour. Grill over hot coals for 15-20 minutes, turning frequently. —*Edna Hoffman Hebron, Indiana*

● Open foil packets cautiously to let steam escape and prevent burns.
—*Dollypearle Martin Douglastown, New Brunswick*

● I could never get my ribs tender enough on the grill—until I tried precooking them in a slow cooker on high heat for 2 to 3 hours. Since racks of ribs don't fit in a slow cooker very well, I roll them up and place them in the pot standing up. —*Loyda Coulombe Federal Way, Washington*

● Venison or turkey burger patties won't stick to the grill when they are coated with nonstick cooking spray.
—*Sue Anderson Wardensville, West Virginia*

● My family enjoys eating veggies grilled in foil packets. After placing vegetables in the center of a piece of aluminum foil, I seal the foil by folding the long sides in to create a seam in the middle, then fold over the sides. The packets can also be baked in the oven on a cookie sheet.
—*Lynna Snider Nipawin, Saskatchewan*

● Don't waste any time scrubbing your grill rack. Instead, put it in a clean plastic trash bag and spray generously with oven cleaner. Tightly close the bag and leave it overnight. The next day, washing the grate is a breeze.
—*Leland Shaver, De Queen, Arkansas*

● Presoak bamboo skewers in water for at least 20 minutes before threading with meat, vegetables or fruit to prevent them from scorching or burning. —*Sally Hook, Houston, Texas*

## Baked Almond Chicken

*Diana Frankford, Sarasota, Florida*

**(Pictured below)**

*This is a tasty dish that my family just loves. The almonds give the chicken a wonderful flavor.*

- 1 broiler-fryer chicken (3 to 3-1/2 pounds), cut up
- 3/4 cup all-purpose flour
- 8 tablespoons butter *or* margarine, melted, *divided*
- 1 teaspoon *each* salt, paprika and celery salt
- 3/4 cup sliced almonds
- 1-1/2 cups half-and-half cream
- 1 cup (8 ounces) sour cream
- 3 tablespoons dry bread crumbs

Place the chicken and flour in a large resealable plastic bag. Seal bag; turn to coat chicken. In a shallow dish, combine 7 tablespoons butter with salt, paprika and celery salt. Add chicken pieces and turn to coat. Transfer to a greased 13-in. x 9-in. x 2-in. baking dish. Sprinkle with almonds. Pour cream around chicken. Cover and bake at 350° for 45 minutes. Drain, reserving 1/2 cup sauce. Stir sour cream into sauce; pour over the chicken. Combine bread crumbs with the remaining butter; sprinkle over chicken. Bake, uncovered, 15 minutes more or until meat juices run clear. **Yield:** 4 servings.

## Mexican Pork Stew

*Mary Lou Kosanke, Hualapai, Arizona*

*This recipe came from a friend, but I added more green chilies to zip it up.*

☑ This tasty dish uses less fat, sugar or salt. Recipe includes Nutritional Analysis and Diabetic Exchanges.

- 2-1/2 pounds lean boneless pork, cut into 1-inch cubes
- 1 garlic clove, minced
- 1 cup chopped onion
- 1 can (14-1/2 ounces) no-salt-added whole tomatoes, undrained and diced
- 1 to 2 cans (4 ounces *each*) chopped green chilies
- 1 tablespoon minced fresh cilantro *or* parsley
- 2 teaspoons dried oregano
- 2 bay leaves
- 1 tablespoon cornstarch
- 1 tablespoon water

In a large skillet that has been coated with non-stick cooking spray, brown pork and garlic. Add onion; saute until tender. Stir in tomatoes, chilies, cilantro, oregano and bay leaves; cover and simmer for 40 minutes or until pork is tender and no longer pink. Combine cornstarch and water; add to skillet. Bring to a boil; boil for 2 minutes, stirring constantly. Remove bay leaves. **Yield:** 10 servings. **Nutritional Analysis:** One 1/2-cup serving equals 199 calories, 97 mg sodium, 69 mg cholesterol, 5 gm carbohydrate, 25 gm protein, 9 gm fat. **Diabetic Exchanges:** 3 lean meat, 1 vegetable.

## Ham and Red Beans

*June Robinson, Bastrop, Louisiana*

*This simple, hearty casserole is complete with corn bread and a green salad.*

☑ This tasty dish uses less fat, sugar or salt. Recipe includes Nutritional Analysis and Diabetic Exchanges.

- 3 cans (15-1/2 ounces *each*) kidney beans, rinsed and drained
- 1 can (14-1/2 ounces) Cajun *or* Mexican stewed tomatoes
- 2 cups diced fully cooked low-fat ham
- 1/2 cup water
- 1/2 teaspoon garlic powder
- 1/2 teaspoon ground cumin
- 1/2 teaspoon dried thyme
- 1/2 teaspoon dried oregano
- 1/4 teaspoon pepper
- 3 dashes hot pepper sauce

In a large saucepan or Dutch oven, bring all in-

gredients to a boil. Reduce heat; cover and simmer for 30 minutes. **Yield:** 10 servings. **Nutritional Analysis:** One 3/4-cup serving equals 207 calories, 474 mg sodium, 13 mg cholesterol, 32 gm carbohydrate, 15 gm protein, 2 gm fat. **Diabetic Exchanges:** 2 starch, 1 lean meat.

## TOASTED APPLE-CHEESE SANDWICHES

*Evelyn Bartolomei, Santa Rosa, California*

*Here's a nice change of pace from traditional grilled cheese sandwiches. Most people are pleasantly surprised at the combination of ingredients. The apple, cheese and bacon really complement each other.*

    6 slices white *or* French bread
    2 tablespoons mayonnaise
    6 slices cheddar cheese
    1 medium tart apple, peeled, cored and cut crosswise into six rings
    1 tablespoon brown sugar
    12 bacon strips, cooked and drained

In a broiler, toast one side of each slice of bread. Spread untoasted side with mayonnaise. Top with cheese and apple; sprinkle with brown sugar. Cross two strips of bacon over each. Broil 6 in. from the heat for 2-3 minutes or until cheese melts. **Yield:** 6 servings.

## POTATO-CRUST PIZZA

*Carol Gorentz, Park Rapids, Minnesota*

**(Pictured above)**

*We grow potatoes and found this recipe is a great way to use up leftover mashed potatoes. This dish is a favorite among our family and friends.*

    3 cups mashed potatoes (prepared with milk)
    1 egg, beaten
    1/2 cup grated Parmesan cheese
    2 tablespoons butter *or* margarine, melted
1-1/2 teaspoons salt
    1 can (8 ounces) pizza sauce
    3 ounces sliced pepperoni
    4 fresh mushrooms, sliced
    1 cup (4 ounces) shredded mozzarella cheese

In a mixing bowl, combine potatoes, egg, Parmesan cheese, butter and salt. Press onto the bottom and up the sides of a greased 10-in. pie plate. Spread pizza sauce over potato mixture to within 1/2 in. of edges. Top with pepperoni and mushrooms. Sprinkle with mozzarella cheese. Bake at 400° for 25-30 minutes or until heated through and cheese is melted. **Yield:** 4-6 servings. **Editor's Note:** An 11-in. x 7-in. x 2-in. baking dish can be used instead of the pie plate.

## GRILLED LAMB CHOPS

*DeLea Lonadier, Montgomery, Louisiana*

*Even folks who don't prefer lamb can't resist these tender chops. The seasoning is easy to prepare and really complements the lamb.*

> 1/2 cup vegetable oil
> 1/4 cup finely chopped onion
> 2 tablespoons lemon juice
> 1 teaspoon ground mustard
> 1/2 teaspoon garlic salt
> 1/2 teaspoon dried tarragon
> 1/8 teaspoon pepper
> 6 loin lamb chops (1-1/2 to 1-3/4 pounds)

In a resealable plastic bag or shallow glass container, combine the first seven ingredients; add lamb chops. Seal bag or cover container and turn to coat. Refrigerate for 10-15 minutes. Drain and discard marinade. Grill chops, covered, over medium-hot coals for 14 minutes, turning once, or until a meat thermometer reads 140° for rare, 150° for medium or 160° for well-done. **Yield:** 3 servings.

﹏﹏﹏﹏﹏﹏﹏﹏﹏﹏﹏

## PORK CHOPS O'BRIEN

*Kathy Dustin, Bedford, Indiana*

**(Pictured above)**

*I like to make this recipe for small holiday gatherings, especially when folks are tired of ham and turkey. It's delicious.*

> 6 pork loin chops (1/2 inch thick)
> 1 tablespoon vegetable oil
> 1 can (10-3/4 ounces) condensed cream of celery soup, undiluted
> 1/2 cup milk
> 1/2 cup sour cream
> 1/4 teaspoon pepper
> 1 cup (4 ounces) shredded cheddar cheese, *divided*
> 1 can (2.8 ounces) french-fried onions, *divided*
> 1 package (24 ounces) frozen O'Brien hash brown potatoes, thawed
> 1/2 teaspoon seasoned salt

In a skillet over medium-high heat, brown pork chops in oil; set aside. Combine the soup, milk, sour cream, pepper, 1/2 cup cheese and 1/2 cup onions; fold in potatoes. Spread in a greased 13-in. x 9-in. x 2-in. baking dish. Arrange chops on top; sprinkle with salt. Cover and bake at 350° for 40-45 minutes or until pork is tender. Uncover; sprinkle with remaining cheese and onions. Return to the oven for 5-10 minutes or until cheese melts. **Yield:** 6 servings.

## RICE-STUFFED ROAST

*Shirley Creamer, Lamar, Colorado*

*We're ranchers who live 23 miles from any town. I like to serve this dish whenever we have visitors—it's a real special roast.*

> 2 packages (6 ounces *each*) long grain and wild rice mix
> 3/4 cup boiling water
> 3/4 cup dried apricots, chopped
> 3/4 cup chopped fresh mushrooms
> 1/2 cup chopped green onions
> 1/2 cup chopped sweet red pepper
> 2 garlic cloves, minced
> 1 tablespoon butter *or* margarine
> 1/3 cup chopped water chestnuts
> 2 tablespoons chopped fresh parsley
> 1/2 teaspoon salt
> 1/4 teaspoon pepper
> 1 boneless rolled pork loin roast (about 4 pounds)
> 1/2 cup apricot preserves

Prepare rice according to package directions. Meanwhile, pour boiling water over apricots; let stand for 20 minutes. Drain and set aside. In a large skillet, saute mushrooms, onions, red pepper and garlic in butter until tender, about 4 minutes. Remove from the heat; stir in rice, apricots, water chestnuts, parsley, salt and pepper. Untie roast and spread 1-1/4 cups of rice mixture inside. Place the remaining stuffing in a covered 2-qt. casserole; set aside. Retie roast and place on a rack in a greased roasting pan. Bake, uncovered, at 350° for 2 to 2-1/2 hours or until a meat thermometer reads 160°-170°. During the last 30 minutes, baste roast with preserves and bake the extra rice stuffing. Let roast stand 10 minutes before slicing. **Yield:** 10-12 servings.

## Cashew Chicken Stir-Fry

*Vicki Hirschfeld, Hartland, Wisconsin*

**(Pictured below)**

*The hardest part of making this dish is keeping the cashews in the cupboard! My family loves them.*

      2 cups chicken broth, *divided*
  1/4 cup cornstarch
      3 tablespoons soy sauce
  1/2 teaspoon ground ginger
      1 pound boneless skinless chicken breasts, cut into 1/2-inch strips
      2 garlic cloves, minced
  1/2 cup thinly sliced carrots
  1/2 cup sliced celery (1/2-inch pieces)
      3 cups broccoli florets
      1 cup fresh *or* frozen snow peas
1-1/2 cups cashews
Hot cooked rice, optional

In a skillet, heat 3 tablespoons of broth. Meanwhile, combine the cornstarch, soy sauce, ginger and remaining broth until smooth; set aside. Add chicken to the skillet; stir-fry over medium heat until no longer pink, about 3-5 minutes. Remove with a slotted spoon and keep warm. Add garlic, carrots and celery to skillet; stir-fry for 3 minutes. Add broccoli and peas; stir-fry for 4-5 minutes or until crisp-tender. Stir broth mixture; add to the skillet with the chicken. Cook and stir for 2 minutes. Stir in cashews. Serve over rice if desired. **Yield:** 4 servings.

## Chicken-Apple Croissants

*Tobi Breternitz, Bay Port, Michigan*

*"Fast foods" are a specialty of mine because I always seem to have drop-in guests. These unique sandwiches can be put together at a moment's notice and taste delicious!*

      2 cups diced cooked chicken
      1 cup diced peeled apple
  3/4 cup mayonnaise *or* salad dressing
  1/2 cup halved green grapes
  1/4 cup sliced almonds, toasted
  1/2 teaspoon seasoned salt
  1/4 teaspoon pepper
      6 croissants *or* hard rolls, split
      6 lettuce leaves

In a bowl, combine the first seven ingredients. Spoon about 1/2 cup onto each croissant; top with lettuce. **Yield:** 6 servings.

## ASPARAGUS SPAGHETTI PIE

*Lorraine Danz, Lancaster, Pennsylvania*

**(Pictured below)**

*I've served this dish at several luncheons and received many compliments. Many people have requested the recipe, so I thought I'd share it with you.*

**CRUST:**
  2 eggs
  1 package (7 ounces) spaghetti, cooked and drained
  1/2 cup grated Parmesan cheese
  2 tablespoons butter *or* margarine, melted
**FILLING:**
  1 cup cubed fully cooked ham
  1 package (8 ounces) frozen asparagus spears, thawed and cut into 1-inch pieces
  1 jar (4-1/2 ounces) sliced mushrooms, drained
  1-1/2 cups (6 ounces) shredded Swiss cheese
  2 eggs
  1/2 cup sour cream
  1 teaspoon dill weed
  1 teaspoon minced chives

In a large bowl, beat eggs; add the spaghetti, Parmesan cheese and butter; mix well. Press onto the bottom and up the sides of a greased 10-in. pie plate. Combine ham, asparagus and mushrooms; spoon into crust. Sprinkle with Swiss cheese. Beat eggs, sour cream, dill and chives; pour over cheese. Bake at 350° for 35-40 minutes or until crust is set and center is lightly browned. Let stand for 10 minutes before serving. **Yield:** 6-8 servings.

## PORK AND APPLE SKEWERS

*Cheryl Plainte, Minot, North Dakota*

**(Pictured on page 32)**

*Necessity was the "mother" of this recipe! I'd already marinated the pork before realizing we were short on kabob vegetables. In place of them, I used apples I had on hand.*

  3/4 cup barbecue sauce
  1/2 cup pineapple juice
  1/4 cup honey mustard*
  1/4 cup packed brown sugar
  2 tablespoons soy sauce
  2 tablespoons olive *or* vegetable oil
1-1/2 pounds pork tenderloin, cut into 3/4-inch cubes
  5 medium unpeeled tart apples

In a large resealable plastic bag or shallow glass container, combine the first six ingredients; mix well. Reserve 1/2 cup for basting and refrigerate. Add pork to remaining marinade and turn to coat. Seal bag or cover container; refrigerate for at least 1 hour. Drain and discard marinade. Cut the apples into 1-1/2-in. cubes. Alternate pork and apples on metal or soaked bamboo skewers. Grill, uncovered, over medium coals, for 3 minutes on each side. Baste with the reserved marinade. Continue turning and basting for 8-10 minutes or until meat juices run clear and apples are tender. **Yield:** 6 servings. *Editor's Note: As a substitute for honey mustard, combine 2 tablespoons Dijon mustard and 2 tablespoons honey.

## PIZZA ON THE GRILL

*Lisa Boettcher, Columbus, Wisconsin*

**(Pictured on page 33)**

*Pizza is such a favorite at our house I make it at least once a week. The barbecue flavor mingling with the cheese tastes delicious.*

**CRUST:**
  1 package (1/4 ounce) active dry yeast
  1 cup warm water (110° to 115°)
  2 tablespoons vegetable oil

Main Dishes

2 teaspoons sugar
1 teaspoon baking soda
1 teaspoon salt
2-3/4 to 3 cups all-purpose flour
TOPPINGS:
    2 cups cubed cooked chicken
    1/2 to 3/4 cup barbecue sauce
    1/2 cup julienned green pepper
    2 cups (8 ounces) shredded Monterey Jack cheese

In a mixing bowl, dissolve yeast in water. Add the oil, sugar, baking soda, salt and 2 cups flour. Stir in enough remaining flour to form a soft dough. Turn onto a floured surface; knead until smooth and elastic, about 6-8 minutes. Cover and let rest for 10 minutes. On a floured surface, roll dough into a 13-in. circle. Transfer to a greased 12-in. pizza pan. Build up edges slightly. Grill, covered, over medium coals for 5 minutes. Remove from grill. Combine chicken and barbecue sauce; spread over the crust. Sprinkle with green pepper and cheese. Grill, covered, 5-10 minutes longer or until crust is golden and cheese is melted. **Yield:** 4 servings.

## MAPLE-GLAZED CHICKEN WINGS

*Janice Henck, Clarkston, Georgia*

**(Pictured on page 33)**

*Some wonderful maple syrup I brought back from my last trip to Vermont is what inspired my recipe. These wings have been a hit with family and friends.*

    2 to 3 pounds whole chicken wings
    1 cup maple syrup
2/3 cup chili sauce
1/2 cup finely chopped onion
    2 tablespoons Dijon mustard
    2 teaspoons Worcestershire sauce
1/4 to 1/2 teaspoon crushed red pepper flakes

Cut chicken wings into three sections; discard wing tip section. In a large resealable plastic bag or shallow glass container, combine remaining ingredients. Reserve 1 cup for basting and refrigerate. Add chicken to remaining marinade and turn to coat. Seal bag or cover container; refrigerate for 4 hours, turning occasionally. Drain and discard marinade. Grill chicken, covered, over medium coals for 12-16 minutes, turning occasionally. Brush with reserved marinade. Grill, uncovered, for 8-10 minutes or until juices run clear, basting and turning several times. **Yield:** 6-8 servings. **Editor's Note:** The wings may be baked in a 375° oven for 30-40 minutes or until juices run clear.

## POTATO-TOPPED CHILI LOAF

*Glenn Schildknecht, Savannah, Missouri*

**(Pictured above)**

*Here's a meat loaf that constitutes a whole meal. The beef, potatoes, corn and beans will satisfy the heartiest of appetites.*

1-1/2 pounds lean ground beef
    3/4 cup diced onion
    1/3 cup saltine crumbs
    1 egg
    3 tablespoons milk
    1 tablespoon chili powder
1/2 teaspoon salt
TOPPING:
    3 cups hot mashed potatoes (with milk and butter)
    1 can (11 ounces) Mexicorn, drained
    1 can (15-1/2 ounces) kidney beans, rinsed and drained
1/4 cup thinly sliced green onions
    1 cup (4 ounces) shredded cheddar *or* taco cheese, *divided*

Combine the first seven ingredients and mix well. Press into an ungreased 9-in. square baking pan. Bake at 375° for 25 minutes or until no longer pink; drain. Combine the potatoes, corn, beans, onions and 1/2 cup of cheese; spread over meat loaf. Sprinkle with the remaining cheese. Bake 15 minutes longer or until the potato layer is lightly browned and heated through. **Yield:** 6 servings.

**WHEN THE KITCHEN** *heats up before you even turn on the oven, cooking outside on the grill is a wonderful way to keep your cool.*

**GREAT GRILLING.** Clockwise from upper right: Pizza on the Grill (p. 30), Teriyaki Beef Kabobs (p. 34), Hawaiian Honey Burgers (p. 34), Spicy Grilled Chicken (p. 35), Campfire Bundles (p. 34), Pork and Apple Skewers (p. 30), Barbecued Chuck Roast (p. 34) and Maple-Glazed Chicken Wings (p. 31).

## TERIYAKI BEEF KABOBS

*Lisa Hector, Estevan, Saskatchewan*

**(Pictured on page 33)**

*My sister-in-law brought this recipe on a family camping trip, and we fixed it for an outdoor potluck. It was so delicious I asked if I could have a copy.*

    1/4 cup vegetable oil
    1/4 cup orange juice
    1/4 cup soy sauce
      1 teaspoon garlic powder
      1 teaspoon ground ginger
1-3/4 pounds beef tenderloin, cut into 1-inch
        cubes
    3/4 pound cherry tomatoes
    1/2 pound fresh whole mushrooms
      2 large green peppers, cubed
      1 large red onion, cut into wedges
Hot cooked rice, optional

In a resealable plastic bag or shallow glass container, combine the first five ingredients and mix well. Reserve 1/2 cup for basting and refrigerate. Add beef to remaining marinade; turn to coat. Seal bag or cover container; refrigerate for 1 hour, turning occasionally. Drain and discard the marinade. On metal or soaked bamboo skewers, alternate beef, tomatoes, mushrooms, green peppers and onions. Grill, uncovered, over medium coals for 3 minutes on each side. Baste with reserved marinade. Continue turning and basting for 8-10 minutes or until meat reaches desired doneness (for rare, a meat thermometer should read 140°; medium, 160°; well-done, 170°). Serve meat and vegetables over rice if desired. **Yield:** 6-8 servings.

## HAWAIIAN HONEY BURGERS

*Sheryl Creech, Lancaster, California*

**(Pictured on page 32)**

*These burgers were a favorite when I was growing up. I now use them as a way to "fancy up" a barbecue without a lot of extra preparation.*

      2 pounds ground beef
    1/2 cup honey
    1/4 teaspoon ground cinnamon
    1/4 teaspoon paprika
    1/4 teaspoon curry powder
    1/8 teaspoon ground ginger
    1/8 teaspoon ground nutmeg
    1/4 cup soy sauce
      1 can (23 ounces) sliced pineapple, drained
      8 hamburger buns, split and toasted
Lettuce leaves, optional

In a bowl, combine the first seven ingredients; mix well. Shape into eight 3/4-in.-thick patties. Grill the burgers, uncovered, over medium-hot coals for 3 minutes on each side. Brush with soy sauce. Continue grilling for 4-6 minutes or until juices run clear, basting and turning several times. During the last 4 minutes, grill the pineapple slices until browned, turning once. Serve burgers and pineapple on buns with lettuce if desired. **Yield:** 8 servings.

## CAMPFIRE BUNDLES

*Lauri Krause, Jackson, Nebraska*

**(Pictured on page 32)**

*A family camping trip's where I "invented" this recipe. I'd brought along a hodgepodge of ingredients, so I just mixed them all together and threw them on the grill. Everyone said the bundles were delicious. Ever since, I've grilled them at home.*

      1 large sweet onion, sliced
      1 *each* large green, sweet red and yellow
        peppers, sliced
      4 medium potatoes, sliced 1/2 inch thick
      6 medium carrots, sliced 1/4 inch thick
      1 small cabbage, sliced
      2 medium tomatoes, chopped
      1 to 1-1/2 pounds fully cooked Polish
        sausage, cut into 1/2-inch pieces
    1/2 cup butter *or* margarine
      1 teaspoon salt
    1/2 teaspoon pepper

Place vegetables in order listed on three pieces of double-layered heavy-duty foil (about 18 in. x 18 in.). Add sausage; dot with butter. Sprinkle with salt and pepper. Fold foil around the mixture and seal tightly. Grill, covered, over medium coals for 30 minutes. Turn and grill 30 minutes longer or until vegetables are tender. **Yield:** 6 servings.

## BARBECUED CHUCK ROAST

*Ardis Gautier, Lamont, Oklahoma*

**(Pictured on page 32)**

*Whether I serve this roast for church dinners, company or family, it is always a hit. If there's ever any left over, it makes good sandwiches, too.*

    1/3 cup cider vinegar
    1/4 cup ketchup
      2 tablespoons vegetable oil
      2 tablespoons soy sauce
      1 tablespoon Worcestershire sauce

1 teaspoon garlic powder
1 teaspoon prepared mustard
1 teaspoon salt
1/4 teaspoon pepper
1 boneless chuck roast (2-1/2 to 3 pounds)
1/2 cup applesauce

In a large resealable plastic bag or shallow glass container, combine the first nine ingredients; mix well. Add roast and turn to coat. Seal bag or cover container; refrigerate for at least 3 hours, turning occasionally. Remove roast. Pour marinade into a small saucepan; bring to a boil. Reduce heat; simmer for 15 minutes. Meanwhile, grill roast, covered, over indirect heat for 20 minutes, turning occasionally. Add applesauce to marinade; brush over roast. Continue basting and turning the roast several times for 1 to 1-1/2 hours or until meat reaches desired doneness (for rare, a meat thermometer should read 140°; medium, 160°; well-done, 170°). **Yield:** 6-8 servings.

## SPICY GRILLED CHICKEN

*Edith Maki, Hancock, Michigan*

**(Pictured on page 32)**

*Very near the top of the list of foods I prepare for company is this chicken. It's easy to fix and has never flopped. It's a family favorite, too.*

3/4 cup finely chopped onion
1/2 cup grapefruit juice
2 tablespoons olive *or* vegetable oil
2 tablespoons soy sauce
1 tablespoon honey
1 garlic clove, minced
1-1/2 teaspoons salt
1-1/2 teaspoons rubbed sage
1-1/2 teaspoons dried thyme
1 teaspoon ground allspice
1 teaspoon garlic powder
1/2 teaspoon ground cinnamon
1/2 teaspoon ground nutmeg
1/4 teaspoon cayenne pepper
1/4 teaspoon pepper
6 boneless skinless chicken breast halves

In a large resealable plastic bag or shallow glass container, combine the first 15 ingredients; mix well. Reserve 1/3 cup for basting and refrigerate. Add chicken to remaining marinade and turn to coat. Seal bag or cover container; refrigerate overnight. Drain and discard marinade. Grill chicken, uncovered, over medium coals for 3 minutes on each side. Baste with reserved marinade. Continue grilling for 6-8 minutes or until juices run clear, basting and turning several times. **Yield:** 6 servings.

## FRESH TOMATO PASTA TOSS

*Cheryl Travagliante, Independence, Ohio*

**(Pictured below)**

*My parents went on vacation one year just as their tomato crop—and mine—was ready to harvest, so I had to come up with new ideas for using tomatoes. My husband loved this creation!*

☑ This tasty dish uses less fat, sugar or salt. Recipe includes Nutritional Analysis and Diabetic Exchanges.

3 pounds tomatoes
2 garlic cloves, minced
1 tablespoon vegetable oil
1 tablespoon minced fresh parsley *or* 1 teaspoon dried parsley flakes
1 tablespoon minced fresh basil *or* 1 teaspoon dried basil
2 teaspoons minced fresh oregano *or* 3/4 teaspoon dried oregano
1 teaspoon salt
1/4 teaspoon sugar
1/8 teaspoon pepper
1/4 cup whipping cream
1 pound tube pasta, cooked and drained
1/4 cup shredded Parmesan *or* Romano cheese

In a saucepan, bring water to a boil; dip tomatoes in water. Peel skins and discard. Chop pulp; set aside. In a skillet over medium heat, saute garlic in oil. Add tomato pulp, parsley, basil, oregano, salt, sugar and pepper; mix well. Bring to a boil; reduce heat. Add cream; heat through. Pour over hot pasta and toss to coat. Sprinkle with cheese. **Yield:** 8 servings. **Nutritional Analysis:** One serving (prepared with Parmesan cheese) equals 277 calories, 244 mg sodium, 13 mg cholesterol, 46 gm carbohydrate, 9 gm protein, 7 gm fat. **Diabetic Exchanges:** 2-1/2 starch, 1-1/2 fat, 1 vegetable.

## HAM 'N' POTATOES AU GRATIN

*Leila Long, Rock Hill, South Carolina*

**(Pictured below)**

*The comforting flavor of ham and potatoes can't be beat. This is a nice recipe to share at covered dish dinners—it's a meal in itself.*

　1/4 cup chopped green onions
　1/4 cup chopped green pepper
　　2 tablespoons butter *or* margarine, *divided*
　　3 cups diced peeled potatoes, cooked
　　1 pound fully cooked ham, cubed
　1/4 cup mayonnaise
　　1 tablespoon all-purpose flour
　1/8 teaspoon pepper
　3/4 cup milk
　　1 cup (4 ounces) shredded cheddar cheese

In a skillet, saute onions and green pepper in 1 tablespoon butter until tender. Combine onions and pepper with potatoes, ham and mayonnaise; pour into an ungreased 11-in. x 7-in. x 2-in. baking dish. In a saucepan, melt remaining butter. Stir in flour and pepper until smooth. Gradually add milk; bring to a boil. Cook and stir for 1 minute. Stir in cheese just until melted. Pour over potato mixture. Cover and bake at 350° for 30 minutes or until bubbly. **Yield:** 8 servings.

## DEEP-DISH CHICKEN POTPIE

*Dixie Terry, Marion, Illinois*

*I remember Sunday dinners at my grandma's farm. Chicken potpie was probably second in popularity only to chicken and dumplings. I like to collect heritage recipes from my area and hope to compile them someday into a cookbook.*

　　2 cups all-purpose flour
　1/2 teaspoon salt
　2/3 cup cold butter *or* margarine
　　6 to 8 tablespoons cold water
FILLING:
　　3 tablespoons butter *or* margarine
　　3 tablespoons all-purpose flour
　　1 cup half-and-half cream
　1/2 cup chicken broth
　1/2 teaspoon salt
　1/2 teaspoon dried thyme
　1/4 teaspoon pepper
2-1/2 cups cubed cooked chicken
　　2 cups fresh *or* frozen peas
　　2 medium potatoes, cut into 1/2-inch
　　　cubes
　　3 medium carrots, thinly sliced
　1/4 cup chopped onion
　　1 teaspoon milk

In a bowl, combine flour and salt; cut in butter until mixture resembles coarse crumbs. Add water, 1 tablespoon at a time, stirring with a fork until a ball forms. Divide pastry into thirds. On a floured surface, roll two-thirds of the pastry to fit an ungreased 2-qt. baking dish; line dish with pastry. For filling, melt butter in a large saucepan; stir in flour until smooth. Add cream, broth, salt, thyme and pepper. Bring to a boil; boil for 2 minutes, stirring constantly. Stir in chicken, peas, potatoes, carrots and onion. Pour into prepared dish. Roll out remaining pastry to fit top of dish. Place over filling; seal edges. Cut slits in top; brush with milk. Bake at 350° for 1 hour or until vegetables are tender. **Yield:** 6 servings.

## HEARTY KRAUTWICHES

*Karen Ann Bland, Gove, Kansas*

*With sauerkraut and liverwurst, this is an ethnic sandwich that you'll find hard to resist. The recipe has strong ties to our German ancestors who settled in this part of Kansas.*

> 4 hard-cooked eggs, *divided*
> 1 can (14 ounces) sauerkraut, well drained
> 1/3 cup Russian salad dressing
> 1 medium red onion
> 6 onion buns, split
> 8 ounces thinly sliced salami
> 6 slices Muenster cheese
> 6 ounces sliced liverwurst
> 6 lettuce leaves
> Additional Russian salad dressing, optional

In a small bowl, chop one egg; stir in sauerkraut and salad dressing. Chop half of the onion; add to sauerkraut mixture. Slice remaining eggs and onion; set aside. On bun bottoms, layer salami, cheese, liverwurst, lettuce, onion and about 1/3 cup of sauerkraut mixture. Top each with sliced eggs and additional salad dressing if desired. Replace bun tops. **Yield:** 6 servings.

## JUICY ROAST TURKEY

*Terrie Herman, N. Myrtle Beach, South Carolina*

**(Pictured above right)**

*I can't wait to serve this juicy turkey at Thanksgiving—so I make it several times a year. It's even more delicious than its aroma while baking!*

> 1/4 cup ground mustard
> 2 tablespoons Worcestershire sauce
> 2 tablespoons olive *or* vegetable oil

> 1/2 teaspoon vinegar
> 1 teaspoon salt
> 1/8 teaspoon pepper
> 1 turkey (10 to 12 pounds)
> 1 medium onion, quartered
> 2 celery ribs, quartered lengthwise
> Fresh parsley sprigs
> 2 bacon strips
> 1/4 cup butter *or* margarine, softened
> Additional olive *or* vegetable oil
> Cheesecloth,* optional
> 2 cups chicken broth
> 1 cup water

Combine the first six ingredients in a small bowl; stir to form a smooth paste. Brush over inside and outside of turkey. Cover or place in a 2-gal. resealable plastic bag; refrigerate for 1-24 hours. Place turkey on a rack in a large roasting pan. Place onion, celery and parsley inside turkey cavity. Lay bacon across breast. Spread butter between legs and body. Tie drumsticks together. Brush turkey with oil, or take a piece of cheesecloth large enough to cover turkey and soak it in oil; place over the turkey. Pour broth and water into pan. Bake, uncovered, at 325° for 3-1/2 to 4 hours or until a meat thermometer reads 185°, basting frequently. Remove from oven; discard cheesecloth and bacon. Let stand 20 minutes before carving. Thicken pan juices for gravy if desired. **Yield:** 10-12 servings. ***Editor's Note:** Cheesecloth is available in the housewares section of your grocery store. This recipe can be prepared without the cheesecloth.

## CUBE STEAK PARMIGIANA

*Kathryn Bray, Westfield, Indiana*

**(Pictured below)**

*I received this recipe from a friend when I was a newlywed. Now my family of six loves it so much I have to double the recipe! I like to serve it with pasta, a tossed salad and homemade bread.*

    3 tablespoons all-purpose flour
    1/2 teaspoon salt
    1/4 teaspoon pepper
    1 egg
    1 tablespoon water
    1/3 cup grated Parmesan cheese
    1/3 cup finely crushed saltines (about 10)
    1/2 teaspoon dried basil
    6 cube steaks (about 4 ounces *each*)
    2 tablespoons vegetable oil
SAUCE:
    1 can (15 ounces) tomato sauce
    1 tablespoon sugar
    1 garlic clove, minced
    1/2 teaspoon dried oregano, *divided*
    3 slices mozzarella cheese, halved
    1/3 cup grated Parmesan cheese

In three shallow bowls, combine flour, salt and pepper; beat egg and water; and combine Parme-san cheese, saltines and basil. Dip steaks in flour mixture and egg mixture, then roll in cheese mixture. In a large skillet, heat 1 tablespoon of oil over medium-high heat. Brown three steaks on both sides. Remove to a greased 13-in. x 9-in. x 2-in. baking pan. Repeat with the remaining steaks, adding additional oil as needed. Bake, uncovered, at 375° for 25 minutes. Drain any pan juices. Combine the tomato sauce, sugar, garlic and 1/4 teaspoon of oregano; pour over steaks. Bake 20 minutes longer. Place mozzarella cheese on steaks. Sprinkle with Parmesan and remaining oregano. Return to the oven for 5 minutes or until cheese is melted. **Yield:** 6 servings.

## MARINATED PORK STRIPS

*Karen Peterson, Hainesville, Illinois*

*Especially if you're having company, this is a good recipe. While it looks like you spent time on it, it's actually easy.*

    5 tablespoons soy sauce
    1/4 cup ketchup
    3 tablespoons vinegar
    3 tablespoons chili sauce
    3 tablespoons sugar
    2 teaspoons salt
    1/8 teaspoon pepper
    3 garlic cloves, minced
    2 cans (12 ounces *each*) lemon-lime soda
    2 pounds pork tenderloin, cut lengthwise
       into 1/2-inch strips

In a large resealable plastic bag or shallow glass container, combine the first nine ingredients. Add pork and turn to coat. Seal bag or cover container; refrigerate overnight. Drain and discard marinade. Thread pork onto metal or soaked bamboo skewers. Grill over hot coals for 12 minutes, turning once. **Yield:** 6-8 servings.

## FLANK STEAK SANTA FE

*Tanya Johnson, San Diego, California*

*This recipe is truly representative of the flavors we enjoy in this region. It's a favorite in my family for that special Saturday night dinner.*

    3/4 pound spicy sausage *or* chorizo, casings
       removed
    2 eggs, beaten
    1-1/2 cups unseasoned croutons
    1/3 cup sliced green onions
    1/3 cup minced fresh parsley

# Ham, Pork Secrets Are in Sauce

IT'S NOT what Kathy Gilmore puts in her pork that gives it such a tantalizing sweet/tart zip—it's what she tops the meat with that sets taste buds tingling!

"These fruity sauces are just right for special occasions and festive meals on holidays like Easter or Christmas," confirms Kathy, a Marshalltown, Iowa farm wife. "They're a pretty and fun way to 'dress up' both pork and ham.

"The recipes came from our local pork producers group," notes Kathy, who advises experimenting with different flavors. "Try various tart jellies—crab apple, cherry or currant—to find your family's favorite."

### NUTMEG ORANGE SAUCE

**1 jar (18 ounces) orange marmalade**
**1/2 cup orange juice**
**1/8 teaspoon ground nutmeg**
**Pinch white pepper**

In a small saucepan, combine the marmalade, orange juice, nutmeg and pepper; simmer until heated through. Serve warm with sliced ham. **Yield:** 2 cups.

### ZIPPY CHERRY SAUCE

**1 can (21 ounces) cherry pie filling**
**1/4 cup lemon juice**
**1 tablespoon brown sugar**
**1/2 teaspoon ground ginger**
**1/4 teaspoon seasoned salt**
**1/4 teaspoon vinegar**

In a small saucepan, combine pie filling, lemon juice, sugar, ginger, salt and vinegar; bring to a boil, stirring constantly. Serve warm with pork roast, pork chops or pork tenderloin. **Yield:** 2-1/4 cups.

---

**1 flank steak (1-1/2 to 2 pounds)**
**3 tablespoons vegetable oil**
**1 jar (16 ounces) picante sauce *or* salsa verde**
**Additional picante sauce *or* salsa, optional**

In a skillet, brown and crumble sausage; drain. Add eggs, croutons, onions and parsley; mix well. Slice steak in half horizontally to within 1/2 in. of end; open steak and pound to 1/2-in. thickness. Spread with sausage mixture. Roll up, jelly-roll style, beginning at a short end; tie with string. In a large skillet, brown steak in oil. Place in a 13-in. x 9-in. x 2-in. baking dish. Spread picante sauce over steak. Cover and bake at 350° for 1-1/2 to 1-3/4 hours or until tender. Garnish with additional picante sauce if desired. **Yield:** 6-8 servings.

### MEXICAN-STYLE CHICKEN KIEV

*Frances Patton, Wichita Falls, Texas*

*This is a recipe our whole family enjoys. I've shared it with friends, who tell me their teenage boys just love it.*

**8 boneless skinless chicken breast halves**
**2 cans (4 ounces *each*) whole green chilies, drained**
**1 block (4 ounces) Monterey Jack cheese**
**1/2 cup dry bread crumbs**
**1/4 cup grated Parmesan cheese**
**2 teaspoons chili powder**
**1/2 teaspoon garlic salt**
**1/2 teaspoon ground cumin**
**1/4 teaspoon pepper**
**2 tablespoons butter *or* margarine, melted**
**Taco sauce, optional**

Flatten chicken to 1/4-in. thickness. Remove seeds from the chilies and cut into eight pieces. Cut cheese into eight 2-1/2-in. x 1/2-in. sticks. Place one cheese stick and one piece of chili in the center of each chicken breast. Fold short sides over and roll up along long sides to enclose filling (secure with a toothpick if necessary). In a shallow bowl, combine bread crumbs, Parmesan cheese, chili powder, garlic salt, cumin and pepper. Dip chicken in butter, then roll in crumb mixture. Place, seam side down, in a greased 13-in. x 9-in. x 2-in. baking dish. Bake, uncovered, at 400° for 25-30 minutes or until chicken juices run clear. Remove toothpicks. Serve with taco sauce if desired. **Yield:** 8 servings.

## SPICY PORK ROAST

*Sandy Birkey, Bloomington, Indiana*

*I enjoy cooking and entertaining friends and family. My husband and I often cook this roast together for these gatherings.*

        2 teaspoons garlic powder
        2 teaspoons salt
        2 teaspoons pepper
    1-1/2 teaspoons ground mustard
    1-1/2 teaspoons onion powder
    1-1/2 teaspoons paprika
        1 teaspoon rubbed sage
    1/4 to 1/2 teaspoon cayenne pepper
        1 boneless pork loin roast (3 to 3-1/2
          pounds)

Combine the first eight ingredients; rub over entire roast. Cover and refrigerate overnight. Place roast on a greased rack in a roasting pan. Bake, uncovered, at 350° for 2-1/4 to 2-3/4 hours or until a meat thermometer reads 160°-170°. Let stand 10 minutes before slicing. **Yield:** 8-10 servings.

## SWEET-AND-SOUR SKEWERED SHRIMP

*Rena Malek, Dubuque, Iowa*

*We prepare these tangy skewers on our portable grill when we go boating. My husband thinks they're great.*

    1/2 cup barbecue sauce
    1/4 cup pineapple preserves
    1/4 cup lemon juice
      4 teaspoons soy sauce
    1/2 teaspoon ground ginger
     30 large fresh shrimp (about 2 pounds),
          shelled and deveined
      1 to 2 large green peppers, cut into 1-inch
          pieces
    1/2 pound fresh mushrooms, halved

Combine the first five ingredients in a small saucepan; bring to a boil over medium heat, stirring frequently. Remove from the heat; cool. Set aside 1/2 cup for basting. Place remaining sauce in a large resealable plastic bag or shallow glass container; add shrimp. Seal bag or cover container; refrigerate for 30 minutes. Drain and discard marinade. Thread shrimp, green peppers and mushrooms alternately on metal or soaked bamboo skewers. Grill, uncovered, over medium-hot coals for 2 minutes on each side. Brush with reserved sauce. Continue grilling for 4-8 minutes or until shrimp are pink throughout, turning and basting several times. **Yield:** 6 servings.

## CHICKEN WITH CRANBERRIES

*Pauline Olsson, Edina, Minnesota*

**(Pictured above)**

*When cranberries are in season, I like to stock the freezer so I can serve this dish year-round. The sauce's tangy flavor complements the chicken very well.*

    3/4 cup all-purpose flour
    1/2 teaspoon salt
    1/4 teaspoon pepper
      6 boneless skinless chicken breast halves
    1/4 cup butter *or* margarine
      1 cup fresh *or* frozen cranberries
      1 cup water
    1/2 cup packed brown sugar
      1 tablespoon red wine vinegar
    Dash ground nutmeg

In a shallow bowl, combine flour, salt and pepper; dredge the chicken. In a large skillet, cook chicken in butter until browned on both sides. Remove chicken and set aside. In the same skillet, combine the cranberries, water, brown sugar, vinegar and nutmeg; cover and simmer for 5 minutes. Place chicken on top; cover and simmer for 30 minutes. To serve, spoon cranberry mixture over chicken. **Yield:** 6 servings.

Main Dishes

## HONEY-GARLIC PORK RIBS

*Patsy Saulnier, South Ohio, Nova Scotia*

*This is a great recipe I discovered recently. I make it often because we really enjoy it...hope you do, too!*

    4 pounds pork spareribs *or* pork loin back
       ribs
    1/2 cup honey
    1/2 cup packed brown sugar
    3 tablespoons soy sauce
    1/2 teaspoon garlic powder
    1/2 teaspoon ground ginger
    1/2 teaspoon ground mustard

Cut ribs into serving-size pieces; place in a large resealable plastic bag. Combine remaining ingredients; pour over ribs. Seal bag; turn once. Refrigerate for several hours or overnight, turning bag occasionally. Drain ribs, reserving marinade. Return marinade to the refrigerator. Place ribs on a rack in a greased shallow baking pan. Cover and bake at 350° for 1-1/2 hours. Drain. Pour the marinade over ribs. Bake, uncovered, 45 minutes longer or until meat is tender, brushing occasionally with pan juices. **Yield:** 4 servings.

## GOLDEN BAKED WHITEFISH

*Polly Habel, Monson, Massachusetts*

*This recipe represents our part of the country as fishing is very big here. We eat a lot of fish, and this is one of our favorite ways to prepare it.*

✓ This tasty dish uses less fat, sugar or salt. Recipe includes Nutritional Analysis and Diabetic Exchanges.

    2 pounds whitefish fillets
    1/8 teaspoon pepper
    1 egg white
    1/2 teaspoon salt, optional
    1/4 cup mayonnaise
    1/4 teaspoon dill weed
    1/2 teaspoon onion juice *or* 1 teaspoon
       grated onion
Fresh dill and lemon wedges, optional

Place fish in a greased 13-in. x 9-in. x 2-in. baking dish; sprinkle with pepper. Beat egg white with salt if desired until stiff peaks form. Fold in mayonnaise, dill and onion juice; spoon over fish. Bake, uncovered, at 425° for 15-20 minutes or until topping is puffed and fish flakes easily with a fork. Garnish with dill and lemon if desired. **Yield:** 8 servings. **Nutritional Analysis:** One serving (prepared with light mayonnaise and without salt) equals 201 calories, 165 mg sodium, 70 mg cholesterol, 1 gm carbohydrate, 23 gm protein, 11 gm fat. **Diabetic Exchanges:** 3 lean meat, 1/2 fat.

## CREAMY PORK TENDERLOIN

*Janice Christofferson*
*Eagle River, Wisconsin*

**(Pictured below)**

*For years, I've been making this recipe both for my husband and me and for guests as well.*

    2 pork tenderloins (about 1 pound *each*)
    1 egg
    1 tablespoon water
    1/2 teaspoon dried rosemary, crushed
    1/4 teaspoon pepper
Dash garlic powder
    1 cup seasoned dry bread crumbs
    3 tablespoons vegetable oil
    1/2 pound fresh mushrooms, sliced
    2 tablespoons butter *or* margarine
    1 can (10-3/4 ounces) cream of chicken
       soup, undiluted
    1 cup (8 ounces) sour cream
    1/4 cup chicken broth

Cut each tenderloin into eight pieces. Place each piece between two pieces of plastic wrap or waxed paper and flatten to 3/4-in. thickness. In a shallow dish, combine the next five ingredients. Dip pork into egg mixture, then into bread crumbs. In a large skillet over medium heat, brown pork in oil for 5 minutes on each side. Remove to a 13-in. x 9-in. x 2-in. baking dish; keep warm. In the same skillet, saute mushrooms in butter until tender. Stir in soup, sour cream and broth; pour over pork. Cover and bake at 325° for 1 hour or until pork is tender. **Yield:** 6-8 servings.

## CAULIFLOWER AND HAM CASSEROLE

*Rosemary Flexman, Waukesha, Wisconsin*

**(Pictured below)**

*My mother made this recipe often while I was growing up. I remember leaning on the table to watch her.*

☑ This tasty dish uses less fat, sugar or salt. Recipe includes Nutritional Analysis and Diabetic Exchanges.

   1 tablespoon chopped onion
   3 tablespoons butter *or* margarine, ***divided***
   2 tablespoons all-purpose flour
1/2 teaspoon salt, optional
Pepper to taste
   1 cup milk
1/2 cup shredded cheddar cheese
   1 medium head cauliflower, cut into florets, cooked and drained
   2 cups cubed fully cooked ham
   1 jar (4-1/2 ounces) sliced mushrooms, drained
   1 jar (2 ounces) diced pimientos, drained
   6 saltines, crumbled

In a saucepan over medium heat, saute onion in 2 tablespoons of butter until tender. Stir in flour, salt if desired and pepper until smooth. Gradually add milk; cook and stir for 2 minutes or until thick and bubbly. Remove from the heat; stir in cheese until melted. Fold in cauliflower, ham, mushrooms and pimientos. Pour into a greased 2-qt. casserole. In a small saucepan, brown cracker crumbs in remaining butter; sprinkle over casserole. Cover and bake at 350° for 20 minutes. Uncover and bake 5-10 minutes longer or until heated through. **Yield:** 6 servings. **Nutritional Analysis:** One serving (prepared with margarine, skim milk and low-fat ham and without salt ) equals 209 calories, 942 mg sodium, 33 mg cholesterol, 11 gm carbohydrate, 15 gm protein, 12 gm fat. **Diabetic Exchanges:** 2 meat, 2 vegetable.

## PORK ROAST WITH APPLE TOPPING

*Paula Neal, Dolores, Colorado*

*This recipe's one my mother-in-law and I developed together. The topping also goes great with pork chops, lean sausage balls or patties and ham.*

   1 boneless pork loin roast (3 to 3-1/2 pounds), trimmed
1/2 teaspoon poultry seasoning
   1 jar (10 ounces) apple jelly
   1 cup apple juice
1/2 teaspoon ground cardamom
   1 cup chopped peeled tart fresh *or* dried apples
   3 tablespoons chopped fresh *or* dried cranberries
   5 teaspoons cornstarch
   2 tablespoons water

Place roast on a rack in a shallow roasting pan and rub with poultry seasoning. Bake, uncovered, at 325° for 2-1/2 hours or until a meat thermometer reads 160°-170°. For topping, combine the apple jelly, juice and cardamom in a saucepan. Cook and stir over low heat until smooth. Add apples and cranberries; cook until tender, about 5-10 minutes. Combine cornstarch and water; stir into apple mixture. Bring to a boil. Cook and stir over medium heat until thickened, about 1-2 minutes. Remove roast from oven and let stand for 10 minutes before slicing. Serve with apple topping. **Yield:** 8-10 servings (about 2 cups topping).

## MULLIGAN STEW

*Beth Schlea, Gibsonburg, Ohio*

*This hearty stew is packed with a colorful combination of vegetables and tender pieces of beef.*

☑ This tasty dish uses less fat, sugar or salt. Recipe includes Nutritional Analysis and Diabetic Exchanges.

1/4 cup all-purpose flour
   1 teaspoon pepper
   1 pound beef stew meat, cut into 1-inch cubes
   1 tablespoon vegetable oil
   2 cans (10-1/2 ounces *each*) beef broth
   1 cup water

2 bay leaves
1/2 teaspoon garlic salt
1/2 teaspoon dried oregano
1/2 teaspoon dried basil
1/2 teaspoon dill weed
3 medium carrots, cut into 1-inch slices
2 medium potatoes, peeled and cubed
2 celery ribs, cut into 1-inch slices
1 onion, cut into eight wedges
1 cup *each* frozen corn, green beans, lima beans and peas
1 tablespoon cornstarch
2 tablespoons cold water
1 tablespoon minced fresh parsley

Combine flour and pepper; toss with beef. In a Dutch oven, brown beef in oil. Add broth, water, bay leaves, garlic salt, oregano, basil and dill; bring to a boil. Reduce heat; cover and simmer until meat is tender, about 2 hours. Add carrots, potatoes, celery and onion; cover and simmer for 40 minutes. Add corn, beans and peas; cover and simmer 15 minutes longer or until vegetables are tender. Combine cornstarch and cold water until smooth; add to stew. Bring to a boil; boil and stir for 2 minutes. Remove bay leaves; add parsley. **Yield:** 8-10 servings. **Nutritional Analysis:** One 1-cup serving (prepared with low-sodium broth) equals 203 calories, 239 mg sodium, 31 mg cholesterol, 25 gm carbohydrate, 15 gm protein, 5 gm fat. **Diabetic Exchanges:** 2 vegetable, 1 starch, 1 meat.

## CRANBERRY-GLAZED PORK ROAST

*Madeline Strauss, Clinton Township, Michigan*

**(Pictured above)**

*Many pork recipes were too spicy for me, so I decided to try this sweeter alternative. That was almost 20 years ago, and it became a family favorite. It tastes great the day after in a cold sandwich, too.*

1 teaspoon salt
1/2 teaspoon pepper
1 boneless rolled pork loin roast (3 pounds)
1 cup jellied cranberry sauce
1/2 cup orange juice
1/4 cup packed brown sugar

Combine salt and pepper; rub over the roast. Place roast, fat side up, on a rack in a greased roasting pan. Bake, uncovered, at 350° for 1-1/2 hours. Meanwhile, combine cranberry sauce, orange juice and brown sugar in a saucepan; cook over medium heat until cranberry sauce melts. Brush a fourth over the roast. Bake 30 minutes longer; brush with another fourth of the glaze. Return to the oven for 15 minutes or until a meat thermometer reads 160°-170°. Let stand for 10 minutes before slicing. Warm remaining glaze; serve with roast. **Yield:** 6-8 servings.

## TURKEY PASTA PRIMAVERA

*Marilyn Schafer, Weidman, Michigan*

*This is a fast, easy and satisfying recipe that uses a wide array of vegetables and leftover turkey. My kids will eat vegetables when they're in a sauce, so I'm always on the lookout for a new way to serve them.*

☑ This tasty dish uses less fat, sugar or salt. Recipe includes Nutritional Analysis and Diabetic Exchanges.

    8 ounces fettuccine *or* spaghetti
    1 cup broccoli florets
    1 cup julienned carrots
  1/2 cup chopped sweet red pepper
    2 tablespoons all-purpose flour
1-3/4 cups milk
    1 package (8 ounces) cream cheese, cubed
  1/2 cup chopped green onions
  3/4 teaspoon Italian seasoning
  1/4 teaspoon garlic powder
  1/8 teaspoon pepper
  1/2 teaspoon salt, optional
    2 cups julienned cooked turkey
  1/2 cup grated Parmesan cheese

Cook pasta according to package directions, adding broccoli, carrots and red pepper during the last 5 minutes. Meanwhile, in a medium saucepan, stir flour and milk until smooth. Add the cream cheese, onions and seasonings; bring to a boil over medium-low heat. Cook and stir 1-2 minutes. Add turkey and Parmesan cheese; heat through. Drain pasta; toss with cheese sauce. **Yield:** 6 servings. **Nutritional Analysis:** One serving (prepared with skim milk, light cream cheese and turkey breast and without salt) equals 333 calories, 348 mg sodium, 50 mg cholesterol, 40 gm carbohydrate, 23 gm protein, 8 gm fat. **Diabetic Exchanges:** 2 starch, 2 meat, 2 vegetable, 1/2 fat.

## CHICKEN BROCCOLI PACKETS

*Lynda Simmons, Fayetteville, North Carolina*

*I like this recipe because it's simple to prepare...and cleanup is a snap!*

    4 boneless skinless chicken breast halves
Seasoned salt
    1 package (10 ounces) frozen broccoli
      spears
    1 medium onion, sliced into rings
    4 teaspoons lemon juice
    4 tablespoons butter *or* margarine

Place each chicken breast in the center of a piece of heavy-duty foil (about 12 in. x 12 in.). Sprinkle with seasoned salt. Top each with 2 broccoli spears, 3-4 onion rings, 1 teaspoon of lemon

## APPLE-HAM GRILLED CHEESE

*Shirley Brazel, Rocklin, California*

**(Pictured above)**

*After finding this recipe years ago, I altered it to fit our tastes by adding the apples and walnuts. Our whole family loves them!*

    1 cup chopped tart apples
  1/3 cup mayonnaise
  1/4 cup finely chopped walnuts
    8 slices process American cheese
    8 slices sourdough bread
    4 slices fully cooked ham
  1/4 cup butter *or* margarine, softened

Combine apples, mayonnaise and walnuts. Place a slice of cheese on four slices of bread. Layer each with 1/3 cup of the apple mixture, a slice of ham and another slice of cheese; cover with remaining bread. Butter the outsides of the sandwiches. Cook in a large skillet over medium heat on each side until bread is golden brown and cheese is melted. **Yield:** 4 servings.

juice and 1 tablespoon of butter. Fold foil around chicken and seal tightly. Grill, covered, over medium-hot coals for 20 minutes or until meat juices run clear. Serve in foil packets if desired. **Yield:** 4 servings.

## HONEY PORK AND PEPPERS

*Carol Heim, Nokesville, Virginia*

**(Pictured below)**

*I'm always trying new recipes on my husband and son. This easy, quick and delicious one is a keeper— a nice change from pork roast or pork chops.*

1-1/2 pounds boneless pork, cut into 1-inch
    cubes
  2 tablespoons vegetable oil
  1 envelope (.87 ounce) brown gravy mix
  1 cup water
1/4 cup honey
  3 tablespoons soy sauce
  2 tablespoons red wine vinegar
1/2 teaspoon ground ginger
1/8 teaspoon garlic powder
  1 medium onion, cut into wedges
  1 medium sweet red pepper, cut into
    1-inch pieces
  1 medium green pepper, cut into 1-inch
    pieces
Hot cooked rice

In a large skillet over medium heat, cook pork in oil until browned, about 15 minutes. Combine gravy mix, water, honey, soy sauce, vinegar, ginger and garlic powder; add to the pork. Cover and simmer for 20 minutes, stirring occasionally. Add onion and peppers; cook 5-10 minutes longer. Serve over rice. **Yield:** 4-6 servings.

## PINE NUT CHICKEN

*Wanda Holoubek, Omaha, Nebraska*

*I like trying new dishes and getting away from the same meals all the time.*

3/4 cup all-purpose flour
1/4 teaspoon salt
1/8 teaspoon pepper
  2 eggs
  6 boneless skinless chicken breast halves
    (1-1/2 pounds)
  2 cups chopped pine nuts *or* almonds
1/3 cup butter *or* margarine

Place flour, salt and pepper in a shallow bowl. Beat eggs in another shallow bowl. Flatten chicken to 1/2-in. thickness. Coat with flour mixture; dip into eggs. Pat the nuts firmly onto both sides of chicken. In a large skillet over medium heat, cook the chicken in butter for 4-5 minutes on each side or until browned and juices run clear. **Yield:** 4-6 servings.

# Secret to Recipe Grows on Trees

BRANCHING OUT, Michelle Hatfield has come up with a deliciously different flavor of barbecued chicken. Her fruity sauce is sweetened with apples!

"I'd heard that people were lining up for the apple butter chicken served at a local restaurant," she writes from her Cincinnati, Ohio home. "Figuring homemade is always better, I decided to try my own version.

"My two daughters—who like low-fat dishes with a lot of taste—think this recipe's a real winner. The sauce is a fun variation on a traditional one, and the recipe's so quick and easy they can get the meal started before I arrive home.

The sauce also refrigerates well, so you can make it days ahead."

Everyone that tries her chicken agrees—Michelle's alternative is "appletizing"!

### APPLE BUTTER BARBECUED CHICKEN

✓ This tasty dish uses less fat, sugar or salt. Recipe includes Nutritional Analysis and Diabetic Exchanges.

4 boneless skinless chicken breast halves (1 pound)
1/3 cup apple butter
2 tablespoons salsa
2 tablespoons ketchup
1 tablespoon vegetable oil
1/2 teaspoon salt, optional
1/4 teaspoon garlic powder
2 drops Worcestershire sauce
2 drops liquid smoke, optional

Place chicken in a greased 8-in. square baking dish. Combine remaining ingredients; pour over chicken. Bake, uncovered, at 375° for 25 minutes or until meat juices run clear. **Yield:** 4 servings. **Nutritional Analysis:** One serving (prepared without salt and liquid smoke) equals 206 calories, 226 mg sodium, 63 mg cholesterol, 14 gm carbohydrate, 23 gm protein, 6 gm fat. **Diabetic Exchanges:** 3 very lean meat, 1-1/2 fruit.

### APRICOT-GLAZED CORNISH HENS

*Ruth Andrewson, Leavenworth, Washington*

*Filled with a well-seasoned stuffing, these savory hens make perfect individual servings. The hens smell so good while baking folks can hardly wait to eat.*

3 tablespoons chopped celery
3 tablespoons chopped onion
1/4 cup butter *or* margarine
3 cups dry bread cubes
1 can (4 ounces) mushroom stems and pieces, drained
1-1/2 teaspoons poultry seasoning
1/2 teaspoon rubbed sage
1/4 teaspoon salt
1/4 teaspoon pepper
3 to 4 tablespoons chicken broth
4 Cornish game hens (1-1/4 pounds *each*)
1 jar (12 ounces) apricot preserves, warmed
4 green onions (green part only), optional
Fresh rosemary sprigs, optional

In a large skillet, saute celery and onion in butter until tender; remove from heat. Add bread, mushrooms and seasonings; mix well. Toss with enough chicken broth just to moisten. Stuff hens; tie drumsticks together. Place on a rack in a large shallow baking pan. Cover and bake at 350° for 1 hour. Brush with preserves. Bake, uncovered, 30 to 45 minutes longer or until meat juices run clear, basting every 10-15 minutes. If using green onions, first soften them in boiling water or the microwave for a few seconds, then tie over the string used to tie the drumsticks together. Garnish platter with fresh rosemary sprigs if desired. **Yield:** 4 servings.

### REUNION BBQ'S

*Margery Bryan, Royal City, Washington*

*I found this recipe in our local Cattlewomen's cookbook. It's a favorite when I need to make lots of sandwiches for a crowd. Piled high on a pretty platter, they're always gobbled up in no time.*

5 pounds ground beef
2 cups chopped onion
3 cups water
2 tablespoons ketchup

2 to 3 tablespoons chili powder
2 tablespoons salt
1 tablespoon pepper
1 teaspoon ground mustard
1 cup quick-cooking oats
24 hamburger buns, split

In a large saucepan or Dutch oven, brown beef and onion over medium heat; drain. Add water, ketchup, chili powder, salt, pepper and mustard; bring to a boil. Add oats; mix well. Reduce heat; cover and simmer for 30 minutes. Serve on buns. **Yield:** 24 (1/2-cup) servings.

## SAVORY CRESCENT BUNDLES

*Margaret Pache, Mesa, Arizona*

*Each time I prepare this full-flavored dish, I'm reminded fondly of my mother, who made it often for me and my seven brothers and sisters. It was her favorite—and now it's ours, too.*

1 package (3 ounces) cream cheese, softened
3 tablespoons butter *or* margarine, melted, *divided*
2 cups cooked cubed chicken *or* turkey
2 tablespoons milk
1 tablespoon chopped chives
1 tablespoon chopped pimientos
1/4 teaspoon salt
1/8 teaspoon pepper
1 tube (8 ounces) refrigerated crescent rolls
1/2 cup seasoned bread crumbs
Additional chives *or* thin ribbon

In a mixing bowl, beat cream cheese and 2 tablespoons butter until smooth. Stir in chicken, milk, chives, pimientos, salt and pepper. Separate crescent dough into four rectangles; firmly press perforations to seal. Spoon 1/2 cup chicken mixture into center of each rectangle. Bring four corners of dough together and twist; pinch edges to seal. Brush tops with remaining butter. Sprinkle with bread crumbs. Place on an ungreased baking sheet. Bake at 350° for 20-25 minutes or until golden brown. Tie a chive or ribbon around each. **Yield:** 4 servings.

## SWEET-AND-SOUR RIBS

*Kate Raleigh, Salt Lake City, Utah*

**(Pictured at right)**

*I like making this for family dinners and potlucks at work. It supplies a nice change from everyday fare.*

4 pounds pork spareribs
1-1/2 teaspoons salt, *divided*
1/2 teaspoon pepper
1/3 cup chopped celery
1/3 cup chopped green pepper
2 tablespoons butter *or* margarine
1 can (20 ounces) pineapple tidbits
2 tablespoons cornstarch
1/3 cup vinegar
2 tablespoons soy sauce
1 tablespoon sugar
1 garlic clove, minced
1/2 teaspoon ground ginger

Cut ribs into serving-size pieces; place with bone side down on a rack in a greased shallow roasting pan. Sprinkle with 1 teaspoon salt and pepper. Cover and bake at 400° for 30 minutes; drain. Reduce heat to 350°; cover and bake 1 hour longer. In a saucepan, saute celery and green pepper in butter until tender. Drain pineapple, reserving juice. Set pineapple aside. Combine juice and cornstarch; add to saucepan and bring to a boil. Cook and stir until thickened, about 2 minutes. Add pineapple, vinegar, soy sauce, sugar, garlic, ginger and remaining salt; mix well. Spoon over ribs. Bake, uncovered, 25-30 minutes longer or until meat is tender. **Yield:** 4 servings.

## POLENTA WITH ITALIAN SAUSAGE

*Peggy Ratliff, North Tazewell, Virginia*

**(Pictured below)**

*This recipe came from my mom, who brought it over from Europe. When I first made it, everyone wanted to know where I got the recipe. I've copied it numerous times for friends.*

 4 cups water
 1 cup cornmeal
 1 teaspoon salt
 1 pound Italian sausage
 2 garlic cloves, minced
 2 tablespoons minced fresh parsley
 1 can (14-1/2 ounces) Italian stewed
   tomatoes
 1 can (6 ounces) tomato paste
 1/4 cup shredded Parmesan cheese

Combine water, cornmeal and salt in a double boiler or heavy saucepan; bring to a boil, stirring constantly. Reduce heat; cover and simmer for 1-1/2 hours, stirring occasionally. Meanwhile, brown the sausage and garlic in a large skillet; drain. Cool slightly. Cut sausage into 1-in. pieces; return to skillet. Add parsley, tomatoes and toma-

to paste; bring to a boil. Remove from the heat. Spread half of the cornmeal mixture in a serving dish; top with half of the sausage mixture. Repeat layers. Sprinkle with Parmesan cheese. Serve immediately. **Yield:** 6-8 servings.

## AUTUMN CHICKEN

*Debbi Jo Mullins, Canoga Park, California*

*My husband loves rich foods but really enjoys this light sweet chicken.*

☑ This tasty dish uses less fat, sugar or salt. Recipe includes Nutritional Analysis and Diabetic Exchanges.

 1 large onion, sliced
 1 tablespoon olive or vegetable oil
 2 cups sliced peeled tart apples
 6 boneless skinless chicken breast halves
   (1-1/2 pounds)
 1-1/2 cups unsweetened apple juice
 2 tablespoons honey

In a skillet, saute onion in oil until tender; add apples and saute 1 minute longer. Place chicken in a greased 13-in. x 9-in. x 2-in. baking dish. Top with onion mixture. Combine apple juice and honey; pour over all. Cover and bake at 350° for 45 minutes or until meat juices run clear. **Yield:** 6 servings. **Nutritional Analysis:** One serving equals 223 calories, 57 mg sodium, 63 mg cholesterol, 21 gm carbohydrate, 23 gm protein, 5 gm fat. **Diabetic Exchanges:** 3 very lean meat, 1-1/2 fruit, 1/2 fat.

## PORK BURGERS DELUXE

*Peggy Bellar, Howard, Kansas*

*I found this recipe in a book I got for my wedding. The flavor of the burgers is fantastic.*

 2 pounds ground pork
 1/3 cup vinegar
 1/4 cup packed brown sugar
 1 small onion, chopped
 2 tablespoons soy sauce
 1 teaspoon salt
 1 teaspoon garlic salt
 1 can (20 ounces) pineapple slices, drained
 10 bacon strips
 10 hamburger buns, split

Combine the first seven ingredients; mix well. Shape into 10 patties. Top each with a pineapple slice; wrap with a bacon strip and secure with a toothpick. Broil or grill over medium-hot coals for 15-20 minutes or until meat is no longer pink, turning once. Serve on buns. **Yield:** 10 servings.

# Tips to Make Pork Perfect

• Leftover barbecued pork chops make wonderful sandwiches. Just remove meat from the bones and chop in a food processor. Reheat the meat and serve on buns.
—*Deborah Imiolo-Schriver*
*Amherst, New York*

• When baking a pork chop casserole, keep it covered for the first 45 minutes. Uncover toward the end of the baking time to add a little browning.
—*Mardel Stenzel, Wells, Minnesota*

• For a no-fuss appetizer, wrap 1 pound bacon around 2 pounds cocktail wieners. Use a toothpick to secure each bacon slice to a wiener. Place in a slow cooker and top with 1 pound brown sugar. Heat on low for 6-8 hours.
—*Deborah Loney*
*Central City, Kentucky*

• For an eight-egg and bacon casserole, I add a can of undiluted cream of potato soup instead of milk to the eggs before beating. It gives the casserole more flavor and body as it cooks.
—*Valerie Trca, Waterloo, Iowa*

• Try this for a quick, freeze-ahead meal: Make your favorite ham ball recipe, placing the balls on a cookie sheet so they are not touching each other. Freeze until firm. Pack into freezer bags, top with additional sauce if desired and return to freezer. To serve, defrost the ham balls and reheat in a matter of minutes. —*Gloria Kaufmann*
*Orrville, Ohio*

• Need an easy holiday ham glaze? Combine 1 cup of canned whole-berry cranberry sauce, 3 tablespoons brown sugar and 1-1/2 teaspoons prepared mustard. Baste ham with glaze as it bakes.

To serve ham with a pretty garnish, line the platter with curly endive, then add canned peach halves, cavity side up and filled with a ball of cream cheese that has been rolled in chopped nuts. —*Sandra Larrick*
*Hanover, Pennsylvania*

• Add some dried marjoram the next time you make your favorite creamy ham casserole. It's just the right complement.
—*Caryn Hasbrouck*
*Wheaton, Illinois*

• To make pork loin roast even tastier, top it with a jar of all-fruit apricot preserves (no sugar added). Pour 1/2 cup apple juice over all and sprinkle with lemon pepper. Bake at 350° until the roast is very tender.
—*Bettyrae Easley, Anchorage, Alaska*

• Here's an easy marinade for grilled pork chops: For four chops, combine 1/2 cup each soy sauce, water and honey. Pour over chops and marinate, covered, in the refrigerator overnight. Grill until done as desired. —*Rhea Lease*
*Colman, South Dakota*

• If you're preparing a pork dish in a slow cooker, add fresh herbs at the end of the cooking time for pleasing taste and pretty color.
—*Elizabeth Mullett*
*Haverhill, Massachusetts*

• Shape ham balls with an ice cream scoop to obtain more uniform sizes and a perfect shape. —*Sharon Fenimore*
*Bethany, Missouri*

## SOUTHWESTERN LASAGNA

*Norma Hoffmaster, Long Beach, California*

**(Pictured above)**

*I first tasted this lasagna at a church potluck more than 20 years ago. I asked for the recipe and have made it many times since. It's one of our favorites.*

1-1/2 pounds ground beef
  1 medium onion, chopped
  1 can (15 ounces) enchilada sauce
  1 can (14-1/2 ounces) diced tomatoes, undrained
  1 can (2-1/4 ounces) sliced ripe olives, drained
  1 teaspoon salt
1/4 teaspoon garlic powder
1/4 teaspoon pepper
  1 cup small-curd cottage cheese
  1 egg
1/2 pound Monterey Jack cheese, thinly sliced
  8 corn tortillas (8 inches), halved
1/2 cup shredded cheddar cheese

In a large skillet, brown beef and onion; drain. Stir in enchilada sauce, tomatoes, olives, salt, garlic powder and pepper; bring to a boil. Reduce heat; simmer, uncovered, for 20 minutes. In a small bowl, combine cottage cheese and egg; set aside. Spread one-third of the meat sauce in a greased 13-in. x 9-in. x 2-in. baking dish. Top with half the Monterey Jack cheese, half the cottage cheese mixture and half the tortillas. Repeat layers, ending with meat sauce. Sprinkle with cheddar cheese. Cover and bake at 350° for 20 minutes. Uncover and bake 10 minutes longer. **Yield:** 6-8 servings.

ꞯꞯꞯꞯꞯꞯꞯꞯꞯꞯꞯꞯꞯ

## SPICY PORK STIR-FRY

*Jane Flatgard, Circle Pines, Minnesota*

*The first time I made this recipe, some years ago, my closest girlfriend came over for dinner. Between the two of us, we managed to finish the entire panful!*

1-1/4 pounds pork tenderloin
  2 tablespoons soy sauce
  1 tablespoon cornstarch
1/4 teaspoon salt
1/4 teaspoon sugar
1/4 teaspoon ground ginger
1/4 teaspoon cayenne pepper

1 medium onion, thinly sliced
1 medium carrot, julienned
1 garlic clove, minced
2 tablespoons vegetable oil
1 package (6 ounces) frozen snow peas, thawed
Boston lettuce leaves *or* hot cooked rice
Toasted sesame seeds, optional

Cut the pork into 1/8-in.-wide slices; cut each slice into 3-in. strips. In a bowl, combine the soy sauce, cornstarch, salt, sugar, ginger and cayenne. Add pork; toss to coat and set aside. In a large skillet or wok, stir-fry onion, carrot and garlic in oil until crisp-tender. Remove with a slotted spoon and keep warm. In the same skillet, stir-fry pork over medium-high heat until browned and no longer pink. Add onion mixture and peas; heat through. Serve in lettuce cups or over rice. Sprinkle with sesame seeds if desired. **Yield:** 4 servings.

### GRILLED LEMON CHICKEN

*Linda Nilsen, Anoka, Minnesota*

*The secret behind the flavor that enhances this poultry dish is a citrusy one. I use lemonade concentrate.*

1 can (6 ounces) frozen lemonade concentrate, thawed
1/3 cup soy sauce
1 garlic clove, minced
1 teaspoon seasoned salt
1/2 teaspoon celery salt
1/8 teaspoon garlic powder
2 broiler-fryer chickens (3 to 3-1/2 pounds *each*), quartered

In a jar with tight-fitting lid, combine the first six ingredients; shake well. Pour half into a shallow glass dish (set remaining sauce aside). Dip chicken on both sides into sauce in dish; discard sauce. Grill chicken, covered, over medium coals for 30 minutes, turning occasionally. Brush with reserved sauce. Continue basting and turning chicken several times for another 10-15 minutes or until juices run clear. **Yield:** 8 servings.

### SHREDDED PORK SANDWICHES

*Judi Jones, Wadsworth, Ohio*

**(Pictured at right)**

*I received this recipe from my sister Linda. Her recipes are always delicious because she's an excellent cook.*

1 boneless pork shoulder roast (3 to 4 pounds)

1-1/4 cups ketchup
1/2 cup water
1/2 cup chopped celery
1/4 cup chopped onion
1/4 cup lemon juice
3 tablespoons vinegar
2 tablespoons Worcestershire sauce
2 tablespoons brown sugar
1-1/2 teaspoons ground mustard
1 teaspoon salt
1/2 teaspoon pepper
12 to 14 hamburger buns, split

Place roast in a Dutch oven or large kettle. In a bowl, combine the ketchup, water, celery, onion, lemon juice, vinegar, Worcestershire sauce, brown sugar, mustard, salt and pepper; pour over roast. Cover and cook over medium-low heat for 4-6 hours or until meat is tender and pulls apart easily. Shred meat with two forks. Serve on buns. **Yield:** 12-14 servings.

**THESE SCRUMPTIOUS** side dishes—
featuring meat, pasta, vegetables or fruit—are
sure to complement all of your favorite meals.

**ON THE SIDE.** Top to bottom: Asparagus Tomato Salad
(p. 54), Potatoes Supreme (p. 53), Fresh Cucumber Salad
(p. 53) and Louisiana Gumbo (p. 53).

# Soups, Salads & Sides

## LOUISIANA GUMBO

*Wilton and Gloria Mason*
*Springhill, Louisiana*

**(Pictured at left)**

*This recipe certainly reflects our area of the country. It really is a meal in itself.*

    1 broiler/fryer chicken (3 to 3-1/2 pounds),
        cut up
    2 quarts water
    3/4 cup all-purpose flour
    1/2 cup vegetable oil
    1/2 cup sliced green onions
    1/2 cup chopped onion
    1/2 cup chopped green pepper
    1/2 cup chopped sweet red pepper
    1/2 cup chopped celery
      2 garlic cloves, minced
    1/2 pound fully cooked smoked sausage, cut
        into 1-inch cubes
    1/2 pound fully cooked ham, cut into
        3/4-inch cubes
    1/2 pound fresh *or* frozen uncooked shrimp,
        peeled and deveined
      1 cup cut fresh *or* frozen okra (3/4-inch
        pieces)
      1 can (15 ounces) kidney beans, rinsed
        and drained
    1/2 teaspoon salt
    1/4 teaspoon pepper
    1/4 teaspoon hot pepper sauce

Place the chicken and water in a Dutch oven; bring to a boil. Skim fat. Reduce heat; cover and simmer 30-45 minutes or until chicken is tender. Remove chicken; cool. Reserve 6 cups broth. Remove chicken from bones; cut into bite-size pieces. In a 4-qt. kettle, mix flour and oil until smooth; cook and stir over medium-low heat until browned, 2-3 minutes. Stir in onions, peppers, celery and garlic; cook for 5 minutes or until vegetables are tender. Stir in the sausage, ham and reserved broth and chicken; cover and simmer for 45 minutes. Add the shrimp, okra, beans, salt, pepper and hot pepper sauce; cover and simmer 10 minutes longer or until shrimp is cooked. **Yield:** 12 servings.

## POTATOES SUPREME

*Mrs. Afton Johnson, Sugar City, Idaho*

**(Pictured at left)**

*Every time my grandson comes home from college, he asks me to make these potatoes. In fact, it's the whole family's favorite potato dish.*

    8 to 10 medium potatoes, peeled and
        cubed
    1 can (10-3/4 ounces) condensed cream of
        chicken soup, undiluted
    3 cups (12 ounces) shredded cheddar
        cheese, *divided*
    1 cup (8 ounces) sour cream
    3 green onions, chopped
Salt and pepper to taste

Place potatoes in a saucepan and cover with water. Bring to a boil; cover and cook until almost tender. Drain and cool. Combine soup, 1-1/2 cups cheese, sour cream, onions, salt and pepper; stir in potatoes. Place in a greased 13-in. x 9-in x 2-in. baking dish. Sprinkle with remaining cheese. Bake, uncovered, at 350° for 25-30 minutes or until heated through. **Yield:** 8-10 servings.

## FRESH CUCUMBER SALAD

*Betsy Carlson, Rockford, Illinois*

**(Pictured at left)**

*Crisp, garden-fresh cukes are always in season when we hold our family reunion…and they really shine in this simple salad. The recipe can easily be expanded to make large quantities, too.*

    3 medium cucumbers, sliced
    1 cup sugar
    3/4 cup water
    1/2 cup vinegar
    3 tablespoons minced fresh dill *or* parsley

Place cucumbers in a 1-1/2-qt. to 2-qt. glass container. In a jar with tight-fitting lid, combine remaining ingredients. Pour over cucumbers. Cover and refrigerate 4 hours or overnight. Serve with a slotted spoon. **Yield:** 10-12 servings.

## MACARONI SALAD

*LaVerna Mjones, Moorhead, Minnesota*

*This hearty noodle salad is sure to please appetites of all ages...and it serves lots!*

2 pounds uncooked elbow macaroni
12 hard-cooked eggs, chopped
2-1/2 pounds fully cooked ham, cubed
1 package (16 ounces) frozen peas, thawed
3 cups sliced celery
1 large green pepper, chopped
1/2 cup chopped onion
1 jar (4 ounces) diced pimientos, drained
1 quart mayonnaise *or* salad dressing

Cook macaroni according to package directions. Rinse in cold water; drain and cool completely. Place in a large bowl; stir in remaining ingredients. Cover and refrigerate for at least 3 hours. **Yield:** 34 (1-cup) servings.

## MAPLE BAKED ONIONS

*Donna Kurant, West Rutland, Vermont*

**(Pictured below)**

*I created this side dish to make use of the great maple syrup we have here in Vermont. My family loves this recipe, and it's so easy to prepare.*

6 large sweet onions, sliced 1/2 inch thick
1/3 cup maple syrup
1/4 cup butter *or* margarine, melted

Layer onions in a greased 13-in. x 9-in. x 2-in. baking dish. Combine syrup and butter; pour over onions. Bake, uncovered, at 425° for 40-45 minutes or until tender. **Yield:** 8-10 servings.

## ASPARAGUS TOMATO SALAD

*Darlene Greulich, Cambridge, Ontario*

**(Pictured on page 52)**

*This is my husband's favorite asparagus recipe. All of our children love it, too. It's perfect for a summer dinner.*

✓ This tasty dish uses less fat, sugar or salt. Recipe includes Nutritional Analysis and Diabetic Exchanges.

1 pound fresh asparagus, cut into 1-inch pieces
4 medium tomatoes, cut into wedges
3 cups sliced fresh mushrooms
1 medium green pepper, julienned
1/4 cup vegetable oil
2 tablespoons cider vinegar
1 garlic clove, minced
1 teaspoon dried tarragon
3/4 teaspoon salt, optional
1/4 teaspoon pepper
1/4 teaspoon hot pepper sauce

Cook asparagus in a small amount of water until crisp-tender, about 3-4 minutes; drain and rinse with cold water. Place in a large bowl; add the tomatoes, mushrooms and green pepper. In a small bowl, combine remaining ingredients; mix well. Pour over vegetable mixture; toss to coat. Cover and refrigerate for 2 hours or overnight. **Yield:** 14 servings. **Nutritional Analysis:** One 1/2-cup serving (prepared without salt) equals 55 calories, 5 mg sodium, 0 cholesterol, 1 gm carbohydrate, 4 gm protein, 4 gm fat. **Diabetic Exchanges:** 1 fat, 1/2 vegetable.

## CALICO BEAN CASSEROLE

*Evelyn Pedersen, West Concord, Minnesota*

*To round out any fireside meal, I make this hearty, meaty bean casserole. I like to serve it with corn bread on a cold winter day.*

1/2 pound sliced bacon, diced
1/2 pound ground beef
1/2 cup chopped onion
1 can (16 ounces) pork and beans

1 can (15-1/2 ounces) kidney beans,
  rinsed and drained
1 can (15-1/4 ounces) lima beans, rinsed
  and drained
1/2 to 3/4 cup packed brown sugar
1/2 cup ketchup
2 teaspoons vinegar
1 teaspoon ground mustard

In a medium skillet, cook bacon until crisp. Remove bacon to paper towel to drain. Discard drippings. In the same skillet, cook beef and onion until beef is no longer pink; drain. Combine bacon, beef, onion and remaining ingredients in an ungreased 2-qt. baking dish. Bake, uncovered, at 350° for 45 minutes. **Yield:** 8-10 servings.

## POCKET VEGGIES

*Judi Garst, Springfield, Illinois*

*Whenever I make burgers on the grill, these vegetable packets are our usual accompaniment.*

✓ This tasty dish uses less fat, sugar or salt. Recipe includes Nutritional Analysis and Diabetic Exchanges.

1 *each* medium green, sweet red and
  yellow peppers, julienned
1 cup fresh baby carrots
1 cup fresh whole green beans
4 medium plum tomatoes, quartered
3 tablespoons olive *or* vegetable oil
3 tablespoons vinegar
2 teaspoons dried oregano
1/2 teaspoon pepper

Combine peppers, carrots and beans; divide between four pieces of heavy-duty foil (about 12 in. x 12 in.). Top with tomatoes. In a jar with tight-fitting lid, combine oil, vinegar, oregano and pepper; shake well. Drizzle over vegetables. Fold foil around vegetables and seal the edges tightly. Grill, covered, over indirect heat for 15-20 minutes or until tender. **Yield:** 12 servings. **Nutritional Analysis:** One 1/2-cup serving equals 59 calories, 9 mg sodium, trace cholesterol, 7 gm carbohydrate, 1 gm protein, 4 gm fat. **Diabetic Exchanges:** 1 vegetable, 1/2 fat.

## SOUTH COAST HOMINY

*Leslie Hampel, Palmer, Texas*

**(Pictured above right)**

*The first time I tasted this hominy dish, I couldn't eat enough. It's something my stepmother has prepared for a long time. Whenever I fix it for friends or family, there are never any leftovers.*

1/2 cup chopped onion
1/2 cup chopped green pepper
5 tablespoons butter *or* margarine, *divided*
3 tablespoons all-purpose flour
1 teaspoon salt
1/2 teaspoon ground mustard
Dash cayenne pepper
1-1/2 cups milk
1 cup (4 ounces) shredded cheddar cheese
1 can (15-1/2 ounces) white hominy,
  drained
1/2 cup sliced ripe olives, optional
1/2 cup dry bread crumbs

In a skillet, saute onion and green pepper in 3 tablespoons butter until tender. Add flour, salt, mustard and cayenne; cook and stir until smooth and bubbly, about 2 minutes. Gradually add milk; bring to a boil. Boil for 2 minutes, stirring constantly. Stir in cheese until melted. Remove from the heat; add hominy and olives if desired. Pour into a greased 1-1/2-qt. baking dish. Melt remaining butter and toss with bread crumbs; sprinkle over hominy mixture. Bake, uncovered, at 375° for 30 minutes or until golden. **Yield:** 6-8 servings.

## CALIFORNIA HARVEST SALAD

*Clara Laub, Fresno, California*

*This delicious recipe has an interesting combination of shrimp, fruit, noodles, onions and walnuts. People can't seem to stop eating this unique salad.*

    12 cups leaf lettuce
     1 pound seedless green grapes
     1 pound seedless red grapes
   1/2 pound cooked medium shrimp, peeled
        and deveined
     1 package (3 ounces) Oriental Ramen
        noodles
     1 cup chow mein noodles
   1/4 cup raisins
   1/4 cup golden raisins
   1/4 cup sliced green onions
   1/4 cup toasted walnuts *or* sunflower kernels
Salad dressing of your choice

In a large bowl, combine lettuce, grapes and shrimp. Break Ramen noodles into small pieces (save the seasoning packet for another use); add to salad with the chow mein noodles, raisins, onions and walnuts. Drizzle with dressing; toss to coat. **Yield:** 16 servings.

## HOT BEAN DISH

*Betti Blair, Farmington, New York*

*What would a family gathering be without a hot bean dish? This recipe combines many kinds of beans with a sauce that's creamier than most.*

     1 can (16 ounces) baked beans
     1 can (16 ounces) kidney beans, rinsed
        and drained
     1 can (15-1/2 ounces) butter beans, rinsed
        and drained
     1 can (15-1/4 ounces) lima beans, rinsed
        and drained
     1 jar (2 ounces) diced pimientos, drained
     8 bacon strips, cooked and crumbled
   1/2 cup ketchup
   1/4 cup chopped onion
     2 tablespoons chopped green pepper
     1 tablespoon Worcestershire sauce
     1 teaspoon ground mustard
     1 package (3 ounces) cream cheese, cut
        into cubes

In a bowl, combine the first 11 ingredients; pour into a greased 2-1/2-qt. baking dish. Cover and bake at 350° for 40 minutes. Stir in cream cheese. Bake, uncovered, 10-15 minutes longer, stirring several times, or until cheese is melted. **Yield:** 12-14 servings.

## TEX-MEX GREEN BEAN SALAD

*Mary Ann Valdez, San Antonio, Texas*

**(Pictured above)**

*This salad is a family favorite at cookouts. It's especially good with barbecued beef, which is so popular here in Texas.*

☑ This tasty dish uses less fat, sugar or salt. Recipe includes Nutritional Analysis and Diabetic Exchanges.

     1 pound fresh green beans
     1 teaspoon salt
     2 tablespoons olive *or* vegetable oil
     2 tablespoons fresh lemon juice
     2 tablespoons sliced green onions
   1/4 teaspoon pepper
   1/4 teaspoon ground cumin
Lettuce leaves
Shredded cheddar *or* Monterey Jack cheese,
   optional

Place the beans and salt in a saucepan; add a small amount of water. Cover and cook for 6-7 minutes or until crisp-tender. Rinse in cold water; drain. In a bowl, combine oil, lemon juice, onions, pepper and cumin. Add beans and toss to coat. Serve on a bed of lettuce. Sprinkle with cheese if desired. **Yield:** 6 servings. **Nutritional Analysis:** One 1/2-cup serving (prepared without cheese) equals 65 calories, 360 mg sodium, 0 cholesterol, 16 gm carbohydrate, 1 gm protein, 5 gm fat. **Diabetic Exchanges:** 1 vegetable, 1 fat.

## CHUNKY APPLESAUCE

*Judy Robertson, Southington, Connecticut*

*This applesauce tastes like apple pie without the crust. It's no surprise my husband gobbles up the whole batch in no time!*

☑ This tasty dish uses less fat, sugar or salt. Recipe includes Nutritional Analysis and Diabetic Exchanges.

**30 medium tart apples, peeled and quartered (about 11 pounds)**
**4 cups water**
**2 tablespoons ground cinnamon**
**Artificial sweetener equivalent to 8 teaspoons sugar**

Place apples and water in a large kettle. Cover and cook over medium-low heat for 30-40 minutes or until apples are tender; remove from the heat. Using a potato masher, mash apples to desired consistency. Stir in cinnamon and sweetener. **Yield: 14 cups. Nutritional Analysis:** One 1/2-cup serving equals 103 calories, trace sodium, 0 cholesterol, 27 gm carbohydrate, trace protein, trace fat. **Diabetic Exchanges:** 1-1/2 fruit.

## GRANDMOTHER'S CORN PUDDING

*Susan Brown Langenstein, Salisbury, Maryland*

**(Pictured below)**

*Corn pudding is a very popular side dish on Maryland's Eastern Shore. My grandmother always served this pudding for holidays and family reunions. Today, my family can't wait for special occasions, so I whip up this comforting dish at least once or twice a month to keep them happy!*

**4 eggs**
**1 cup milk**
**1 can (15 ounces) cream-style corn**
**1/2 cup sugar**
**5 slices day-old bread, crusts removed**
**1 tablespoon butter *or* margarine, softened**

In a bowl, beat eggs and milk. Add corn and sugar; mix well. Cut bread into 1/2-in. cubes and place in a greased 9-in. square baking dish. Pour egg mixture over bread. Dot with butter. Bake, uncovered, at 350° for 50-60 minutes or until a knife inserted near the center comes out clean. **Yield:** 9 servings.

## HONEY APPLE SALAD

*Mary Lou Hawkins, Brook Park, Ohio*

**(Pictured below)**

*All my favorite recipes are quick, simple and tasty. I came across this salad while looking for something to make with honey. Substituting several of the ingredients, I served it to my husband and two daughters. It was a hit!*

3-1/2 cups diced red apples
  2 tablespoons lemon juice
  2 cups green grapes
  1 cup thinly sliced celery
1/2 cup chopped dates
1/2 cup mayonnaise
1/4 cup honey
  2 tablespoons sour cream
1/2 teaspoon salt
1/2 cup chopped walnuts

In a large bowl, toss apples with lemon juice. Add grapes, celery and dates. In a small bowl, combine mayonnaise, honey, sour cream and salt; mix well. Pour over apple mixture and toss to coat. Stir in the walnuts. Serve immediately. **Yield:** 6-8 servings.

## COLORFUL ANTIPASTO

*Linda Fredal, Warren, Michigan*

*This zippy, zesty recipe is easy to double and pour into glass jars decorated with ribbons for holiday presents or family occasions throughout the year.*

  3 ounces cheddar cheese, cut into 1/4-inch cubes
  3 ounces Monterey Jack cheese, cut into 1/4-inch cubes
2-1/2 ounces sliced pepperoni
1/2 cup pitted ripe olives
1/2 cup broccoli florets
1/2 cup cauliflowerets
1/2 cup diced green pepper
1/4 cup *each* diced sweet red pepper, yellow pepper, onion and celery
**DRESSING:**
1/3 cup white wine vinegar
1/4 cup olive *or* vegetable oil
  1 tablespoon chopped fresh parsley *or* 1 teaspoon dried parsley flakes
  1 tablespoon sugar
  1 teaspoon dried oregano
1/4 to 1/2 teaspoon crushed red pepper flakes
1/4 teaspoon minced garlic
1/4 teaspoon salt

In a large bowl, combine cheeses, pepperoni, olives and vegetables. In a small bowl, combine dressing ingredients; mix well. Stir into vegetable mixture. Cover and refrigerate for at least 4 hours. Store in the refrigerator for up to 5 days. **Yield:** 10 servings (5 cups).

## SOUP BAR

*Lynn Conlon, Provo, Utah*

*With all of its ingredients, this should be called "Surprise Soup"! Hearty, unique and fun to serve, it's a dish even children like.*

  4 cups chicken broth
  2 cans (14-1/2 ounces *each*) stewed tomatoes
  1 teaspoon chili powder
  1 teaspoon garlic powder
1/4 teaspoon salt
1/8 teaspoon pepper
**CONDIMENTS:**
  1 to 2 cups *each* of any of the following:
Shredded cheddar cheese
Frozen broccoli, carrots *and/or* cauliflower, thawed and chopped
Frozen corn *or* peas, thawed

Cubed cooked chicken, ham *or* sliced smoked
  sausage
Cooked crumbled bacon
Chopped fresh mushrooms
Minced fresh parsley
Cooked pasta *or* rice
Sour cream

In a medium kettle, combine the first six ingredients; bring to a boil. Reduce heat; cover and
simmer for 30 minutes. Meanwhile, arrange
condiments in individual serving dishes. To serve,
spoon desired condiments into soup bowl; top
with hot soup. **Yield:** 6-8 servings.

## OLD-FASHIONED POTATOES ANNA

*Megan Gerritsen, Bridgewater, Maine*

*Cheddar cheese, onion and sweet red pepper make
these potatoes extra-special and flavorful.*

  3 eggs, separated
  2 cups mashed potatoes (without added
    butter *or* milk)
3/4 cup shredded cheddar cheese
  2 teaspoons finely chopped green onion
  2 teaspoons finely chopped sweet red
    pepper
Salt and pepper to taste

In a bowl, beat egg yolks. Add potatoes, cheese,
onion and red pepper. In a mixing bowl, beat egg
whites until stiff peaks form; fold into potato mixture. Add salt and pepper. Place in a greased 1-
1/2-qt. baking dish. Cover and bake at 400° for 20
minutes. **Yield:** 4-6 servings.

## GRILLED FRUIT KABOBS

*Mrs. Travis Baker, Litchfield, Illinois*

*Instead of making a traditional fruit salad, why not try
these quick and easy kabobs?*

1/2 fresh pineapple, trimmed and cut into
    1-inch chunks
  3 nectarines, cut into 1-inch chunks
  3 pears, cut into 1-inch chunks
  3 peaches, cut into 1-inch chunks
  3 to 4 plums, cut into 1-inch chunks
 10 apricots, halved
Honey *or* corn syrup

Thread fruit alternately onto metal or soaked
bamboo skewers. Grill, uncovered, over medium-hot coals until fruit is heated through, about
6 minutes, turning often. Brush with honey or
corn syrup during the last minute of grilling
time. **Yield:** 4-6 servings.

## ALMOND POTATO PUFF

*Carol Ann Hass, Des Moines, Iowa*

**(Pictured above)**

*Our garden produces an abundance of potatoes so
we eat them often. This recipe is a refreshing change
from fried or mashed potatoes. My children love the
almond topping.*

1-1/2 pounds potatoes, peeled and quartered
  1 small onion, chopped
  2 tablespoons butter *or* margarine
  2 eggs
3/4 cup whipping cream, warmed
1/2 cup ground almonds
1/2 teaspoon salt
Dash ground nutmeg
1/2 cup shredded cheddar cheese
1/4 cup slivered almonds

Cook potatoes in boiling water until tender, about
15 minutes; drain and place in a mixing bowl. In
a skillet, saute onion in butter until tender; add to
potatoes. On low speed, beat in eggs, one at a
time, until smooth. Beat in cream (the mixture
will be thin). Add the ground almonds, salt and
nutmeg. Spoon into a greased 1-1/2-qt. baking
dish. Sprinkle with the cheese and slivered almonds. Bake, uncovered, at 400° for 20 minutes.
**Yield:** 6 servings.

## ROBBIE'S RED RICE

*Robbie Joyce, Moncks Corner, South Carolina*

**(Pictured above)**

*Upon my move to the Low Country of South Carolina, I was introduced to red rice, a traditional Deep South dish. I experimented with a recipe and this is the result.*

☑ This tasty dish uses less fat, sugar or salt. Recipe includes Nutritional Analysis and Diabetic Exchanges.

    1 package (12 ounces) bulk pork *or* turkey
      sausage
1-1/2 cups water
    1 cup uncooked long grain rice
    1 cup chopped onion
  1/3 cup *each* chopped green, yellow and
      sweet red pepper
  1/4 cup butter *or* margarine, melted
  1/4 teaspoon pepper
    4 bacon strips, cooked and crumbled,
      optional
  1/2 teaspoon salt, optional

    1 can (14-1/2 ounces) diced tomatoes,
      undrained

In a skillet, cook sausage until no longer pink; drain. Transfer to an ungreased 2-qt. casserole; stir in the water, rice, onion, peppers, butter and pepper. Add bacon and salt if desired. Cover and bake at 350° for 45 minutes. Stir in tomatoes. Bake 15 minutes longer. **Yield:** 10 servings. **Nutritional Analysis:** One 1/2-cup serving (prepared with turkey sausage and margarine and without bacon or salt) equals 103 calories, 243 mg sodium, 22 mg cholesterol, 6 gm carbohydrate, 5 gm protein, 7 gm fat. **Diabetic Exchanges:** 1 meat, 1/2 starch.

## SESAME ASPARAGUS SALAD

*Mrs. A. Squair, Salmon Arm, British Columbia*

*The sesame seeds give this refreshing side dish a taste we all enjoy. I often serve breadsticks with it for even more crunch.*

1 pound fresh asparagus, cut into 1-inch
   pieces
1/4 cup water
8 cups torn romaine
1 green onion, chopped
2 tablespoons chopped pimientos
1/4 cup sesame seeds, toasted
2 tablespoons lemon juice
2 tablespoons vegetable oil
1/4 teaspoon pepper
1/4 teaspoon dried basil
1/8 teaspoon salt

In a saucepan, combine asparagus and water; bring to a boil. Reduce heat; cover and simmer for 4-8 minutes or until asparagus is crisp-tender. Drain. Place asparagus in a large bowl and chill. Just before serving, add romaine, onion and pimientos. In a small bowl, whisk sesame seeds, lemon juice, oil, pepper, basil and salt; pour over salad and toss. **Yield:** 10-12 servings.

## BUTTERNUT SOUP BOATS

*Evelyn Bentley, Ames, Iowa*

*This thick and creamy soup became a part of my recipe collection, thanks to my grown daughter, Jane. We share recipes back and forth all the time. To make it extra fun, use the squash shells as serving bowls.*

3 small butternut squash (about 1-1/2
   pounds *each*)
4 large leeks (white portion only), sliced
1 teaspoon dried thyme
5 tablespoons butter *or* margarine
3 cups chicken broth
1-1/4 teaspoons salt
1/2 teaspoon pepper
1/2 cup sour cream
Chopped chives *or* parsley

Cut squash in half; remove and discard seeds. Place with cut side down in a greased 13-in. x 9-in. x 2-in. baking pan. Add 1/4 in. of water to pan. Cover and bake at 375° for 40 minutes or until tender. Scoop out pulp, leaving about a 1/4-in. shell. Set shells and pulp aside. In a large saucepan, saute leeks and thyme in butter until tender. Add pulp, broth, salt and pepper; simmer for 20 minutes. Remove from the heat; cool slightly. Puree in a blender; return to pan and heat through. Spoon into squash shells. Place sour cream in a heavy-duty resealable plastic bag; cut a small hole in the corner of the bag. Pipe a coil of sour cream over squash filling. Beginning at the center, use a toothpick to draw right angles across the piped lines about 1/2 in. apart. Sprinkle with chives. **Yield:** 6 servings.

## SCALLOPED TURNIPS

*Mrs. Eldon Larabee, Clearmont, Missouri*

**(Pictured below)**

*My husband and I have five grown children and 13 grandchildren. This is the only kind of cooked turnips our kids will eat.*

✓ This tasty dish uses less fat, sugar or salt. Recipe includes Nutritional Analysis and Diabetic Exchanges.

3 cups diced peeled turnips
2 cups water
1 teaspoon sugar
2 tablespoons butter *or* margarine
3 tablespoons all-purpose flour
3/4 teaspoon salt, optional
1-1/2 cups milk
1/4 cup crushed cornflakes
2 tablespoons grated cheddar *or* Parmesan
   cheese, optional
Chopped fresh parsley, optional

Place the turnips, water and sugar in a saucepan; simmer for 5-8 minutes or until tender. Drain and set aside. In another saucepan, melt butter; stir in flour and salt if desired. Gradually add milk; bring to a boil. Cook and stir for 1-2 minutes. Stir in turnips. Pour into a greased 1-qt. baking dish; sprinkle with cornflakes and cheese if desired. Bake, uncovered, at 350° for 20 minutes or until bubbly. Garnish with parsley if desired. **Yield:** 5 servings. **Nutritional Analysis:** One serving (prepared with margarine and skim milk and without salt and cheese) equals 128 calories, 187 mg sodium, 1 mg cholesterol, 18 gm carbohydrate, 4 gm protein, 5 gm fat. **Diabetic Exchanges:** 1 starch, 1 fat.

## REFRESHING
## RHUBARB SALAD

*Sharon Hegland, McIntosh, Minnesota*

**(Pictured below)**

*Nearly everyone I know has rhubarb in their garden, so it is indeed plentiful each spring. I've had this recipe in my scrapbook for years and serve it often at potlucks.*

    4 cups diced fresh *or* frozen rhubarb
1-1/2 cups water
  1/2 cup sugar
    1 package (6 ounces) strawberry gelatin
    1 cup orange juice
    1 teaspoon grated orange peel
    1 cup sliced fresh strawberries
Mayonnaise, fresh mint and additional
    strawberries, optional

In a saucepan over medium heat, bring the rhubarb, water and sugar to a boil. Cook, uncovered, until rhubarb is tender, about 6-8 minutes. Remove from the heat; stir in gelatin until dissolved. Add orange juice and peel; mix well. Chill until mixture begins to thicken. Fold in strawberries. Pour into a 2-qt. bowl; chill until set. If desired, garnish with a dollop of mayonnaise, mint and strawberries. **Yield:** 12-14 servings.

## WARM BEEF SALAD
## IN POTATO BASKETS

*Marian Platt, Sequim, Washington*

*This succulent salad is so striking in taste and appearance when served in edible baskets made from potatoes. The baskets can be used for other salads— like chicken or tuna—too.*

**POTATO BASKETS:**
    6 egg whites
    8 cups shoestring potato sticks
**SALAD:**
    1 cup sliced fresh mushrooms
    1 cup chopped tomatoes
  1/2 cup finely sliced celery
  1/4 cup chopped green pepper
  1/2 cup sliced red onion
    3 tablespoons red wine vinegar
    4 teaspoons olive *or* vegetable oil
1-1/2 teaspoons Worcestershire sauce
  3/4 teaspoon *each* dried parsley flakes, basil
      and oregano
  1/4 teaspoon salt
  1/4 teaspoon pepper
    2 cups sliced cooked roast beef, cut into
      strips
    1 cup garbanzo beans, drained
    2 tablespoons crumbled blue cheese

In a mixing bowl, beat egg whites until stiff. Fold in potato sticks. Grease eight 10-oz. custard cups. Using the back of a spoon, press potato mixture onto the bottom and up the sides of each cup. Bake at 375° for 25 minutes. Meanwhile, in a bowl, combine mushrooms, tomatoes, celery and green pepper; set aside. In a skillet, saute onion in vinegar and oil until tender; add onion to vegetable mixture. Add Worcestershire sauce, herbs, salt and pepper to skillet; mix well. Add beef and beans; heat through. Add to vegetable mixture and toss. Remove baskets from cups with a sharp knife; fill with salad. Top with blue cheese. **Yield:** 8 servings.

## THREE-PEPPER SALAD

*Joanne Nischuk, Lacombe, Alberta*

*Fresh-picked peppers form the foundation of this colorful salad. It's our favorite dish. If you can't find yellow peppers, use only red and green varieties. The salad will be just as pretty.*

  2 medium green peppers, julienned
  2 medium cucumbers, sliced
  2 jars (4-1/2 ounces *each*) whole
    mushrooms, halved
  1 medium sweet red pepper, julienned
  1 medium sweet yellow pepper, julienned
  1 can (6 ounces) pitted ripe olives, halved
1/2 cup chopped onion
DRESSING:
  2/3 cup Italian salad dressing
  1 tablespoon lemon juice
  1 tablespoon olive *or* vegetable oil
1/2 teaspoon seasoned salt
1/4 teaspoon salt

In a large salad bowl, combine the first seven ingredients. In a small bowl or jar with tight-fitting lid, combine dressing ingredients; mix or shake well. Pour over salad. Refrigerate for at least 1 hour, stirring occasionally. Serve with a slotted spoon. **Yield:** 16 servings.

## HAM AND BEAN CHOWDER

*Joe Ann Heavrin, Memphis, Tennessee*

**(Pictured above right)**

*We also call this 2-Day Bean Chowder, since it can be started in the afternoon, chilled overnight and finished off the next day—if you can wait to taste it!*

**1 pound dried great northern beans**

  2 cups chopped onion
  1 cup sliced celery
  2 garlic cloves, minced
  3 tablespoons butter *or* margarine
  1 meaty ham bone
  2 cups water
  1 can (14-1/2 ounces) chicken broth
  1 can (14-1/2 ounces) stewed tomatoes
  2 bay leaves
  2 whole cloves
1/2 teaspoon pepper
  2 cups milk
  2 cups (8 ounces) shredded cheddar
    cheese

Place beans in a Dutch oven or soup kettle; add water to cover by 2 in. Bring to a boil; boil for 2 minutes. Remove from the heat; cover and let stand for 1 hour. Drain beans and discard liquid. In the same kettle, saute onion, celery and garlic in butter until tender. Add beans, ham bone, water, broth, tomatoes, bay leaves, cloves and pepper; bring to a boil. Reduce heat; cover and simmer for 2 hours. Remove ham bone, bay leaves and cloves. When cool enough to handle, remove ham from bone; cut into small pieces and return to soup. Chill for 8 hours or overnight. Skim fat from soup. Stir in milk; cook on low until heated through. Just before serving, stir in cheese. **Yield:** 12-14 servings (3-1/4 quarts).

1/2 cup sliced almonds, toasted, optional
Cantaloupe, optional

In a large bowl, combine the first five ingredients. Fold in rice, celery, green pepper, onion, pineapple, water chestnuts and cheese. Add almonds just before serving if desired. Serve on cantaloupe halves or wedges if desired, or use as a sandwich spread. **Yield:** 8 servings.

## BOW TIE GARDEN PASTA

*Miriam Hershberger, Holmesville, Ohio*

*Just-picked veggies, pleasing bow tie pasta and flavorful seasonings mix together to make a delicious dish. To top if off, it's easy and fun to fix.*

> 1 cup Italian salad dressing
> 2 tablespoons olive or vegetable oil
> 1 cup packed fresh basil leaves
> 2 tablespoons grated Parmesan cheese
> 2 tablespoons chopped walnuts
> 1 tablespoon minced garlic
> 2 cups quartered fresh mushrooms
> 1 cup broccoli florets
> 1 cup cauliflowerets
> 1 medium onion, julienned
> 1 small green pepper, julienned
> 1 small zucchini, sliced
> 1 small yellow squash, sliced
> 3 carrots, julienned
> 1 can (14 ounces) water-packed artichoke hearts, drained and quartered
> 4 cups cooked multicolor cheese-filled tortellini
> 2 cups cooked bow tie pasta

In a blender or food processor, combine the first six ingredients; process until smooth. Pour 1/2 cup into a large skillet; saute all of the vegetables until crisp-tender, about 3-5 minutes. Add tortellini, pasta and remaining dressing; heat through. **Yield:** 14 (1-cup) servings. **Editor's Note:** This recipe may easily be doubled.

## SWEET POTATO ORANGE CUPS

*Melonie Bowers, Sugarcreek, Ohio*

*Serve this refreshingly sweet side dish to your guests in separate cups made from oranges! All you have to do is cut oranges in half, scoop out the fruit and fill the peel with the sweet potato mixture.*

> 3 large sweet potatoes (2 to 2-1/2 pounds), peeled and cubed
> 1 can (6 ounces) orange juice concentrate, thawed

## CROWD-PLEASING CHICKEN SALAD

*Jackie Anderson, Richfield, Utah*

**(Pictured above)**

*I combined parts of several recipes to come up with this one. I'm a busy mother of five and like to fix meals that are quick and easy. I've served this salad at banquets and received many requests for the recipe.*

> 3 cups cubed cooked chicken *or* turkey
> 1 cup mayonnaise
> 1/4 cup sour cream
> 1/4 teaspoon salt
> Dash pepper
> 2 cups cooked rice
> 1 cup chopped celery
> 1/2 cup chopped green pepper
> 1/4 cup chopped onion
> 1 can (20 ounces) pineapple tidbits, drained
> 1 can (8 ounces) sliced water chestnuts, drained
> 1 cup (4 ounces) shredded cheddar cheese

Soups, Salads & Sides

1/4 cup packed brown sugar
1/4 cup half-and-half cream
2 tablespoons butter *or* margarine
3/4 cup miniature marshmallows
1/4 cup chopped pecans
4 large oranges, halved
32 additional miniature marshmallows

In a covered saucepan, cook sweet potatoes in boiling water until tender, about 25-30 minutes; drain. In a mixing bowl, beat sweet potatoes, concentrate, sugar, cream and butter on low until smooth. Stir in marshmallows and pecans; set aside. Remove pulp from oranges, leaving a shell. (Discard pulp or save for another use.) Spoon sweet potato mixture into shells. Place four marshmallows on top of each. Place in a greased 15-in. x 10-in. x 1-in. baking pan. Bake, uncovered, at 350° for 20 minutes or until heated through. **Yield:** 8 servings.

## SCALLOPED CORN

*Kathy Smith, Remsen, New York*

*You'll hear an earful from guests when you offer this creamy corn dish. My mother made this recipe all the time when I was young. Now, it's a favorite at my house—especially during the holidays.*

1 can (15 ounces) cream-style corn
2 eggs, beaten
1/2 cup crushed saltines (about 14 crackers)
1/4 cup butter *or* margarine, melted
1/4 cup grated carrot
1/4 cup evaporated milk
1/4 cup chopped sweet red pepper
1 tablespoon chopped celery
1 tablespoon chopped onion
1/2 teaspoon salt
1/2 teaspoon pepper
1/2 cup shredded cheddar cheese
Paprika

In a large bowl, combine the first 11 ingredients. Spoon into four greased 8-oz. baking dishes. Sprinkle with cheese and paprika. Bake, uncovered, at 350° for 25-30 minutes or until set. **Yield:** 4 servings. **Editor's Note:** A 1-qt. baking dish may be used in place of the individual baking dishes.

## HARVEST SQUASH SOUP

*Mrs. H.L. Sosnowski*
*Grand Island, New York*

**(Pictured at right)**

*This soup is perfect for a group after an autumn out-*ing. The combination of squash, applesauce and spices gives it an appealing flavor.

☑ This tasty dish uses less fat, sugar or salt. Recipe includes Nutritional Analysis and Diabetic Exchanges.

1-1/2 cups chopped onion
1 tablespoon vegetable oil
4 cups mashed cooked butternut squash
3 cups chicken broth
2 cups unsweetened applesauce
1-1/2 cups milk
1 bay leaf
1 tablespoon lime juice
1 tablespoon sugar
1 teaspoon curry powder
1/2 teaspoon ground cinnamon
1/2 teaspoon salt, optional
1/4 teaspoon pepper
1/4 teaspoon ground nutmeg
**Additional cinnamon and bay leaves, optional**

In a large saucepan or Dutch oven, saute onion in oil until tender. Add the next 12 ingredients; simmer, uncovered, for 30 minutes. Remove bay leaf before serving. Garnish with cinnamon and bay leaves if desired. **Yield:** 10 servings (2-1/2 quarts). **Nutritional Analysis:** One 1-cup serving (prepared with low-sodium broth and skim milk and without salt) equals 113 calories, 60 mg sodium, 1 mg cholesterol, 22 gm carbohydrate, 4 gm protein, 2 gm fat. **Diabetic Exchanges:** 1 starch, 1 vegetable.

## APPLE LUNCHEON SALAD

*Audrey Marsh, Arva, Ontario*

**(Pictured above)**

*While this salad is a delicious way to use leftover beef,
I sometimes serve it with cold ham and cheese instead.
It's always been a success at potlucks!*

   3 cups diced red apples
   1 cup julienned cooked roast beef
   1 cup thinly sliced celery
   4 green onions, thinly sliced
1/4 cup minced fresh parsley
1/3 cup vegetable oil
   2 tablespoons cider vinegar
   1 garlic clove, minced
1/2 teaspoon salt
1/4 teaspoon pepper
Lettuce leaves

In a bowl, combine the first five ingredients. In a
small bowl, combine oil, vinegar, garlic, salt and
pepper; mix well. Pour over apple mixture; toss
to coat. Cover and refrigerate for at least 1 hour.
Serve on lettuce. **Yield:** 4-6 servings.

## PASTA SALAD WITH POPPY SEED DRESSING

*Susie Eckert, Acworth, Georgia*

*This pasta salad is frequently requested at family get-
togethers. The poppy seed dressing is also delicious in
coleslaw or with a tossed salad.*

   1 package (16 ounces) bow tie *or* small
      tube pasta
   1 cup (4 ounces) shredded cheddar cheese
   2 cups broccoli florets
   1 cup sliced carrots
   1 cup diced cucumber
   1 cup halved cherry tomatoes
1/2 cup chopped green onions
DRESSING:
1/2 cup cider vinegar
1/2 cup sugar
   1 garlic clove, minced
   1 green onion, chopped
1/2 teaspoon ground mustard
1/2 teaspoon salt
   1 cup vegetable oil
   4 teaspoons poppy seeds

Cook pasta according to package directions; rinse with cold water and drain. Place in a large bowl; add cheese, broccoli, carrots, cucumber, tomatoes and onions. In a blender, combine vinegar, sugar, garlic, onion, mustard and salt; gradually add oil, blending until smooth. Add poppy seeds. Pour over pasta mixture and toss. Cover and refrigerate for at least 1 hour. **Yield:** 16-18 servings.

## MARINATED FRESH VEGETABLES

*Wanda Jones, Ridgedale, Missouri*

*This recipe has been in our family for several years. I like to make it for holidays when the whole clan gets together.*

    3 cups cauliflowerets
2-1/2 cups broccoli florets
    2 cups sliced fresh mushrooms
   3/4 cup sliced celery
   1/2 cup chopped green pepper
**DRESSING:**
   1/2 cup vegetable oil
   1/2 cup sugar
   1/4 cup vinegar
    2 tablespoons grated onion
    1 tablespoon poppy seed
1-1/4 teaspoons ground mustard
1-1/4 teaspoons salt

In a large bowl, combine the cauliflower, broccoli, mushrooms, celery and green pepper. In a small bowl, combine all of the dressing ingredients; mix well. Pour over vegetables and toss to coat. Cover and refrigerate for at least 3 hours. **Yield:** 8-10 servings.

## VIDALIA CASSEROLE

*Libby Bigger, Dunwoody, Georgia*

*Georgia is famous for the sweet onions grown in the Vidalia area. My family looks forward to when these onions are available to use in salads and casseroles.*

 4 to 5 Vidalia *or* sweet onions, sliced 1/4
    inch thick
1/4 cup butter *or* margarine
1/4 cup sour cream
3/4 cup grated Parmesan cheese
 10 butter-flavored crackers, crushed

In a skillet over medium heat, saute onions in butter until tender. Remove from the heat; stir in sour cream. Spoon half into a greased 1-qt. baking dish. Sprinkle with cheese. Top with remaining onion mixture and crackers. Bake, uncovered, at 350° for 20-25 minutes. **Yield:** 4-6 servings.

## CREAM OF CRAB SOUP

*Wanda Weller, Westminster, Maryland*

**(Pictured below)**

*One of our Chesapeake Bay delicacies is the Maryland Blue Crab. It's abundant from May through October and used in a variety of dishes, like this rich soup.*

1/2 cup butter *or* margarine
1/2 cup all-purpose flour
  1 to 2 tablespoons seafood seasoning
   1 teaspoon salt
1/2 teaspoon curry powder
   4 cups milk
   1 pound cooked crabmeat *or* 3 cans
    (6 ounces *each*) crabmeat, drained
   2 tablespoons minced fresh parsley
**Additional milk and parsley, optional**

Melt butter in a 3-qt. saucepan; stir in flour, seafood seasoning, salt and curry powder. Cook until thickened and bubbly. Gradually add milk; cook and stir until mixture is hot (do not boil). Remove cartilage from crab if necessary. Add crab and parsley to soup; cook and stir just until crab is heated. If desired, thin soup with additional milk; garnish with parsley. **Yield:** 6-8 servings.

## SPIRAL PASTA SALAD

*Darlene Kileel, Riverview, New Brunswick*

**(Pictured below)**

*I have two kids and am always on the go, so I appreciate recipes that I can make ahead of time. This dish is easy to fix and perfect for taking along on picnics.*

☑ This tasty dish uses less fat, sugar or salt. Recipe includes Nutritional Analysis and Diabetic Exchanges.

   3 cups cooked spiral pasta
   1/2 cup chopped green pepper
   1/2 cup sliced celery
   1/2 cup chopped tomato
   1/2 cup shredded carrot
**DRESSING:**
   1/4 cup vegetable oil
   1/4 cup cider vinegar
   1/4 cup chopped onion
   2 tablespoons ketchup
   4 teaspoons sugar
   1/2 teaspoon salt, optional
   1/4 teaspoon ground mustard
   1/4 teaspoon paprika
   1/4 teaspoon garlic powder
   1/4 teaspoon dried oregano

In a large bowl, combine pasta, green pepper, celery, tomato and carrot. In a jar with tight-fitting lid, combine dressing ingredients; shake well. Pour over salad and toss. Chill. **Yield:** 8 servings. **Nutritional Analysis:** One 1/2-cup serving (prepared without salt) equals 181 calories, 62 mg sodium, trace cholesterol, 27 gm carbohydrate, 3 gm protein, 7 gm fat. **Diabetic Exchanges:** 1-1/2 starch, 1 vegetable, 1 fat.

## DANISH FRUIT SOUP

*Ellie Marsh, Lewistown, Pennsylvania*

*I've been making this colorful, sweet soup since 1961, and my whole family just loves it. It's a great way to enjoy fruit in winter.*

   1 package (3 ounces) raspberry gelatin
   1/8 teaspoon salt
   1 cup boiling water
   1 package (12 ounces) frozen raspberries
      without syrup
1-1/2 cups cold water
   2 tablespoons lemon juice
**Sour cream and ground nutmeg, optional**

In a large bowl, combine gelatin and salt. Gradually stir in boiling water until gelatin is dissolved. Add the raspberries, cold water and lemon juice; mix well. Refrigerate for 15-20 minutes. Just before serving, stir soup. Garnish with sour cream and nutmeg if desired. **Yield:** 4-6 servings.

## RED SCALLOPED POTATOES

*Clara Honeyager, Mukwonago, Wisconsin*

*Here's a different way to serve red potatoes. Their slightly tangy flavor always appeals to a crowd, making this a perfect dish for a potluck picnic.*

   3 pounds small red potatoes, quartered
   2 cans (10-3/4 ounces *each*) condensed
      cream of mushroom soup, undiluted
   2 cups sliced onion
   1 cup milk
   1/4 cup thinly sliced green onions
   1 teaspoon dill weed
   1 teaspoon dried marjoram
   3/4 teaspoon salt
   1/2 teaspoon pepper

Place potatoes in an ungreased 13-in. x 9-in. x 2-in. baking pan. Combine remaining ingredients; pour over potatoes. Cover and bake at 350° for 1-1/4 hours. Uncover and bake 10-20 minutes longer or until bubbly and potatoes are tender. **Yield:** 10-12 servings.

## Chutney-Filled Acorn Squash

*Arline Blanchard, Stockton Springs, Maine*

*Tart cranberries and acorn squash—two autumn favorites—are paired perfectly in this colorful autumn dish. It's tangy and tasty, and eye-catching as well!*

 3 to 4 acorn squash (about 1 pound *each*)
 4 cups fresh *or* frozen cranberries
 2 cups sugar
 1 cup fresh orange segments
 1 cup chopped unpeeled apple
 1/2 cup orange juice
 1/2 cup raisins
 1/4 cup chopped walnuts
 1 tablespoon vinegar
 1/2 teaspoon ground ginger
 1/2 teaspoon ground cinnamon

Cut squash in half; remove and discard seeds. Level bottoms. Place with hollow side down in an ungreased 13-in. x 9-in. x 2-in. baking pan. Add 1/4 in. of water to pan. Cover and bake at 350° for 45 minutes. Meanwhile, in a large saucepan, combine remaining ingredients; bring to a boil. Reduce heat; simmer for 10 minutes. Remove squash from oven; turn over and fill with chutney. Bake, uncovered, 10 minutes longer or until squash is tender. **Yield:** 6-8 servings.

## Blushing Apples

*Marion Tarkington, Lexington, North Carolina*

*The first time I tasted this dish was over 40 years ago, at a Girl Scout dinner. The individual red apples, arranged on the banquet table, were beautiful and so appealing to little girls. Since then, this has been one of my special-occasion recipes. I especially like to make it at Christmastime.*

 3 cups water
 2 cups sugar
 1 cup red-hot candies
10 to 12 small tart apples, peeled and cored
 1 package (8 ounces) cream cheese, softened
 3 tablespoons mayonnaise
 3 tablespoons chopped pecans

In a large saucepan, bring water, sugar and candies to a boil, stirring occasionally; boil for 3 minutes. Add apples; reduce heat to medium. Cover and cook for 8-12 minutes or until apples are tender but retain their shape. Remove apples with a slotted spoon. Cool. In a mixing bowl, combine cream cheese, mayonnaise and pecans; mix well. Spoon into center of apples. Chill. **Yield:** 10-12 servings.

## Pimiento Potato Salad

*Angie Alcock, Palmer, Alaska*

**(Pictured above and on cover)**

*I experimented with ingredients to come up with this creamy, tasty potato salad. Our children even like it, and that's a big step for them.*

☑ This tasty dish uses less fat, sugar or salt. Recipe includes Nutritional Analysis and Diabetic Exchanges.

1-1/2 pounds potatoes, cooked, peeled and cubed
 1 cup sliced celery
 1 jar (4 ounces) chopped pimientos, drained
 2 tablespoons minced chives
 2 tablespoons minced fresh parsley
 1 cup plain yogurt
1/4 cup mayonnaise
 1 teaspoon white wine vinegar
1/4 teaspoon white pepper
1/4 teaspoon paprika
1/2 teaspoon salt, optional

In a large bowl, combine potatoes, celery, pimientos, chives and parsley. Combine remaining ingredients. Pour over potatoes; toss. Chill. **Yield:** 8 servings. **Nutritional Analysis:** One 1/2-cup serving (prepared with low-fat yogurt and fat-free mayonnaise and without salt) equals 92 calories, 91 mg sodium, 2 mg cholesterol, 19 gm carbohydrate, 3 gm protein, 1 gm fat. **Diabetic Exchanges:** 1 starch.

## OKRA PILAF

*Ruby Hubbard, Cleveland, Oklahoma*

*This is my very favorite rice recipe. I've served it many times, and it's always received rave reviews. I hope you will enjoy it as much as I do.*

☑ This tasty dish uses less fat, sugar or salt. Recipe includes Nutritional Analysis and Diabetic Exchanges.

    4 bacon strips, cut into 1/2-inch pieces
    1 medium onion, chopped
  1/2 cup chopped green pepper
    1 cup sliced fresh *or* frozen okra
    2 medium tomatoes, peeled, seeded and chopped
  1/2 teaspoon salt, optional
  1/4 teaspoon pepper
    3 cups cooked rice

In a skillet, cook the bacon until crisp; remove with a slotted spoon to paper towel to drain. Saute onion and green pepper in drippings for 6-8 minutes or until tender. Stir in the okra, tomatoes, salt if desired and pepper; cook over medium heat for 5 minutes. Add rice; cook for 10-15 minutes or until okra is tender and liquid is absorbed. Crumble bacon; stir into rice mixture and serve immediately. **Yield:** 8 servings. **Nutritional Analysis:** One 1/2-cup serving (prepared with turkey bacon and without salt) equals 134 calories, 97 mg sodium, 6 mg cholesterol, 26 gm carbohydrate, 4 gm protein, 2 gm fat. **Diabetic Exchanges:** 1-1/2 starch, 1 vegetable.

## SHRIMP POTATO SALAD

*Gladys Wolff, Coventry, Rhode Island*

**(Pictured above)**

*Since Rhode Island is known as the Ocean State, I think this recipe represents my state well. Shrimp add a new twist to traditional potato salad.*

    1 pound fresh *or* frozen cooked shrimp, peeled and deveined
    2 tablespoons lemon juice
    4 cups cubed peeled potatoes, cooked and cooled
  1/4 cup sliced green onions
  1/4 cup minced fresh parsley
    1 cup (8 ounces) sour cream
    1 teaspoon salt
  1/4 teaspoon white pepper
  1/4 teaspoon dried tarragon
  1/4 teaspoon ground mustard
  1/8 teaspoon celery seed
    1 garlic clove, minced, optional

In a large bowl, toss shrimp with lemon juice; refrigerate. Add potatoes, onions and parsley. In a small bowl, combine sour cream, salt, pepper, tarragon, mustard, celery seed and garlic if desired; pour over potato mixture and toss. Cover and refrigerate until ready to serve. **Yield:** 4-6 servings.

## SUMMER GARDEN SOUP

*Patsy Bell Hobson, Liberty, Missouri*

*This soup is very tasty, and the best part is that all of the main ingredients come straight from my garden.*

☑ This tasty dish uses less fat, sugar or salt. Recipe includes Nutritional Analysis and Diabetic Exchanges.

    1 cup chopped onion
    4 to 6 garlic cloves, minced
    2 tablespoons olive *or* vegetable oil
    3 cups chopped fresh tomatoes
    1 cup fresh *or* frozen cut green beans
    1 tablespoon minced fresh basil *or* 1 teaspoon dried basil
    1 teaspoon minced fresh tarragon *or* 1/4 teaspoon dried tarragon
  1/2 teaspoon minced fresh dill *or* pinch dill weed
  1/4 teaspoon pepper
  1/4 teaspoon salt, optional
3-1/2 cups chicken broth
    1 cup fresh *or* frozen peas

1 cup sliced zucchini *or* yellow summer
squash

In a saucepan, saute onion and garlic in oil until
onion is tender. Add tomatoes, beans, basil, tarragon, dill, pepper and salt if desired; simmer for
10 minutes. Add broth, peas and zucchini; simmer
for 5-10 minutes or until vegetables are crisp-
tender. **Yield:** 8 servings (2 quarts). **Nutritional
Analysis:** One 1-cup serving (prepared with low-
sodium chicken broth and without salt) equals 86
calories, 77 mg sodium, 2 mg cholesterol, 10 gm
carbohydrate, 4 gm protein, 5 gm fat. **Diabetic Exchanges:** 2 vegetable, 1 fat.

## CREAMY APPLE SALAD

*Brenda Hildebrandt, Moosomin, Saskatchewan*

*This family favorite is especially good with pork
chops or ham. The quick and easy side dish is one I
serve often that we never tire of.*

    1 cup whipping cream
    1 tablespoon sugar
    3 medium tart apples, peeled and diced

In a mixing bowl, whip cream until soft peaks
form. Add sugar; continue beating until stiff peaks
form. Fold in the apples. **Yield:** 6-8 servings.

## TWO-BREAD DRESSING

*Vanessa Leeson, Bishop, Texas*

**(Pictured below)**

*I'm originally from Oregon and was raised on herb
stuffing, but my Southern husband would eat only
his mother's corn bread stuffing. So I created this
recipe as a compromise and have received many
compliments on it.*

    9 bacon strips, diced
    1 cup chopped celery
  1/4 cup chopped onion
    6 slices bread, toasted and cubed
    3 cups coarse corn bread crumbs
  1/3 cup minced fresh parsley
1-1/2 teaspoons rubbed sage
    1 teaspoon dried thyme
    1 teaspoon dried rosemary, crushed
1-1/2 cups chicken broth

In a skillet, cook bacon until crisp. Drain, reserving 2 tablespoons drippings; set bacon aside. Saute
celery and onion in drippings until tender. In a
large bowl, toss bread, parsley, sage, thyme and
rosemary. Add celery, onion, broth and bacon;
mix gently. Spoon into a greased 2-qt. baking dish.
Bake, uncovered, at 350° for 30-35 minutes or until heated through. **Yield:** 6-8 servings.

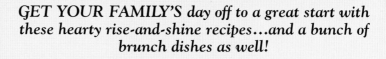

**GET YOUR FAMILY'S** *day off to a great start with these hearty rise-and-shine recipes...and a bunch of brunch dishes as well!*

**TOP O' THE MORNING.** Clockwise from top left: Breakfast Pockets (p. 74), No-Fry Doughnuts (p. 73), True Belgian Waffles (p. 73) and Farmer's Casserole (p. 74).

# Breakfast & Brunch

## TRUE BELGIAN WAFFLES

*Rose Delemeester, St. Charles, Michigan*

**(Pictured at left)**

*It was on a visit to my husband's relatives in Belgium when I was given this recipe. We love these waffles with any kind of topping—blueberries, strawberries, raspberries, fried apples or powdered sugar.*

　2 cups all-purpose flour
　3/4 cup sugar
3-1/2 teaspoons baking powder
　2 eggs, separated
1-1/2 cups milk
　1 cup butter (no substitutes), melted
　1 teaspoon vanilla extract
**Sliced fresh strawberries *or* syrup**

In a bowl, combine flour, sugar and baking powder. In another bowl, lightly beat egg yolks. Add milk, butter and vanilla; mix well. Stir into dry ingredients just until combined. Beat egg whites until stiff peaks form; fold into batter. Bake in a preheated waffle iron according to manufacturer's directions until golden brown. Serve with strawberries or syrup. **Yield:** 10 waffles (about 4-1/2 inches).

## NO-FRY DOUGHNUTS

*Susie Baldwin, Columbia, Tennessee*

**(Pictured at left)**

*These doughnuts never last long at our house. I like making them because I don't have to clean up a greasy mess like with deep-fried doughnuts.*

　2 packages (1/4 ounce *each*) active dry
　　yeast
1/4 cup warm water (110° to 115°)
1-1/2 cups warm milk (110° to 115°)
1/3 cup shortening
1/2 cup sugar
　2 eggs
　1 teaspoon salt
　1 teaspoon ground nutmeg
1/4 teaspoon ground cinnamon

4-1/2 to 5 cups all-purpose flour
　1/4 cup butter *or* margarine, melted
**GLAZE:**
　1/2 cup butter *or* margarine
　　2 cups confectioners' sugar
　　5 teaspoons water
　　2 teaspoons vanilla extract

In a mixing bowl, dissolve yeast in water. Add milk and shortening; stir for 1 minute. Add sugar, eggs, salt, nutmeg, cinnamon and 2 cups flour; beat on low speed until smooth. Stir in enough remaining flour to form a soft dough (do not knead). Cover and let rise in a warm place until doubled, about 1 hour. Punch dough down. Turn onto a floured surface; roll out to 1/2-in. thickness. Cut with a 2-3/4-in. doughnut cutter; place 2 in. apart on greased baking sheets. Brush with butter. Cover and let rise in a warm place until doubled, about 30 minutes. Bake at 350° for 20 minutes or until lightly browned. Meanwhile, in a saucepan, melt butter; stir in sugar, water and vanilla. Stir over low heat until smooth (do not boil). Keep warm. Dip warm doughnuts, one at a time, into glaze and turn to coat. Drain on a wire rack. Serve immediately. **Yield:** 2 dozen.

## BREAKFAST SKEWERS

*Bobi Raab, St. Paul, Minnesota*

*These kabobs are fun, different and delicious, plus they go well with any egg dish.*

　1 package (7 ounces) brown-and-serve
　　sausage links
　1 can (20 ounces) pineapple chunks,
　　drained
10 medium fresh mushrooms
　2 tablespoons butter *or* margarine, melted
**Maple syrup**

Cut sausages in half; alternately thread sausages, pineapple and mushrooms onto metal or soaked bamboo skewers. Brush with butter and syrup. Grill, uncovered, over medium-hot coals, turning and basting with syrup, for 8 minutes or until sausages are lightly browned and fruit is heated through. **Yield:** 5 servings.

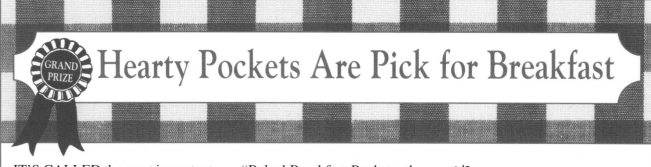

# Hearty Pockets Are Pick for Breakfast

IT'S CALLED the most important meal of the day. Sadly, though, some folks find breakfast just plain boring. Who wouldn't be bored with a piece of toast or a bowl of cold cereal?

Breakfast boredom is no problem for Dolores Jantzen of Plymouth, Nebraska. With her eye-opening Breakfast Pockets, the morning meal is what it was meant to be—a flavorful foundation to the whole day's activities.

"They do look somewhat plain on the outside, but the cheesy, meaty filling is far from ho-hum," Dolores promises. "I like being able to serve a complete breakfast inside a tidy pocket of dough. Just add fresh fruit, juice or fruit-flavored gelatin on the side."

The recipe is versatile as well. With alternate fillings from pizza sauce to tuna or salmon to vegetables in a white sauce, the pockets are suitable for any meal. Or divide the dough and filling into smaller portions to make tasty hors d'oeuvres for family get-togethers.

"Baked Breakfast Pockets also freeze well," Dolores assures. "I've made them ahead to serve at breakfast for overnight guests with delicious results."

## BREAKFAST POCKETS

(Pictured on page 72)

2 packages (1/4 ounce *each*) active dry yeast
1/2 cup warm water (110° to 115°)
3/4 cup warm evaporated milk (110° to 115°)
1/2 cup vegetable oil
1/4 cup sugar
1 egg
1 teaspoon salt
3 to 4 cups all-purpose flour
FILLING:
1 pound bulk pork sausage
1/2 cup chopped onion
2-1/2 cups frozen shredded hash browns, thawed
7 eggs, lightly beaten
3 tablespoons milk
1/2 teaspoon salt
1/2 teaspoon pepper
1/2 teaspoon garlic salt
Pinch cayenne pepper
3 cups (12 ounces) shredded cheddar cheese

In a mixing bowl, dissolve yeast in water. Add evaporated milk, oil, sugar, egg, salt and 2 cups flour; beat until smooth. Add enough remaining flour to form a soft dough (do not knead). Cover and let rise in a warm place until doubled, about 1 hour. Meanwhile, in a skillet, cook the sausage and onion over medium heat until sausage is no longer pink; drain. Add hash browns, eggs, milk and seasonings. Cook and stir until the eggs are completely set. Sprinkle with cheese; keep warm. Punch dough down; divide into 14 pieces. On a floured surface, roll out dough into 7-in. circles. Top each with about 1/3 cup filling; fold dough over filling and pinch the edges to seal. Place on greased baking sheets. Bake at 350° for 15-20 minutes or until golden brown. **Yield:** 14 servings.

## PANCAKE SYRUP

*Lorrie McCurdy, Farmington, New Mexico*

*My husband has fond memories of this recipe. Every Sunday morning, his dad would get up early to make the family pancakes and this sweet syrup.*

1 cup packed brown sugar
1 cup sugar
1 cup water
1 teaspoon maple flavoring

In a medium saucepan, combine sugars and water; bring to a boil. Cook and stir for 2 minutes. Remove from the heat; stir in maple flavoring. **Yield:** 2 cups.

## FARMER'S CASSEROLE

*Nancy Schmidt, Center, Colorado*

(Pictured on page 72)

*This casserole is handy—you can put it together the night before, let the flavors blend, then bake it in the morning. It's elegant enough to serve for a ladies' brunch but hearty enough to satisfy a man-sized appetite.*

3 cups frozen shredded hash browns
3/4 cup shredded Monterey Jack cheese
1 cup diced fully cooked ham
1/4 cup chopped green onions
4 eggs
1 can (12 ounces) evaporated milk

1/4 teaspoon pepper
1/8 teaspoon salt

Place potatoes in an 8-in. square baking dish. Sprinkle with cheese, ham and onions. Beat eggs, milk, pepper and salt; pour over all. Cover and refrigerate for several hours or overnight. Remove from refrigerator 30 minutes before baking. Bake, uncovered, at 350° for 55-60 minutes or until a knife inserted near the center comes out clean. **Yield:** 6 servings.

## SYRUPY APPLES

*Cindy Walstedt, Maidstone, Ontario*

*This fresh, fruity syrup adds delicious flavor to our family's favorite pancake recipe.*

- **2 tablespoons butter *or* margarine**
- **2 medium baking apples, peeled and thinly sliced**
- **1/3 cup packed brown sugar**

Melt butter in a saucepan over medium-low heat. Add apple slices; cook and stir for 5 minutes. Stir in sugar; cook and stir over low heat for 5 minutes. **Yield:** 1-1/3 cups.

## MAKE-AHEAD SCRAMBLED EGGS

*Diane Sackfield, Kingston, Ontario*

**(Pictured above right)**

*I appreciate the convenience of this dish. I've served it for breakfast and also as part of a full brunch buffet along with breads and side salads.*

- **5 tablespoons butter *or* margarine, *divided***
- **1/4 cup all-purpose flour**
- **2 cups milk**
- **2 cups (8 ounces) shredded cheddar cheese**
- **1 cup sliced fresh mushrooms**
- **1/4 cup finely chopped onion**
- **12 eggs, beaten**
- **1 teaspoon salt**
- **1 package (10 ounces) frozen chopped broccoli, cooked and drained**
- **1 cup soft bread crumbs**

In a saucepan, melt 2 tablespoons butter. Add flour; cook and stir until the mixture begins to bubble. Gradually stir in milk; bring to a boil. Cook and stir for 2 minutes. Remove from the heat. Stir in cheese until melted; set aside. In a large skillet, saute mushrooms and onion in 2 tablespoons butter until tender. Add eggs and salt; cook and stir until the eggs are completely set.

Add the cheese sauce and broccoli; mix well. Pour into a greased 11-in. x 7-in. x 2-in. baking dish. Melt the remaining butter and toss with bread crumbs. Sprinkle over egg mixture. Cover and refrigerate overnight. Remove from refrigerator 30 minutes before baking. Bake, uncovered, at 350° for 25-30 minutes or until top is golden brown. **Yield:** 6-8 servings.

## SAUSAGE CHEESE BISCUITS

*Marlene Neideigh, Myrtle Point, Oregon*

*These breakfast-in-a-biscuit goodies will appeal to the young...and the young at heart. They will be equally appealing to the cook. It's one of my favorite recipes because it doesn't require special ingredients.*

- **1 tube (10 ounces) refrigerated buttermilk biscuits**
- **1 package (8 ounces) brown-and-serve sausage links**
- **2 eggs**
- **1/2 cup shredded cheddar cheese**
- **3 tablespoons chopped green onions**

Roll out each biscuit into a 5-in. circle; place each in an ungreased muffin cup. Cut sausages into fourths; brown in a skillet. Drain. Divide sausages among cups. In a small bowl, combine eggs, cheese and onions; spoon 1 tablespoon into each cup. Bake at 400° for 10-12 minutes or until browned. **Yield:** 10 servings.

# Quick & Easy Breakfast & Brunch

THE MORNING won't be awasting when your menu's made up of any of these express recipes for breakfast and brunch eating. Thanks to their especially easy preparation, all are guaranteed to get the cook out of the kitchen—and on to enjoying the day—extra quickly.

### BREAKFAST IN A CUP

*Donna Chapman, Anchor Point, Alaska*

*I usually double this recipe and freeze some cups after baking to reheat for a future meal.*

> 3 cups cooked long grain rice
> 1 cup (4 ounces) shredded cheddar cheese, *divided*
> 1 can (4 ounces) chopped green chilies, drained
> 1 jar (2 ounces) diced pimientos, drained
> 1/3 cup milk
> 2 eggs
> 1/2 teaspoon ground cumin
> 1/2 teaspoon salt
> 1/4 teaspoon pepper

In a large bowl, combine rice, 1/2 cup cheese, chilies, pimientos, milk, eggs, cumin, salt and pepper. Spoon into 12 greased muffin cups. Sprinkle with remaining cheese. Bake at 400° for 15 minutes or until eggs are set. **Yield:** 12 servings.

### CHICKEN A LA KING

*Polly Hurst, Flemingsburg, Kentucky*

*I copied this out of a magazine years ago while traveling with my husband, who was in the army. This is also delicious served over biscuits.*

> 1/4 cup butter *or* margarine
> 1/3 cup all-purpose flour
> 1/2 teaspoon salt
> 1 cup chicken broth

> 1 cup milk
> 2 cups diced cooked chicken
> 1 can (4 ounces) mushroom stems and pieces, drained
> 1 jar (2 ounces) diced pimientos, drained

Toast points

In a saucepan, melt butter; stir in flour and salt until smooth. Add the broth and milk; bring to a boil over medium heat. Cook and stir for 2 minutes or until thickened. Stir in the chicken, mushrooms and pimientos; heat through. Serve over toast points. **Yield:** 4 servings.

### SPINACH FRITTATA

*Betty Breeden, Elko, Nevada*

*I make this recipe year-round but especially enjoy it with fresh spinach from our garden.*

> 1/2 cup chopped green onions
> 2 tablespoons olive *or* vegetable oil
> 10 eggs
> 1/2 cup milk
> 1 package (10 ounces) frozen chopped spinach, thawed and drained
> 1/2 cup sliced fresh mushrooms
> 1/4 teaspoon garlic powder

Salt and pepper to taste

In an ovenproof skillet, saute onions in oil until tender. Beat eggs and milk; add to onions with the remaining ingredients. Cook over medium heat for 5 minutes. Bake, uncovered, at 325° for 15 minutes or until a knife inserted near the center comes out clean. **Yield:** 6-8 servings.

### APPLE 'N' HONEY SCONES

*Bernadette Colvin, Houston, Texas*

*These scones take little time to prepare and are wonderfully moist with lots of flavor.*

2 cups all-purpose flour
2/3 cup wheat germ
2 teaspoons baking powder
1 teaspoon ground cinnamon
1/4 teaspoon baking soda
1/4 teaspoon salt
1/4 teaspoon ground nutmeg
1/3 cup cold butter *or* margarine
1 large tart apple, peeled and chopped
1/2 cup milk
1/4 cup honey
TOPPING:
2 teaspoons wheat germ
2 teaspoons sugar
1/4 teaspoon ground cinnamon

In a large bowl, combine flour, wheat germ, baking powder, cinnamon, baking soda, salt and nutmeg. Cut in the butter until mixture resembles coarse crumbs. Combine apple, milk and honey; add to dry ingredients just until moistened. Turn onto a floured surface and knead gently 5-6 times. Gently pat dough into a 9-in. circle, 1/2 in. thick. Combine topping ingredients; sprinkle over dough. Cut into eight wedges and place on a greased baking sheet. Bake at 400° for 15-18 minutes. **Yield:** 8 scones.

## GERMAN FARMER'S BREAKFAST

*Mary Lou Welsh, Hinsdale, Illinois*

*This casserole can be quickly prepared for a holiday breakfast or weekend brunch.*

6 bacon strips, diced
3 large potatoes, peeled, cooked and cubed
1 small green pepper, diced
2 tablespoons finely chopped onion
Salt and pepper to taste
1/2 cup shredded cheddar cheese
6 eggs
1/4 cup milk

In a skillet over low heat, cook bacon until crisp; remove to paper towel. Reserve 2 tablespoons drippings; add potatoes, green pepper, onion, salt and pepper. Cook and stir over medium heat for 6-8 minutes or until the potatoes are golden brown. Stir in cheese and bacon; remove mixture to a bowl and set aside. Beat eggs and milk; pour into the same skillet. Cook and stir gently over medium heat until eggs are completely set, about 3-5 minutes. Add the potato mixture; cook and stir gently until heated through. **Yield:** 4-6 servings.

## SUNSHINE SALAD

*Margaret Ulrich, Braidwood, Illinois*

**(Pictured below)**

*I found this recipe years ago. When I prepare it for an evening meal, I call it "Sunset Salad".*

1 can (20 ounces) pineapple tidbits
1 can (11 ounces) mandarin oranges
1 package (3.4 ounces) instant lemon pudding
1 cup quartered strawberries
1 cup sliced ripe bananas

Drain pineapple and oranges, reserving liquid. In a large bowl, combine pudding mix with reserved fruit juices. Fold in pineapple, oranges and strawberries; chill for at least 2 hours. Add bananas just before serving. **Yield:** 8-10 servings.

## BAKED BREAKFAST BURRITOS

*Carol Towey, Pasadena, California*

**(Pictured above)**

*Every week, I try a minimum of three new recipes. This is one I clipped from the paper. When I served it to my five grown children, not a morsel was left!*

6 to 8 bacon strips
8 fresh mushrooms, sliced
6 green onions, sliced
1/3 cup chopped green pepper
1 garlic clove, minced
8 eggs
1/4 cup sour cream
3/4 cup shredded cheddar *or* Monterey Jack
    cheese, *divided*
3 tablespoons enchilada *or* taco sauce
1 tablespoon butter *or* margarine
4 large flour tortillas (9 inches)
Sour cream and additional enchilada *or* taco
  sauce, optional

In a skillet, cook bacon until crisp; remove to paper towel to drain. Reserve 1 tablespoon of drippings. Saute mushrooms, onions, green pepper and garlic in drippings until tender; set aside and keep warm. In a bowl, beat eggs and sour cream. Stir in 1/4 cup cheese and enchilada sauce. In a skillet, melt butter; add egg mixture. Cook over low heat, stirring occasionally until eggs are set. Remove from the heat. Crumble the bacon; add to eggs with mushroom mixture. Spoon down center of tortillas; roll up. Place, seam side down, in an 11-in. x 7-in. x 2-in. baking dish. Sprinkle with remaining cheese. Bake at 350° for 5 minutes or until cheese melts. Serve with sour cream and enchilada sauce if desired. **Yield:** 4 servings.

# Breakfast and Brunch Tips

● When I make my cinnamon rolls, I find the easiest way to evenly cut them is to use unwaxed dental floss or thread. Simply place a 10-inch section of thread under the roll where you want to cut it. Bring the ends of the thread together and crisscross so that the thread cuts through the dough. Repeat until all of the rolls are cut—then enjoy a neat treat!
—*Sandra Ziegel*
*Wausau, Wisconsin*

● For perfectly fried doughnuts, be sure to keep the oil at 375°. If it is too hot, the doughnuts will not be cooked through to the inside. If the oil is cooler, the doughnuts will absorb it and end up greasy.
—*Beth Kime*
*Gordon, Nebraska*

● For a tasty change from apples and raisins, I add chopped peaches and a dash of cinnamon while cooking oatmeal.

When you need to prepare breakfast sausages for a crowd, brown them a day ahead. Drain and place in a baking dish; cover with 1 inch of water and refrigerate. The next day, about 30 minutes before serving, place in a 350° oven to warm through.
—*Paulette Reyenga, Brantford, Ontario*

● If company is coming and you haven't a thing to serve with morning coffee, here's a quick way to "dress up" plain old refrigerator biscuits.

Separate several tubes of biscuits. Generously grease a 10-inch fluted tube pan and sprinkle with chopped nuts. In a microwave-safe bowl, melt 1/2 cup butter. Combine sugar and cinnamon in another bowl. Dip the biscuits into melted butter and roll in the cinnamon-sugar. Layer the biscuits in the pan and bake as directed on the package.
—*Vivian Kelsey*
*Wadena, Minnesota*

● On Easter morning, I love to make creamed eggs on toast. To keep the toast warm while I'm working on other parts of the meal, I put it in the oven at 180° (warm). Then, when I'm ready to fix the platter, everything is ready at the same time—no more cold toast!
—*Kari Caven, Moscow, Idaho*

● Turn plain smoked sausage into a breakfast treat by wrapping each slice with half of a bacon strip. Secure it with a toothpick, then place in a baking dish and sprinkle with brown sugar. Bake at 350° for 1 hour.
—*Julie Hinkebein*
*Wentzville, Missouri*

● Tired of your pie pastry shrinking down into the pan when prebaking for quiche? Place your unbaked pastry shell in a pie plate and flute edges. Take the same-size disposable foil pie pan and punch holes in the bottom with a sharp object (such as a clean nail). Turn up the crimped edge of the foil pan so it won't ruin the fluted edge of your pie shell. Place the foil pan over your pastry and press firmly. Bake as usual.
—*Faye Peachey, Bay Tree, Alberta*

● To add pizzazz to your buttermilk pancakes, spread each one with butter while still hot, then sprinkle them with brown sugar and top with sliced bananas. Finally, drizzle with a little bit of hot coffee just to make the sugar melt. Serve and enjoy! —*Shirley Noorlun*
*Battle Ground, Washington*

## AMISH BAKED OATMEAL

*Colleen Butler, Inwood, West Virginia*

**(Pictured below)**

*The first time I had this warm, wonderful treat was at a bed-and-breakfast in Lancaster, Pennsylvania. To me, it tasted just like a big warm-from-the-oven oatmeal cookie!*

1-1/2 cups quick-cooking oats
1/2 cup sugar
1/2 cup milk
1/4 cup butter *or* margarine, melted
1 egg
1 teaspoon baking powder
3/4 teaspoon salt
1 teaspoon vanilla extract
**Warm milk**
**Fresh fruit** *and/or* **brown sugar, optional**

Combine the first eight ingredients; mix well. Spread evenly in a greased 13-in. x 9-in. x 2-in. baking pan. Bake at 350° for 25-30 minutes or until edges are golden brown. Immediately spoon into bowls; add milk. Top with fruit and/or brown sugar if desired. **Yield:** 6 servings.

## CRUSTLESS SPINACH QUICHE

*Melinda Calverley, Janesville, Wisconsin*

*I served this dish at a church luncheon, and I had to laugh when one gentleman said to me, "This is good, and I don't even like broccoli!" I replied, "Sir, it isn't broccoli. It's spinach." He quickly answered, "Oh, I don't like spinach either, but this is good!"*

1 cup chopped onion
1 cup sliced fresh mushrooms
1 tablespoon vegetable oil
1 package (10 ounces) frozen chopped spinach, thawed and well drained
2/3 cup finely chopped fully cooked ham
5 eggs
3 cups (12 ounces) shredded Muenster *or* Monterey Jack cheese
1/8 teaspoon pepper

In a large skillet, saute onion and mushrooms in oil until tender. Add spinach and ham. Cook and stir until the excess moisture is evaporated. Cool slightly. Beat eggs; add cheese and mix well. Stir in spinach mixture and pepper; blend well. Spread evenly into a greased 9-in. pie plate or quiche dish. Bake at 350° for 40-45 minutes or until a knife inserted near the center comes out clean. **Yield:** 6-8 servings.

## CREAMED HAM ON TOAST

*Robin Morton, Ripley, Mississippi*

*Whether for breakfast or brunch—or lunch or supper—this recipe has been popular in our family for years. It is one that my grandmother passed down. The ham, green pepper and celery mixture is delicious!*

1 cup chopped fully cooked ham
1/3 cup chopped green pepper
1/4 cup sliced celery
2 tablespoons butter *or* margarine
3 tablespoons all-purpose flour
1-1/2 cups milk
1/4 teaspoon pepper
1/4 teaspoon celery seed
1 hard-cooked egg, chopped
5 slices process American cheese, quartered
3 slices toast, cut into triangles

In a skillet, saute the ham, green pepper and celery in butter for 4-5 minutes. Sprinkle with flour; stir until smooth and bubbly. Add the milk, pepper and celery seed; bring to a boil. Cook and stir for 2 minutes. Remove from the heat. Add egg and cheese; stir until cheese melts. Serve over toast. **Yield:** 2-3 servings.

## APPLE PANCAKES

*Fern Motzinger, Omaha, Nebraska*

*My husband loves pancakes and is a hearty eater. When we both became diabetics, I revised the recipe to fit our dietary needs.*

☑ This tasty dish uses less fat, sugar or salt. Recipe includes Nutritional Analysis and Diabetic Exchanges.

2 cups reduced-fat biscuit/baking mix
Artificial sweetener equivalent to 2 teaspoons sugar
1 teaspoon baking powder
1 teaspoon ground cinnamon
1/4 teaspoon salt
Egg substitute equivalent to 1 egg
1 cup skim milk
2 teaspoons vanilla extract
1 tart apple, peeled and grated

In a bowl, combine biscuit mix, sweetener, baking powder, cinnamon and salt. In another bowl, combine egg substitute, milk and vanilla; stir into dry ingredients. Fold in apple. Pour batter by 1/4 cupfuls onto a hot skillet coated with nonstick cooking spray; turn when bubbles form on top. Cook until second side is golden brown. **Yield:** 10 servings. **Nutritional Analysis:** One serving (one pancake) equals 117 calories, 420 mg sodium, 1 mg cholesterol, 21 gm carbohydrate, 3 gm protein, 2 gm fat. **Diabetic Exchanges:** 1-1/2 starch, 1/2 fat.

## BREAKFAST PIZZA

*Peggy Sisson, Hot Springs Village, Arkansas*

*I often bake this the day before and then reheat and enjoy it the next day.*

1 pound regular, sage *or* hot bulk pork sausage
1-1/4 cups frozen shredded hash brown potatoes, thawed
1 cup (4 ounces) shredded cheddar cheese
5 eggs
1/2 cup milk
1/4 teaspoon salt
1/8 teaspoon pepper
Grated Parmesan cheese
Paprika, optional

In a skillet, brown sausage; drain. Spoon into an ungreased 10-in. pie pan. Top with potatoes and cheddar cheese. In a bowl, beat eggs, milk, salt and pepper; pour over cheese. Sprinkle with Parmesan cheese and paprika if desired. Bake, uncovered, at 375° for 30-35 minutes or until golden brown. **Yield:** 6 servings.

## FRENCH TOAST CUSTARD

*Pamela Hamp, Arroyo Grande, California*

**(Pictured above)**

*I usually make this dish for brunch, but it's also wonderful for breakfast or dinner. Guests have said it just melts in their mouth.*

8 to 10 slices day-old French bread (1 inch thick)
5 tablespoons butter *or* margarine, melted
4 eggs
2 egg yolks
3 cups milk
1 cup whipping cream
1/2 cup sugar
1 tablespoon vanilla extract
1/4 teaspoon ground nutmeg
Confectioners' sugar, optional

Brush both sides of bread with butter; place in a greased 13-in. x 9-in. x 2-in. baking dish. In a large bowl, beat eggs and yolks. Add milk, cream, sugar, vanilla and nutmeg; mix well. Pour over the bread. Cover and chill overnight. Remove from the refrigerator 30 minutes before baking. Bake, uncovered, at 350° for 55-60 minutes or until a knife inserted near the center comes out clean. Cool 10 minutes before serving. Dust with confectioners' sugar if desired. **Yield:** 8-10 servings.

# Tasty Ways to Use Up Eggcess Easter Eggs!

WHAT in the world can you do with all those hard-cooked eggs the Easter Bunny leaves behind each year?

Here's a delicious solution to your annual dilemma, thanks to the folks at the American Egg Board. Try some of these delightful recipes—all of them featuring hard-cooked eggs—to add a timely taste of the season to an Easter brunch or springtime luncheon.

## CREATE-YOUR-OWN EGG SALAD

**(Pictured at right)**

1/4 to 1/3 cup bottled salad dressing*
1/4 to 1/2 teaspoon dried herbs (dill, basil, thyme *or* tarragon)
1/4 teaspoon salt, optional
1/8 teaspoon pepper
  6 hard-cooked eggs, chopped *or* sliced
  1 to 1-1/2 cups cooked rice *or* pasta with your choice of chopped fruits *and/or* vegetables (apples, grapes, avocados, carrots, cucumbers, green or sweet red pepper, onion, olives, zucchini)

In a bowl, combine dressing, herbs, salt if desired and pepper. Gently stir in eggs and 1 to 1-1/2 cups total of rice, pasta, fruits and vegetables. Cover and chill for at least 1 hour. **Yield:** about 3 cups. ***Editor's Note:** In place of bottled salad dressing, you can use mayonnaise, sour cream or plain yogurt.

## DILLY DEVILED EGGS

**(Pictured above right)**

1 small cucumber, shredded
1 teaspoon salt
6 hard-cooked eggs
1/4 cup sour cream
1/4 teaspoon dill weed
**Fresh dill *and/or* parsley, optional**

Combine cucumber and salt; let stand 15 minutes.

Drain and squeeze out excess liquid; set aside. Slice eggs in half lengthwise; remove yolks and set whites aside. In a bowl, mash yolks; stir in sour cream and dill weed. Add cucumber. Evenly fill egg whites. Garnish with dill and/or parsley if desired. Chill until ready to serve. **Yield:** 1 dozen.

## GOLDEN GRILLS

**(Pictured above)**

  6 hard-cooked eggs, chopped
1/2 cup diced fully cooked ham
1/3 cup diced onion
1/4 cup shredded Swiss cheese
  2 tablespoons sweet pickle relish
  2 tablespoons mayonnaise *or* salad dressing
1/2 teaspoon salt
**Butter *or* margarine, softened**
  12 slices rye bread

In a bowl, combine the first seven ingredients. Butter one side of each slice of bread. Place six slices on a griddle or skillet, buttered side down. Spread about 1/3 cup filling on each slice. Top with remaining bread, buttered side up. Cook each side until golden brown and cheese is melted. **Yield:** 6 servings.

## LASAGNA FLORENTINE

### (Pictured at left)

1 egg
1 package (10 ounces) frozen chopped spinach, cooked and drained
1 cup cottage cheese
1 can (15 ounces) Italian-style tomato sauce
6 lasagna noodles, cooked and drained
8 hard-cooked eggs, sliced
1 cup (4 ounces) shredded mozzarella cheese
1/4 cup dry bread crumbs
2 tablespoons grated Parmesan cheese
2 tablespoons butter *or* margarine, melted
1 garlic clove, minced

In a bowl, combine egg, spinach and cottage cheese; set aside. In a greased 11-in. x 7-in. x 2-in. baking dish, layer half of the tomato sauce, noodles, spinach mixture, hard-cooked eggs and mozzarella. Repeat layers. Combine the crumbs, Parmesan cheese, butter and garlic; sprinkle over top. Cover and bake at 350° for 35 minutes; uncover and bake 10 minutes longer or until heated through. **Yield:** 6-8 servings.

## PICKLED EGGS

2 cups vinegar
1 medium onion, thinly sliced
2 tablespoons sugar
2 teaspoons mixed pickling spices
2 teaspoons curry powder
1 teaspoon salt
12 hard-cooked eggs, peeled

In a medium saucepan, combine the first six ingredients; bring to a boil. Reduce heat; simmer, uncovered, until onion is tender, about 5 minutes. Place six eggs each in two 1-qt. jars with tight-fitting lids. Pour half of the hot vinegar mixture into each jar; cover with lids. Refrigerate several hours or overnight. **Yield:** 1 dozen.

## BRUNCH ENCHILADAS

8 hard-cooked eggs, chopped
1 can (8-1/2 ounces) cream-style corn
2/3 cup shredded cheddar cheese
1 can (4 ounces) chopped green chilies, undrained
2 teaspoons taco seasoning mix
1/4 teaspoon salt
8 corn tortillas, warmed
1 bottle (8 ounces) mild taco sauce
Sour cream, optional

Combine the first six ingredients; spoon 1/2 cup down the center of each tortilla. Roll up tightly. Place, seam side down, in a greased 13-in. x 9-in. x 2-in. baking dish. Top with taco sauce. Bake, uncovered, at 350° for 15 minutes or until heated through. Serve with sour cream if desired. **Yield:** 8 servings.

## EASY DOES IT WITH HARD-COOKED EGGS

IF YOU find it difficult to peel hard-cooked eggs, you may be using eggs that are too fresh. Store eggs in cartons in the refrigerator for about a week before hard-cooking them.

Cook, don't boil, eggs. Follow this foolproof method for tender hard-cooked eggs: In a saucepan, place eggs in a single layer (for better circulation and even cooking). Add enough tap water to come at least 1 inch above eggs. Cover and quickly bring to a boil. Turn heat off and remove pan from the burner. Let eggs stand, covered, for 15 minutes for large eggs. (Adjust time up or down by 3 minutes for each size larger or smaller.) Immediately run cold water over eggs until completely cooled. Refrigerate until ready to serve.

To easily remove the hard-cooked egg's shell, crack it by tapping it gently all over. Roll the egg between your hands to loosen the shell, then begin to peel. It may be helpful to hold the egg under running water or dip it in a bowl of water to ease off the shell.

## HAM 'N' CHEESE STRATA

*Marilyn Kroeker, Steinbach, Manitoba*

**(Pictured below)**

*Our daughter wouldn't mind if I made this every weekend! I do prepare it for each holiday, serving it alongside fresh cinnamon buns and a fruit salad.*

  12 slices white bread, crusts removed
   1 pound fully cooked ham, diced
   2 cups (8 ounces) shredded cheddar
     cheese
   6 eggs
   3 cups milk
   2 teaspoons Worcestershire sauce
   1 teaspoon ground mustard
1/2 teaspoon salt
1/4 teaspoon pepper
Dash cayenne pepper
1/4 cup minced onion
1/4 cup minced green pepper
1/4 cup butter *or* margarine, melted
   1 cup crushed cornflakes

Arrange six slices of bread in the bottom of a greased 13-in. x 9-in. x 2-in. baking dish. Top with ham and cheese. Cover with remaining bread. In a bowl, beat eggs, milk, Worcestershire sauce, mustard, salt, pepper and cayenne. Stir in onion and green pepper; pour over all. Cover and refrigerate overnight. Remove from the refrigerator 30 minutes before baking. Pour butter over bread; sprinkle with cornflakes. Bake, uncovered, at 350° for 50-60 minutes or until a knife inserted near the center comes out clean. Let stand 10 minutes before serving. **Yield:** 8-10 servings.

## HERBED WAFFLES WITH CREAMED BEEF

*Lois McCormick, Muncy, Pennsylvania*

*This is a nice recipe to whip up when you come home from church. I adapted it from one I saw in an old cookbook. It's a little different way to use herbs.*

   2 cups all-purpose flour
   1 tablespoon baking powder
1/2 teaspoon salt
1-3/4 cups milk
   6 tablespoons butter *or* margarine, melted
   2 eggs, *separated*
   1 tablespoon chopped fresh parsley
   1 tablespoon grated onion
1/2 teaspoon rubbed sage
1/2 teaspoon dried thyme
**CREAMED BEEF:**
   6 tablespoons butter *or* margarine
   6 tablespoons all-purpose flour
2-1/2 cups milk
1/4 teaspoon dried thyme
   1 package (4 ounces) shredded dried beef
Chopped fresh parsley, optional

Combine the first three ingredients; set aside. In a mixing bowl, beat milk, butter, egg yolks, parsley, onion, sage and thyme. Gradually add dry ingredients; mix well. Beat egg whites until stiff peaks form; fold into batter. Bake in a preheated waffle iron according to manufacturer's directions until golden brown. Meanwhile, in a saucepan, melt butter; add flour. Whisk in milk and thyme; bring to a boil. Cook and stir for 2 minutes or until thick. Add the beef and heat through. Serve over waffles. Sprinkle with parsley if desired. **Yield:** 7 waffles (6 inches).

## BRUNCH EGG CASSEROLE

*Mavis McBride, Mena, Arkansas*

*Make sure to include this easy dish on your menu— it features hard-cooked eggs, which you're likely to have in abundance at Easter.*

  10 hard-cooked eggs, chopped
1-1/2 cups diced celery

2/3 cup mayonnaise
1/2 cup chopped pecans *or* walnuts
  2 tablespoons chopped green pepper
  1 teaspoon finely chopped onion
1/2 teaspoon salt
1/4 teaspoon pepper
  1 cup (4 ounces) shredded cheddar cheese
1/2 cup crushed potato chips

In a bowl, combine eggs, celery, mayonnaise, nuts, green pepper, onion, salt and pepper; mix well. Pour into a greased 11-in. x 7-in. x 2-in. baking dish. Sprinkle with cheese and potato chips. Bake, uncovered, at 375° for 25 minutes or until heated through. **Yield:** 6-8 servings.

## APPLE NUT HOTCAKES

*Barbara Nowakowski*
*North Tonawanda, New York*

**(Pictured above)**

*Not only are these an old family favorite, they're a neighborhood favorite as well. We have several bachelor neighbors who all rave about them.*

  1 cup all-purpose flour
  2 tablespoons sugar

  2 teaspoons baking powder
1/2 teaspoon salt
1/2 teaspoon ground cinnamon
3/4 cup milk
  3 tablespoons butter *or* margarine, melted
  2 teaspoons vanilla extract
  2 egg whites
1/2 cup shredded peeled apple
1/2 cup chopped walnuts
**APPLE SYRUP:**
  1/4 cup sugar
    4 teaspoons cornstarch
  1/4 teaspoon ground allspice
1-1/2 cups apple juice

In a large bowl, combine flour, sugar, baking powder, salt and cinnamon. In another bowl, combine milk, butter and vanilla; mix well. Stir into dry ingredients just until combined. Beat egg whites until stiff peaks form; fold into batter with apple and nuts. Pour batter by 1/4 cupfuls onto a lightly greased hot griddle; turn when bubbles form on top. Cook until second side is golden brown. For syrup, combine sugar, cornstarch and allspice in a medium saucepan; stir in apple juice. Cook and stir over medium heat until thickened, about 6-8 minutes. Serve over hotcakes. **Yield:** 10-12 hotcakes.

THE MOUTH-WATERING *aroma of bread baking in the oven is irresistible. And the flavor of these homemade rolls, muffins, breads and biscuits is equally unbeatable!*

**OVEN-FRESH GOODNESS.** Top to bottom: Rhubarb Muffins (p. 88), Whole Wheat Braids (p. 87) and Southern Banana Nut Bread (p. 87).

# Breads & Rolls

## SOUTHERN BANANA NUT BREAD

*Viva Forman, Tallahassee, Florida*

**(Pictured at left)**

*I found this banana bread recipe in an old church recipe book. It really is good with pecans in the bread and in the topping, which makes it unique.*

1/2 cup butter-flavored shortening
1-1/2 cups sugar
2 eggs
1 cup mashed ripe bananas (about 2 medium)
1 teaspoon vanilla extract
2 cups self-rising flour*
1/2 cup buttermilk
3/4 cup chopped pecans
TOPPING:
1/4 to 1/3 cup mashed ripe bananas
1-1/4 cups confectioners' sugar
1 teaspoon lemon juice
Additional chopped pecans

In a mixing bowl, cream shortening and sugar; beat in eggs. Blend in bananas and vanilla. Add flour alternately with buttermilk. Fold in pecans. Pour into two greased 8-in. x 4-in. x 2-in. loaf pans. Bake at 350° for 45-55 minutes or until a toothpick inserted near the center comes out clean. Cool in pan for 10 minutes before removing to a wire rack; cool completely. For topping, combine bananas, confectioners' sugar and lemon juice; spread over loaves. Sprinkle with pecans. **Yield:** 2 loaves. **\*Editor's Note:** As a substitute for each cup of self-rising flour, place 1-1/2 teaspoons baking powder and 1/2 teaspoon salt in a measuring cup; add all-purpose flour to equal 1 cup.

## WHOLE WHEAT BRAIDS

*Suella Miller, LaGrange, Indiana*

**(Pictured at left)**

*There's nothing like fresh bread to complete a meal.*

*I've had very good results with this recipe. Braiding the dough makes a pretty presentation.*

☑ This tasty dish uses less fat, sugar or salt. Recipe includes Nutritional Analysis and Diabetic Exchanges.

3 packages (1/4 ounce *each*) active dry yeast
3 cups warm water (110° to 115°)
1/2 cup sugar
3 eggs
1/3 cup vegetable oil
1 tablespoon salt
5 cups whole wheat flour
4 to 4-1/2 cups all-purpose flour

In a mixing bowl, dissolve yeast in warm water. Add the sugar, eggs, oil, salt and whole wheat flour; beat until smooth. Add enough all-purpose flour to form a soft dough. Turn onto a floured surface; knead until smooth and elastic, about 6-8 minutes. Place in a greased bowl, turning once to grease top. Cover and let rise in a warm place until doubled, about 1 hour. Punch dough down. Divide into nine pieces; shape each piece into a 14-in. rope and braid three ropes together. Place in three greased 8-in. x 4-in. x 2-in. loaf pans. Cover and let rise until doubled, about 30 minutes. Bake at 350° for 40-45 minutes. Remove from pans to cool on wire racks. **Yield:** 3 loaves (16 slices each). **Nutritional Analysis:** One slice equals 112 calories, 138 mg sodium, 13 mg cholesterol, 20 gm carbohydrate, 3 gm protein, 2 gm fat. **Diabetic Exchanges:** 1-1/2 starch.

## SWEET HONEY ALMOND BUTTER

*Evelyn Harris, Waynesboro, Virginia*

*This homemade butter makes a nice gift along with a fresh-from-the-oven loaf of bread.*

1 cup butter *or* margarine, softened
3/4 cup honey
3/4 cup confectioners' sugar
3/4 cup finely ground almonds
1/4 to 1/2 teaspoon almond extract

In a mixing bowl, combine all ingredients; mix well. Store in the refrigerator. **Yield:** 2 cups.

surface; knead until smooth and elastic, about 6-8 minutes. Place in a greased bowl, turning once to grease top. Cover and let rise in a warm place until doubled, about 1 hour. For filling, beat egg whites in a mixing bowl until foamy; gradually add sugar and beat well. Stir in nuts and butter; mix well. Punch dough down; divide into eight balls. Roll each into an 8-in. circle; brush with melted butter. Spread about 2/3 cup filling on each circle. Roll up tightly into loaves; seal ends. Place on greased baking sheets. Cover and let rise until doubled, about 50 minutes. Brush with egg. Bake at 350° for 20-25 minutes or until golden brown. Cool on wire racks. **Yield:** 8 loaves.

## RHUBARB MUFFINS

*Evelyn Winchester, Hilton, New York*

**(Pictured on page 86)**

*I had several rhubarb plants on our farm in Iowa. Even though I moved East to be closer to my children and grandchildren, I still make these muffins. I even won a ribbon with them at the 4-H bake sale here.*

> 1 egg
> 1-1/4 cups packed brown sugar
> 1 cup buttermilk
> 1/2 cup vegetable oil
> 2 teaspoons vanilla extract
> 2-1/2 cups all-purpose flour
> 1 teaspoon baking soda
> 1 teaspoon baking powder
> 1/2 teaspoon salt
> 1-1/2 cups diced fresh rhubarb
> 1/2 cup chopped walnuts
> TOPPING:
> 1/3 cup sugar
> 1 teaspoon ground cinnamon
> 1 teaspoon butter *or* margarine, melted

In a mixing bowl, beat egg. Add brown sugar, buttermilk, oil and vanilla; beat for 1 minute. Combine dry ingredients; stir into sugar mixture just until moistened. Fold in rhubarb and walnuts. Fill greased or paper-lined muffin cups three-fourths full. Combine topping ingredients; sprinkle over muffins. Bake at 375° for 20-25 minutes or until muffins test done. **Yield:** 1 dozen.

## FRUIT 'N' NUT LOAF

*Janet Boulger, Botwood, Newfoundland*

*I enjoy all kinds of cooking, but especially like baking delicious breads like this! It's chock-full of good things like apricots, almonds and bananas.*

## NUT SWIRL BREAD

*Darlene Simmons, Newfield, New Jersey*

**(Pictured above)**

*The best way that I can describe these nutty loaves is to say they taste like a celebration. Cooking from scratch like this is an easy way to cut a few corners on my food budget.*

> 2 packages (1/4 ounce *each*) active dry yeast
> 1/4 cup warm water (110° to 115°)
> 2 cups warm milk (110° to 115°)
> 1/2 cup sugar
> 1/2 cup butter *or* margarine, softened
> 2 eggs
> 2 teaspoons salt
> 7 to 7-1/2 cups all-purpose flour
> FILLING:
> 5 egg whites
> 1 cup sugar
> 5 cups finely chopped walnuts *or* pecans (about 1-1/2 pounds)
> 1 tablespoon butter *or* margarine, melted
> Additional melted butter
> 1 egg, beaten

In a large mixing bowl, dissolve yeast in water. Add milk, sugar, butter, eggs, salt and 3-1/2 cups of flour; beat until smooth. Add enough remaining flour to form a soft dough. Turn onto a floured

This tasty dish uses less fat, sugar or salt. Recipe includes Nutritional Analysis and Diabetic Exchanges.

1 cup all-purpose flour
1 cup whole wheat flour
1 cup raisins
2/3 cup instant nonfat dry milk powder
1/2 cup packed brown sugar
1/2 cup finely chopped dried apricots
1/3 cup wheat germ
1/4 cup chopped toasted almonds
2 teaspoons baking powder
1/2 teaspoon baking soda
1/2 teaspoon salt
Egg substitute equivalent to 3 eggs
3/4 cup orange juice
1/2 cup vegetable oil
1/2 cup molasses
2 large ripe bananas, mashed

In a large bowl, combine the first 11 ingredients. In another bowl, beat the egg substitute, juice, oil, molasses and bananas; stir into dry ingredients just until moistened. Pour into two 8-in. x 4-in. x 2-in. loaf pans that have been coated with non-stick cooking spray. Bake at 325° for 1 hour or until bread tests done. Cool for 10 minutes; remove from pans to wire racks to cool. **Yield:** 2 loaves (14 slices each). **Nutritional Analysis:** One slice equals 158 calories, 136 mg sodium, trace cholesterol, 25 gm carbohydrate, 3 gm protein, 6 gm fat. **Diabetic Exchanges:** 1 starch, 1 fat, 1/2 fruit.

## APPLE LADDER LOAF
*Norma Foster, Compton, Illinois*

**(Pictured at right)**

*I first served my family this rich bread with its spicy apple filling years ago. From the very first bite, it was a hit with everyone. Now I bake it often for church groups, potluck dinners and parties with friends. It makes a nice breakfast pastry or—with a scoop of ice cream—a lovely dessert.*

1 package (1/4 ounce) active dry yeast
1/4 cup warm water (110° to 115°)
1/2 cup warm milk (110° to 115°)
1/2 cup butter *or* margarine, softened
1/3 cup sugar
4 eggs
4-1/2 to 4-3/4 cups all-purpose flour
FILLING:
1/3 cup packed brown sugar
2 tablespoons all-purpose flour
1-1/4 teaspoons ground cinnamon
1/2 teaspoon ground nutmeg
1/8 teaspoon ground allspice
4 cups thinly sliced peeled tart apples

1/4 cup butter *or* margarine, softened
ICING:
1 cup confectioners' sugar
1 to 2 tablespoons orange juice
1/4 teaspoon vanilla extract

In a mixing bowl, dissolve yeast in water; let stand for 5 minutes. Add milk, butter, sugar, eggs and 1 cup flour. Beat on low speed for 3 minutes. Stir in enough remaining flour to form a soft dough. Knead on a floured surface until smooth and elastic, about 6-8 minutes. Place in a greased bowl, turning once to grease top. Cover and refrigerate for 6-24 hours; punch down after 1-2 hours. For filling, combine sugar, flour, cinnamon, nutmeg and allspice in a small bowl. Add apples; toss to coat. Set aside. Punch dough down; divide in half. Roll each half into a 12-in. x 9-in. rectangle. Place each rectangle on a greased baking sheet. Spread with butter. Spread filling down center third of each rectangle. On each long side, cut 1-in.-wide strips 3 in. into center. Starting at one end, fold alternating strips at an angle across filling; seal ends. Cover and let rise for 45-60 minutes or until nearly doubled. Bake at 350° for 25-30 minutes or until golden brown. Combine icing ingredients until smooth; drizzle over warm loaves. Serve warm or at room temperature. **Yield:** 2 loaves.

## SOUTHWESTERN SAVORY MUFFINS

*Laura Parker, Los Alamos, New Mexico*

**(Pictured below)**

*When I was first married, I found a muffin recipe that called for bacon. I modified it through the years and came up with this recipe. It's become a favorite breakfast treat for my husband and me. He grew up in northern New Mexico and thinks most foods benefit from the addition of green chilies.*

    10 bacon strips
     2 cups all-purpose flour
    1/4 cup sugar
     1 tablespoon baking powder
    3/4 cup milk
     1 egg
    1-1/2 cups (6 ounces) shredded cheddar
        cheese
    1/4 cup diced green chilies

In a skillet, cook the bacon until crisp; reserve 1/3 cup drippings. Crumble bacon and set aside. In a large bowl, combine flour, sugar and baking powder. In a mixing bowl, beat milk, egg and drippings; stir into dry ingredients just until moistened. Fold in the cheese, chilies and bacon. Fill greased or paper-lined muffin cups three-fourths full. Bake at 400° for 15-20 minutes or until golden brown. Serve warm. **Yield:** 14 servings.

## CINNAMON ROLLS

*Kim Marie VanRheenan, Mendota, Illinois*

*This recipe is simplified by starting with frozen bread dough. Chopped apple contributes to the texture and taste. I've made these for family reunions and other gatherings, and they're always warmly received.*

☑ This tasty dish uses less fat, sugar or salt. Recipe includes Nutritional Analysis and Diabetic Exchanges.

     1 loaf (1 pound) frozen white bread
        dough, thawed
     2 tablespoons reduced-fat margarine,
        softened
     1 tablespoon ground cinnamon
     1 small tart apple, peeled and chopped
    3/4 cup raisins
    1/2 cup chopped pecans

Roll dough into a 12-in. x 9-in. rectangle. Brush with margarine; sprinkle with cinnamon. Sprinkle apple, raisins and pecans evenly over dough. Roll up jelly roll style, starting at a long side. Cut into 12 slices, 1 in. each. Place rolls, cut side down, in a greased 11-in. x 7-in. x 2-in. baking dish. Cover and let rise until doubled, about 1 hour. Bake at 350° for 25-30 minutes or until golden brown. Cool on a wire rack. **Yield:** 1 dozen. **Nutritional Analysis:** One serving (one roll) equals 183 calories, 234 mg sodium, 0 cholesterol, 30 gm carbohydrate, 5 gm protein, 6 gm fat. **Diabetic Exchanges:** 2 starch, 1 fat.

## BANANA STREUSEL MUFFINS

*Robin Perry, Seneca, Pennsylvania*

*I often make muffins for my husband and our two teenage sons. I like to use whatever fruit is in season, and since bananas are available year-round, I make this recipe frequently. Everyone loves the banana flavor and the streusel topping.*

     2 cups all-purpose flour
     1 cup sugar
     1 teaspoon baking powder
    1/2 teaspoon salt

1/2 teaspoon baking soda
1/4 teaspoon ground cinnamon
   2 eggs
   1 cup (8 ounces) sour cream
1/4 cup butter *or* margarine, melted
   2 medium ripe bananas, mashed (1 cup)
STREUSEL:
1/4 cup sugar
   3 tablespoons all-purpose flour
1/4 teaspoon ground cinnamon
   2 tablespoons butter *or* margarine

In a large bowl, combine the flour, sugar, baking powder, salt, baking soda and cinnamon. In a small bowl, beat eggs, sour cream, butter and bananas; stir into dry ingredients just until moistened. Fill greased or paper-lined muffin cups three-fourths full. For streusel, combine sugar, flour and cinnamon in a small bowl; cut in butter. Sprinkle over muffins. Bake at 375° for 20-25 minutes. **Yield:** about 1 dozen.

## OPEN FIRE BREAD

*Kathy Thye Dewbre, Kimberley, South Africa*

*I was raised on a farm in Gowrie, Iowa, but my husband and I have been missionaries in Africa since 1989. We were introduced to this bread at a street fair, where it was cooked over an open fire, then served with meaty farm sausages. We quickly learned how to make it from a retired farm family.*

   2 packages (1/4 ounce *each*) active dry
      yeast
   2 teaspoons honey
   3 cups warm water (110° to 115°),
      *divided*
   2 teaspoons salt
   1 tablespoon vegetable oil
   7 to 8 cups all-purpose flour

In a mixing bowl, combine yeast, honey and 2/3 cup water; mix well. Let stand 5 minutes. Add salt, oil, remaining water and 6 cups flour; mix well. Add enough remaining flour to form a soft dough. Turn onto a floured surface; knead until smooth and elastic, about 6-8 minutes. (Dough will be soft and slightly sticky.) Place in a greased bowl, turning once to grease top. Cover and let rise in a warm place until doubled, about 1 hour. Punch dough down. On a heavily floured surface, roll out dough to 3/4-in. thickness. Cut into 4-in. x 1-in. strips with a pizza cutter; sprinkle with flour. Place on a floured baking sheet. Let rise until doubled, about 25-30 minutes. Place strips directly on grill. Grill, uncovered, over medium-hot coals until golden brown, about 6-8 minutes, turning often. **Yield:** about 3 dozen.

## CRANBERRY PUMPKIN BREAD

*Lydia Fenton Piper, Valatie, New York*

**(Pictured above)**

*This tasty bread is perfect for a Thanksgiving meal or any time of the year. I plant pumpkins in my garden, and this is one of my favorite ways to use them.*

   1 cup canned *or* cooked pumpkin
   1 cup sugar
1/2 cup milk
   2 eggs
1/4 cup butter *or* margarine, melted
   2 cups all-purpose flour
   2 teaspoons baking powder
   1 teaspoon ground cinnamon
1/2 teaspoon baking soda
1/2 teaspoon ground nutmeg
1/2 teaspoon ground ginger
   1 cup chopped walnuts
   1 cup fresh *or* frozen cranberries

In a mixing bowl, beat pumpkin, sugar, milk, eggs and butter. Combine dry ingredients; stir into pumpkin mixture. Fold in walnuts and cranberries. Pour into a greased 9-in. x 5-in. x 3-in. loaf pan. Bake at 350° for 70 minutes or until a toothpick inserted in the center comes out clean. Cool in pan for 10 minutes; remove to a wire rack to cool completely. **Yield:** 1 loaf.

1 cup vegetable oil
2 teaspoons vanilla extract
3 cups all-purpose flour
1 teaspoon salt
1/2 teaspoon baking powder
1/2 teaspoon baking soda
2 teaspoons ground cinnamon
1-1/2 teaspoons ground nutmeg
2 cups shredded zucchini
1 can (8 ounces) crushed pineapple, undrained

In a mixing bowl, beat eggs, sugar, oil and vanilla. Combine dry ingredients; stir into egg mixture just until moistened. Fold in zucchini and pineapple. Pour into two greased 8-in. x 4-in. x 2-in. loaf pans. Bake at 350° for 60-70 minutes or until a toothpick inserted near the center comes out clean. Cool in pans 10 minutes before removing to a wire rack. **Yield:** 2 loaves.

## SAUSAGE CORN BREAD

*Annie South, Tishomingo, Mississippi*

**(Pictured above)**

*Corn bread is a staple here in the South. I added sausage and cheddar cheese to a corn bread recipe and came up with this satisfying dish. It goes especially well with soup.*

1 pound bulk pork sausage
1 large onion, chopped
1-1/2 cups self-rising cornmeal
1 can (14-3/4 ounces) cream-style corn
3/4 cup milk
2 eggs
1/4 cup vegetable oil
2 cups (8 ounces) shredded sharp cheddar cheese

In a skillet, cook the sausage and onion until meat is browned and onion is tender; drain. In a bowl, combine cornmeal, corn, milk, eggs and oil. Pour half into a greased 10-in. ovenproof iron skillet. Sprinkle with the sausage mixture and cheese. Spread remaining cornmeal mixture on top. Bake at 425° for 45-50 minutes or until corn bread tests done. **Yield:** 8-10 servings.

## PINEAPPLE ZUCCHINI BREAD

*Sharon Lafferty, Partlow, Virginia*

*The pineapple and zucchini make a nice combination in this flavorful bread.*

2 eggs
2 cups sugar

## WHOLE WHEAT BISCUITS

*Margie Thomason, Belvidere, Kansas*

**(Pictured on cover)**

*This quick and easy recipe adds a special touch to everyday meals. See if you don't get a lot of compliments when you serve these fluffy biscuits fresh from the oven.*

1-1/2 cups all-purpose flour
1/2 cup whole wheat flour
2 tablespoons sugar
1 tablespoon baking powder
1/2 teaspoon cream of tartar
1/4 teaspoon salt
1/2 cup shortening
1 egg
1/2 cup milk
1 tablespoon butter, melted

In a bowl, combine flours, sugar, baking powder, cream of tartar and salt. Cut in shortening until mixture resembles coarse crumbs. Beat egg and milk; stir into dry ingredients until a ball forms. Turn onto a floured surface, knead 5-6 times. Roll to 1/2-in. thickness; brush with butter. Cut with a 2-in. biscuit cutter. Place on an ungreased baking sheet. Bake at 450° for 10-12 minutes or until golden brown. **Yield:** about 1 dozen.

## CINNAMON SWIRL QUICK BREAD

*Helen Richardson, Shelbyville, Michigan*

*I always take this bread—which I've been making for over 20 years—to potlucks and parties.*

Breads & Rolls

1-1/2 cups sugar, *divided*
1 tablespoon ground cinnamon
2 cups all-purpose flour
1 teaspoon baking soda
1/2 teaspoon salt
1 cup buttermilk
1 egg
1/4 cup vegetable oil
GLAZE:
1/4 cup confectioners' sugar
1-1/2 to 2 teaspoons milk

Combine 1/2 cup sugar and cinnamon; set aside. Combine flour, baking soda, salt and remaining sugar. Combine buttermilk, egg and oil; stir into dry ingredients just until combined. Grease the bottom only of a 9-in. x 5-in. x 3-in. loaf pan. Pour half of the batter into pan; sprinkle with half of the cinnamon-sugar. Carefully spread with remaining batter and sprinkle with remaining cinnamon-sugar; swirl knife through batter. Bake at 350° for 45-50 minutes or until a toothpick inserted near the center comes out clean. Cool in pan 10 minutes before removing to a wire rack to cool completely. Combine glaze ingredients; drizzle over bread. **Yield:** 1 loaf.

## HONEY WHOLE WHEAT ROLLS

*Celecia Stoup, Hobart, Oklahoma*

*Most of the farmers in our area grow wheat, so this recipe definitely represents my region. I bake these rolls often, especially when I'm making soup or stew. The honey gives these whole wheat rolls a pleasantly sweet flavor.*

2 packages (1/4 ounce *each*) active dry yeast
1 cup warm water (110° to 115°)
1/4 cup butter *or* margarine, melted
1/4 cup honey
1 egg
3/4 cup whole wheat flour
1/2 cup old-fashioned oats
1 teaspoon salt
2-1/4 to 2-3/4 cups all-purpose flour
Additional melted butter *or* margarine

In a mixing bowl, dissolve yeast in water. Stir in the butter, honey, egg, whole wheat flour, oats, salt and 1 cup of all-purpose flour; beat until smooth. Add enough remaining all-purpose flour to form a soft dough. Turn onto a floured surface; knead dough until smooth and elastic, about 6-8 minutes. Place in a greased bowl, turning once to grease top. Cover and let rise in a warm place until doubled, about 1 hour. Punch dough down. Shape into 15 rolls. Place in a greased 13-in. x 9-

in. x 2-in. baking pan. Cover and let rise until doubled, about 45 minutes. Bake at 375° for 20 minutes or until golden brown. Brush with butter. **Yield:** 15 rolls.

## PECAN BITES

*Pat Schrand, Enterprise, Alabama*

**(Pictured below)**

*While these are delicious year-round, you could easily turn them into an edible Christmas gift. They look festive on a decorative tray wrapped in red or green cellophane or tucked into a giveaway cookie plate. And don't forget to include the recipe so your recipient can enjoy this treat over and over again!*

1 cup packed brown sugar
1/2 cup all-purpose flour
1 cup chopped pecans
2/3 cup butter (no substitutes), melted
2 eggs, beaten

In a bowl, combine brown sugar, flour and pecans; set aside. Combine butter and eggs; mix well. Stir into flour mixture. Fill greased and floured miniature muffin cups two-thirds full. Bake at 350° for 22-25 minutes. Remove immediately to cool on wire racks. **Yield:** about 2-1/2 dozen. **Editor's Note:** This recipe uses only 1/2 cup flour.

## CRANBERRY SWEET ROLLS

*Germaine Stank, Pound, Wisconsin*

**(Pictured below)**

*Christmas morning will be sweeter than ever when you serve these festive rolls topped with a rich and creamy frosting. They rise nice and high and hold their shape. Plus, the tart cranberry filling is a nice change of pace from cinnamon rolls.*

1-1/4 cups sugar, *divided*
  1/2 cup water
    2 cups cranberries
    1 teaspoon grated orange peel
    2 packages (1/4 ounce *each*) active dry
      yeast
  1/2 cup warm water (110° to 115°)
  1/2 cup butter *or* margarine, softened
  1/2 cup milk
    2 eggs
    1 teaspoon salt
    1 teaspoon ground cinnamon
  1/2 teaspoon ground nutmeg
4-1/2 to 5 cups all-purpose flour
Melted butter *or* margarine
**CREAM CHEESE FROSTING:**
    1 cup confectioners' sugar
  1/2 of a 3-ounce package cream cheese,
      softened
  1/4 cup butter *or* margarine, softened
  1/2 teaspoon vanilla extract
  1/2 teaspoon milk

In a saucepan, bring 3/4 cup sugar and water to a boil. Add cranberries; return to a boil. Boil, uncovered, for 20 minutes, stirring occasionally. Stir in orange peel; cover and chill. In a mixing bowl, dissolve yeast in warm water. Add the next six ingredients, remaining sugar and 3 cups flour; beat until smooth. Add enough remaining flour to form a soft dough. Turn onto a floured surface; knead until smooth and elastic, about 6-8 minutes. Place in a greased bowl, turning once to grease top. Cover and let rise in a warm place until doubled, about 1 hour. Punch dough down. Roll into a 15-in. x 10-in. rectangle; brush with butter. Spread cranberry filling over dough to within 1 in. of edges. Roll up, jelly roll style, starting at a long side. Cut into 15 slices; place, cut side down, in a greased 13-in. x 9-in. x 2-in. baking pan. Cover and let rise until doubled, about 30 minutes. Bake at 375° for 25-30 minutes. Cool in pan 5 minutes; remove to a wire rack to cool. Beat frosting ingredients until smooth; spread over warm rolls. **Yield:** 15 servings.

## WALNUT-DATE QUICK BREAD

*Yvonne Covey, Haver Hill, Massachusetts*

*I can remember my Aunt Emma making this bread when I was a young girl, and I always loved a slice of it right from the oven. This recipe must be 60 or more years old. But it still tastes as good as ever today!*

    1 cup chopped dates
    1 cup boiling water
    3 tablespoons butter *or* margarine,
      softened
    1 cup packed brown sugar
    1 egg
1-3/4 cups all-purpose flour
    1 teaspoon baking soda
  1/4 teaspoon salt
    1 cup chopped walnuts

In a small bowl, combine the dates and water; let stand for 15 minutes (do not drain). In a mixing bowl, cream butter and brown sugar; add egg and mix well. Combine flour, baking soda and salt; add to the creamed mixture alternately with dates and liquid. Stir in walnuts. Pour into a greased 8-in. x 4-in. x 2-in. loaf pan. Bake at 350° for 60-65 minutes or until a toothpick inserted near the center comes out clean. Cool on a wire rack. **Yield:** 1 loaf.

## BUTTERMILK BROWN BREAD

*Ruby Williams, Bogalusa, Louisiana*

*This recipe is nearly 200 years old, having come over from England in the early 19th century.*

2 cups whole wheat flour
1 cup cornmeal
2 teaspoons baking soda
1 teaspoon salt
2-1/2 cups buttermilk
1/2 cup molasses

In a large bowl, combine dry ingredients. Stir in buttermilk and molasses until well blended. Pour into a large well-greased coffee can.* Cover with foil; tie securely with string. Place the can on a rack in a deep kettle. Fill kettle with 3 in. of water; bring to a boil. Reduce heat; cover kettle and simmer for 4 hours. Cool 10 minutes before removing bread from can to a wire rack. **Yield:** 1 loaf. **\*Editor's Note:** Coffee can sizes that will work for this recipe are 2.25 lb., 2 lb. 7 oz. and 1 lb. 8 oz.

## APPLE CINNAMON MUFFINS

*Serena Verboom, Providence Bay, Ontario*

*I make these mouth-watering muffins at least once a week and receive many recipe requests.*

1-1/2 cups all-purpose flour
3/4 cup sugar
3/4 teaspoon baking soda
1/2 teaspoon baking powder
3/4 teaspoon ground cinnamon
1 egg
1/3 cup orange juice
1/4 cup butter *or* margarine, melted
2 cups chopped peeled tart apples

In a large bowl, combine flour, sugar, baking soda, baking powder and cinnamon; set aside. Beat egg; add orange juice and butter. Stir into the dry ingredients just until moistened (batter will be thick). Fold in apples. Fill greased or paper-lined muffin cups two-thirds full. Bake at 350° for 20-25 minutes or until muffins test done. **Yield:** about 1 dozen.

## SAUSAGE CHEESE BRAID

*Christena Weed, Levant, Kansas*

**(Pictured above right)**

*Our daughters, grandchildren and great-grandchildren all love this bread. It's good for a snack anytime.*

2 packages (1/4 ounce *each*) active dry yeast
1-1/4 cups warm water (110° to 115°)
2 tablespoons sugar
1-1/2 teaspoons salt
1 teaspoon Italian seasoning
2 eggs, *divided*
1/4 cup butter *or* margarine, softened
4 to 4-1/2 cups all-purpose flour
1 pound bulk hot pork sausage
1 cup (4 ounces) shredded mozzarella *or* cheddar cheese

In a large mixing bowl, dissolve yeast in warm water. Add sugar, salt, Italian seasoning, 1 egg, butter and 2 cups of the flour; beat until smooth. Add enough remaining flour to form a soft dough. Turn onto a floured board; knead until smooth and elastic, about 6-8 minutes. Place in a greased bowl, turning once to grease top. Cover and let rise in a warm place until doubled, about 1 hour. Meanwhile, in a skillet, cook pork sausage until brown; drain and set aside to cool. Punch the dough down; divide in half. On a floured surface, roll each half into a 14-in. x 12-in. rectangle. Cut each one into three 14-in. x 4-in. strips. Combine mozzarella or cheddar cheese and sausage; spoon 1/2 cup down the center of each strip. Bring long edges together over filling; pinch to seal. Place three strips with seam side down on greased baking sheets. Braid strips together; secure ends. Cover and let rise until doubled, about 45 minutes. Beat remaining egg and brush over the loaves. Bake at 400° for 20-25 minutes or until golden. Immediately remove from baking sheets to wire racks. Serve warm. **Yield:** 2 loaves.

PASS A COOKIE JAR brimming with these *tasty morsels and a platter stacked with generous slices of cake—they make great snacks or a sweet ending to your meal.*

**TASTY TREATS.** Top to bottom: Lemon Poppy Seed Cake (p. 97), Super Brownies (p. 97) and Soft Oatmeal Apricot Cookies (p. 99).

# Cakes & Cookies

## LEMON POPPY SEED CAKE

*Brenda Wood, Egbert, Ontario*

**(Pictured at left)**

*I got this luscious, lemony cake recipe from Betty Bjarnason, whose delicious recipe also appears in a reunion cookbook.*

1 package (18-1/4 ounces) lemon cake mix
1 package (3.4 ounces) instant lemon
   pudding mix
3/4 cup warm water
1/2 cup vegetable oil
4 eggs
1 teaspoon lemon extract
1 teaspoon almond extract
1/3 cup poppy seeds
1/2 cup confectioners' sugar
Juice of 1 lemon
Additional confectioners' sugar, optional

In a mixing bowl, combine cake and pudding mixes. Add the water, oil, eggs and extracts. Beat for 30 seconds on low speed. Beat for 3 minutes on medium speed. Stir in poppy seeds. Pour into a greased 12-cup fluted tube pan. Bake at 350° for 50-60 minutes or until a toothpick inserted near the center comes out clean. Cool in pan 10 minutes before inverting onto a serving plate. Combine confectioners' sugar and lemon juice; brush over the warm cake. Cool. Dust with confectioners' sugar if desired. **Yield:** 12-16 servings.

## SUPER BROWNIES

*Bernice Muilenburg, Molalla, Oregon*

**(Pictured at left)**

*Even though he's not a chocolate fan, my husband really likes these brownies.*

1/2 cup butter *or* margarine
1-1/2 cups sugar
4-2/3 cups (28 ounces) semisweet chocolate
   chips, *divided*
3 tablespoons hot water
4 eggs

5 teaspoons vanilla extract
1-1/2 cups all-purpose flour
1/2 teaspoon baking soda
1/2 teaspoon salt
2 cups coarsely chopped macadamia nuts
   or pecans, *divided*

In a saucepan over medium heat, melt butter and sugar. Remove from the heat; stir in 2 cups chocolate chips until melted. Pour into a mixing bowl; beat in water. Add eggs, one at a time, beating well after each addition. Add vanilla. Combine flour, baking soda and salt; beat into the chocolate mixture until smooth. Stir in 2 cups of chocolate chips and 1 cup of nuts. Pour into a greased 13-in. x 9-in. x 2-in. baking pan. Sprinkle with remaining chips and nuts. Bake at 325° for 55 minutes or until the center is set (do not overbake). **Yield:** about 3-1/2 dozen.

## JUMBO CHOCOLATE CHIP COOKIES

*Lori Sporer, Oakley, Kansas*

*These huge cookies are a family favorite. No one can resist their sweet chocolaty taste.*

2/3 cup shortening
2/3 cup butter *or* margarine, softened
1 cup sugar
1 cup packed brown sugar
2 eggs
2 teaspoons vanilla extract
3-1/2 cups all-purpose flour
1 teaspoon baking soda
1 teaspoon salt
2 cups (12 ounces) semisweet chocolate
   chips
1 cup chopped pecans

In a mixing bowl, cream shortening, butter and sugars. Add eggs and vanilla. Combine the flour, baking soda and salt; add to creamed mixture and mix well. Fold in the chocolate chips and pecans. Chill for at least 1 hour. Drop by 1/4 cupfuls at least 1-1/2 in. apart onto greased baking sheets. Bake at 375° for 13-15 minutes or until golden brown. Cool for 5 minutes before removing to a wire rack. **Yield:** 2 dozen.

## APPLE SNACK SQUARES

*Julia Quintrell, Sumerco, West Virginia*

**(Pictured below)**

*As soon as I was old enough to stand on a chair, I started cooking. This recipe came from my sister-in-law. It's a favorite at our large family gatherings.*

2 cups sugar
2 eggs
3/4 cup vegetable oil
2-1/2 cups self-rising flour*
1 teaspoon ground cinnamon
3 cups diced peeled tart apples
1 cup chopped walnuts
3/4 cup butterscotch chips

In a bowl, combine sugar, eggs and oil; mix well. Stir in flour and cinnamon (batter will be thick). Stir in apples and nuts. Spread into a greased 13-in. x 9-in. x 2-in. baking pan. Sprinkle with chips. Bake at 350° for 35-40 minutes or until golden and a toothpick inserted near the center comes out clean. Cool before cutting. **Yield:** 2 dozen.

**\*Editor's Note:** As a substitute for each cup of self-rising flour, place 1-1/2 teaspoons of baking powder and 1/2 teaspoon of salt in a measuring cup. Add all-purpose flour to equal 1 cup.

## BEET BUNDT CAKE

*Vermadel Kirby, Milford, Delaware*

*I found this recipe handwritten in my grandmother's well-worn cookbook. I've made it many times, and my four grandchildren love it. Our state is known as the beet-growing capital.*

1 cup butter *or* margarine, softened, *divided*
1-1/2 cups packed dark brown sugar
3 eggs
4 squares (1 ounce *each*) semisweet chocolate
2 cups pureed cooked beets
1 teaspoon vanilla extract
2 cups all-purpose flour
2 teaspoons baking soda

1/4 teaspoon salt
Confectioners' sugar

In a mixing bowl, cream 3/4 cup butter and brown sugar. Add eggs; mix well. Melt chocolate with remaining butter; stir until smooth. Cool slightly. Blend chocolate mixture, beets and vanilla into the creamed mixture (mixture will appear separated). Combine flour, baking soda and salt; add to the creamed mixture and mix well. Pour into a greased and floured 10-in. fluted tube pan. Bake at 375° for 45-55 minutes or until a toothpick inserted near the center comes out clean. Cool in pan 10 minutes before removing to a wire rack. Cool completely. Before serving, dust with confectioners' sugar. **Yield:** 16-20 servings.

## Soft Oatmeal Apricot Cookies

*Eileen Milacek, Waukomis, Oklahoma*

**(Pictured on page 96)**

*These cookies are a real attention-getter because of their spicy flavor. They are the perfect snack for a cool fall day.*

  1 cup shortening
1-1/2 cups packed dark brown sugar
  1/3 cup molasses
    3 eggs
    3 cups quick-cooking oats
    2 cups all-purpose flour
    1 tablespoon ground cinnamon
    1 teaspoon ground nutmeg
    1 teaspoon ground cloves
    1 teaspoon baking soda
  1/2 teaspoon salt
    1 package (6 ounces) dried apricots, chopped

In a mixing bowl, cream shortening and brown sugar. Beat in molasses. Add the eggs, one at a time, beating well after each. Combine remaining ingredients; stir into batter. Cover and refrigerate for at least 2 hours. Shape into 1-in. balls and place 2 in. apart on greased baking sheets. Bake at 350° for 10 minutes or until browned. **Yield:** 7 dozen.

## Chocolate Chip Meringue Bars

*Elaine Swenson, Kindred, North Dakota*

**(Pictured above right)**

*My husband and I are sugar beet farmers in the great Red River Valley. I've made these bars many times for my family, and we all love them.*

  1 cup shortening
1-1/2 cups packed brown sugar, *divided*
  1/2 cup sugar
    3 eggs, *separated*
    1 tablespoon cold water
    1 tablespoon vanilla extract
    2 cups all-purpose flour
    1 teaspoon baking soda
  1/8 teaspoon salt
    1 cup (6 ounces) semisweet chocolate chips
    1 cup ground salted peanuts

In a mixing bowl, cream shortening, 1/2 cup of brown sugar and sugar. Add egg yolks; mix well. Combine the water and vanilla. Combine flour, baking soda and salt; add to creamed mixture alternately with water mixture. Mix well. Spread into a greased 15-in. x 10-in. x 1-in. baking pan. Sprinkle with chocolate chips. In a small mixing bowl, beat egg whites until soft peaks form. Add the remaining brown sugar, 2 tablespoons at a time, beating well after each addition. Beat until stiff peaks form. Spread over chocolate chips. Top with peanuts. Bake at 350° for 30-35 minutes. **Yield:** about 3 dozen.

In a mixing bowl, cream the butter and brown sugar; add the egg and mix well. Combine dry ingredients; add alternately with milk to creamed mixture. Stir in zucchini, nuts, raisins and orange peel. Drop by teaspoonfuls 2 in. apart onto greased baking sheets. Bake at 350° for 12-14 minutes or until edges are lightly browned and cookies are set. **Yield:** about 4 dozen.

## GINGER BARS

*Deborah Haake, Minnetonka, Minnesota*

*We always had dessert when we visited my grandparents' farm, and these spicy bars were one of our favorites. During harvesttime, my brothers and sisters and I would take them out to the field for the workers.*

>     1 cup shortening
>     1 cup sugar
>     2 eggs
>     1 cup water
>     1/2 cup molasses
> 2-1/2 cups all-purpose flour
>     1 teaspoon baking soda
>     1 teaspoon ground cinnamon
>     1/2 teaspoon ground cloves
>     1/2 teaspoon ground ginger
>     1/2 teaspoon salt
> **Confectioners' sugar, optional**

In a mixing bowl, cream shortening and sugar. Add eggs; beat well. Beat in water and molasses. Combine flour, baking soda, cinnamon, cloves, ginger and salt; add to molasses mixture and mix well. Spread into a greased 15-in. x 10-in. x 1-in. baking pan. Bake at 350° for 20-22 minutes or until bars test done. Cool. Dust with confectioners' sugar if desired. **Yield:** 16-20 servings.

## BITE-SIZE FRUITCAKES

*Alma Stearns, Lansing, Michigan*

*Because I didn't care for fruitcake, I had to have the recipe for this after I found out what it was I'd been enjoying at the office over the holidays! I like these tasty treats because each bite is packed with dates, nuts and candied pineapple and cherries.*

>     1/2 cup butter *or* margarine, softened
>     1 cup packed brown sugar
>     3 eggs
>     2 cups all-purpose flour
>     1 teaspoon baking soda
>     1 cup (8 ounces) sour cream
>     2 packages (8 ounces *each*) chopped dates
>     1 pound Brazil nuts, coarsely chopped

## SOFT ZUCCHINI SPICE COOKIES

*Milli Seemar, Chatham, New Jersey*

**(Pictured above)**

*These cookies don't last very long at my house. Why don't you see how long they last at yours?*

>     1/2 cup butter *or* margarine, softened
>     1 cup packed brown sugar
>     1 egg
> 1-3/4 cups all-purpose flour
>     2 teaspoons baking powder
>     3/4 teaspoon ground cinnamon
>     1/2 teaspoon salt
>     1/4 teaspoon ground nutmeg
>     1/8 teaspoon ground cloves
>     1/4 cup milk
> 1-1/2 cups grated zucchini
>     1/2 cup chopped walnuts
>     1/2 cup raisins
>     1 teaspoon grated orange peel

Cakes & Cookies

1 pound pecans, coarsely chopped
3/4 pound chopped candied pineapple
3/4 pound candied cherries, halved
1 cup raisins
GLAZE:
1 egg, beaten
1/2 cup evaporated milk
1/4 cup water
Additional candied cherries, optional

In a large mixing bowl, cream the butter and sugar. Add eggs and mix well. Combine the flour and baking soda; add alternately to the creamed mixture with sour cream. Stir in the dates, nuts, pineapple, cherries and raisins. Fill paper-lined miniature muffin cups three-fourths full. Bake at 300° for 40-50 minutes or until lightly browned and set. For glaze, combine egg, milk and water; mix well. Brush over fruitcakes. Bake 10 minutes longer. Decorate with candied cherries if desired. Cool on wire racks. **Yield:** about 10 dozen.

## REALLY ROCKY ROAD BROWNIES

*Brenda Wood, Egbert, Ontario*

*My niece Olivia Fallon sent this rich fudgy dessert recipe to me for a family reunion cookbook that I compiled. It's good to make for family gatherings because it's easy to make and you get 4 dozen brownies!*

8 squares (1 ounce *each*) unsweetened chocolate
1-1/2 cups butter *or* margarine
6 eggs
3 cups sugar
1 tablespoon vanilla extract
1-1/2 cups all-purpose flour
1 cup chopped walnuts, optional
TOPPING:
2 cups miniature marshmallows
1 square (1 ounce) unsweetened chocolate, melted

In a heavy saucepan over medium heat, cook and stir chocolate and butter until melted; cool slightly. In a mixing bowl, beat eggs for 2 minutes. Gradually add sugar; beat until thick, about 3 minutes. Stir in chocolate mixture and vanilla. Fold in flour and nuts if desired. Pour into two greased and floured 9-in. square baking pans. Bake at 350° for 25-30 minutes or until a toothpick inserted in the center comes out with moist crumbs (do not overbake). Sprinkle each pan with 1 cup of marshmallows. Broil until marshmallows are golden brown, about 30-60 seconds. Drizzle with melted chocolate. **Yield:** 4 dozen. **Editor's Note:** For easier cutting, refrigerate brownies for several hours.

## AUSTRIAN NUT COOKIES

*Marianne Weber, South Beach, Oregon*

**(Pictured below)**

*These are my family's favorite Christmas cookies. If you arrange the slivered almonds in pinwheel fashion, the cookie looks like a poinsettia.*

1 cup all-purpose flour
2/3 cup finely chopped almonds
1/3 cup sugar
1/2 cup cold butter (no substitutes)
1/2 cup raspberry jam
FROSTING:
1 square (1 ounce) unsweetened chocolate, melted and cooled
1/3 cup confectioners' sugar
2 tablespoons butter *or* margarine, softened
Slivered almonds

In a bowl, combine flour, chopped almonds and sugar. Cut in butter until mixture resembles coarse crumbs. Form into a ball; cover and refrigerate for 1 hour. On a floured surface, roll the dough to 1/8-in. thickness. Cut with a 2-in. round cutter and place 1 in. apart on greased baking sheets. Bake at 375° for 7-10 minutes or until the edges are lightly browned. Remove to wire racks to cool completely. Spread 1/2 teaspoon jam on half of the cookies; top with another cookie. For frosting, combine chocolate, confectioners' sugar and butter. Spread on tops of cookies. Decorate with slivered almonds. **Yield:** 20 sandwich cookies.

## DUTCH APPLE CAKE

*Elizabeth Peters, Martintown, Ontario*

**(Pictured below)**

*My husband and I came to Canada over 40 years ago from Holland. This recipe, a family favorite, is one I found in a Dutch cookbook. It frequently goes along with me to potluck suppers.*

- 3 medium peeled tart apples, sliced 1/4 inch thick (3 cups)
- 1 cup plus 3 tablespoons sugar, *divided*
- 1 teaspoon ground cinnamon
- 2/3 cup butter *or* margarine, softened
- 4 eggs
- 1 teaspoon vanilla extract
- 2 cups all-purpose flour
- 1/8 teaspoon salt

In a bowl, combine the apples, 3 tablespoons sugar and cinnamon; let stand for 1 hour. In a mixing bowl, cream butter and remaining sugar. Add eggs, one at a time, beating well after each. Add vanilla. Combine flour and salt; gradually add to creamed mixture and beat until smooth. Pour into a greased 9-in. x 5-in. x 3-in. loaf pan. Push apple slices vertically into batter, placing them close together. Bake at 300° for 1 hour and 40 minutes or until a toothpick inserted near the center comes out clean. Cool for 10 minutes on a wire rack. Remove from pan. Serve warm. **Yield:** 10-12 servings.

## NUTTY CHEESECAKE SQUARES

*Ruth Simon, Buffalo, New York*

*I grew up on a farm and have had a lot of good recipes handed down to me. This is one of my favorite desserts to serve guests.*

- 2 cups all-purpose flour
- 1 cup finely chopped walnuts
- 2/3 cup packed brown sugar
- 1/2 teaspoon salt
- 2/3 cup butter *or* margarine

**FILLING:**

- 2 packages (8 ounces *each*) cream cheese, softened
- 1/2 cup sugar
- 2 eggs
- 1/4 cup milk
- 1 teaspoon vanilla extract

In a bowl, combine flour, walnuts, brown sugar and salt; cut in butter until the mixture resembles coarse crumbs. Set half aside; press remaining crumb mixture onto the bottom of a greased 13-in. x 9-in. x 2-in. baking pan. Bake at 350° for 10-15 minutes or until lightly browned. In a mixing bowl, beat cream cheese, sugar, eggs, milk and vanilla until smooth; pour over crust. Sprinkle with reserved crumb mixture. Bake at 350° for 20-25 minutes or until a knife inserted near the center comes out clean. Cool completely. Store in the refrigerator. **Yield:** 16-20 servings.

## CHEWY PECAN PIE BARS

*Judy Taylor, Shreveport, Louisiana*

*This is one of my husband's favorite recipes. I've been making it for many years.*

- 1/4 cup butter *or* margarine, melted
- 2 cups packed brown sugar
- 2/3 cup all-purpose flour
- 4 eggs
- 2 teaspoons vanilla extract
- 1/4 teaspoon baking soda
- 1/4 teaspoon salt
- 2 cups chopped pecans

Confectioners' sugar

Pour butter into a 13-in. x 9-in. x 2-in. baking pan; set aside. In a mixing bowl, combine brown sugar, flour, eggs, vanilla, baking soda and salt; mix well. Stir in pecans. Spread over butter. Bake at 350° for 30-35 minutes. Remove from the oven; immediately dust with confectioners' sugar. Cool before cutting. **Yield:** about 2 dozen.

# Cookies Are the Dairy Best

THE HOLIDAYS wouldn't be complete without a plateful of homemade cookies to give family and friends. Whip up a batch of these melt-in-your-mouth morsels from the folks at the American Dairy Association to spread some Christmas cheer.

### CANDY CANE BUTTER COOKIES

    1 cup butter (no substitutes), softened
1/2 cup sugar
    1 egg yolk
    1 teaspoon almond extract
    1 teaspoon anise extract
1/4 teaspoon salt
2-1/4 cups all-purpose flour
   10 to 12 drops red food coloring

In a mixing bowl, cream butter, sugar, egg yolk, extracts and salt until light and fluffy. Gradually add flour. Remove half of dough from mixing bowl. Add food coloring to remaining half; mix well. Wrap doughs separately in plastic wrap. Refrigerate for 1 hour or up to 2 days. Shape teaspoonfuls of dough from each portion into 4-in. ropes. Place ropes side by side; press together gently and twist. Place 2 in. apart on lightly greased baking sheets. Curve one end to form a cane. Refrigerate for 5 minutes or until firm. Bake at 350° for 12-15 minutes. Cool for 5 minutes; remove from pan to wire racks to cool completely. **Yield:** 3 dozen.

### CRANBERRY SLICES

    1 cup butter (no substitutes), softened
1/2 cup sugar
    1 egg yolk
    1 teaspoon vanilla extract
1/2 teaspoon salt
2-1/4 cups all-purpose flour
1/2 cup dried cranberries, chopped

In a mixing bowl, cream butter, sugar, egg yolk, vanilla and salt until light and fluffy. Gradually add flour. Stir in cranberries. Divide the dough in half; form each half into a 6-in. x 3-in. x 1-in. block. Cover with plastic wrap and refrigerate for 3 hours or up to 2 days. To bake, cut the dough into 1/4-in.-thick slices; place on ungreased parchment-lined baking sheets. Bake at 350° for 12-15 minutes or until edges are golden. **Yield:** 4 dozen.

### BUTTERY NUT COOKIES

    1 cup butter (no substitutes), softened
1/2 cup sugar
    1 egg yolk
    1 teaspoon vanilla extract
1/4 teaspoon salt
2-1/4 cups all-purpose flour
    1 cup ground pecans

In a mixing bowl, cream butter, sugar, egg yolk, vanilla and salt until light and fluffy. Combine flour and pecans; gradually add to creamed mixture. Cover and refrigerate for 1 hour or up to 2 days. Shape into 1-in. balls. Place 1-1/2 in. apart on ungreased baking sheets. Bake at 350° for 12-15 minutes or until firm. If desired, roll warm cookies in confectioners' sugar; or cool cookies and drizzle with melted chocolate. **Yield:** 4 dozen.

## RAINBOW SHERBET CAKE ROLL

*Karen Edland, McHenry, North Dakota*

*This light and easy cake roll can be prepared year-round...it's especially nice to have a dessert ready to serve in the freezer for unexpected company.*

☑ This tasty dish uses less fat, sugar or salt. Recipe includes Nutritional Analysis and Diabetic Exchanges.

**1 package (14-1/2 ounces) angel food cake mix**
**1/2 gallon rainbow sherbet**

Coat two 15-in. x 10-in. x 1-in. baking pans with nonstick cooking spray; line pans with waxed paper and spray the paper. Prepare cake mix according to package directions; spread batter into prepared pans. Bake at 375° for 18-22 minutes or until the cake springs back when lightly touched. Cool in pans for 10 minutes. Turn each cake onto a linen towel dusted with confectioners' sugar. Remove waxed paper; trim off dry edges. Roll up each cake in the towel, starting with a narrow end. Cool on a wire rack. When cooled, unroll cakes; spread each with 4 cups sherbet. Roll up carefully; place with seam side down on aluminum foil. Wrap securely; freeze until firm, about 6 hours. Remove from freezer 15 minutes before serving. Cut into 1-in. slices. **Yield:** 20 servings. **Nutritional Analysis:** One serving equals 183 calories, 187 mg sodium, 4 mg cholesterol, 41 gm carbohydrate, 3 gm protein, 2 gm fat. **Diabetic Exchanges:** 2 starch, 1/2 fat.

## OAT-RAGEOUS CHOCOLATE CHIP COOKIES

*Jaymie Noble, Kalamazoo, Michigan*

**(Pictured above)**

*My aunt gave me this recipe, and my family thinks these cookies are delicious. We enjoy all different kinds of cookies—this recipe combines three of our favorites!*

**1/2 cup butter *or* margarine, softened**
**1/2 cup creamy peanut butter**
**1/2 cup sugar**
**1/3 cup packed brown sugar**
**1 egg**
**1/2 teaspoon vanilla extract**
**1 cup all-purpose flour**
**1/2 cup quick-cooking oats**
**1 teaspoon baking soda**
**1/4 teaspoon salt**
**1 cup (6 ounces) semisweet chocolate chips**

In a mixing bowl, cream butter, peanut butter and sugars; beat in egg and vanilla. Combine flour, oats, baking soda and salt. Add to the creamed mixture and mix well. Stir in chocolate chips. Drop by rounded teaspoonfuls onto ungreased baking sheets. Bake at 350° for 10-12 minutes or until lightly browned. **Yield:** about 3 dozen.

## HAMBURGER COOKIES

*Pat Carter, Clearwater, Florida*

*Children can help create this sweet treat. My daughters and I form an assembly line to put them together.*

**1/2 cup vanilla frosting**
**Red and green liquid *or* paste food coloring**
**1 cup flaked coconut**
**80 vanilla wafers (about 12 ounces)**
**40 chocolate-coated mint cookies (about 12 ounces)**

Divide frosting into two bowls; add red food coloring to one bowl. Place coconut in a resealable plastic bag; add green food coloring and shake to coat. Frost the bottoms of 40 vanilla wafers with white frosting; set aside. Frost the bottoms of remaining wafers with red frosting. Sprinkle coconut over red frosting; top with a chocolate cookie. Place white-frosted wafers, frosting side down, on top of cookies. Squeeze wafers together, forming sandwich cookies, and invert. **Yield:** 40 cookies.

## MACADAMIA FUDGE CAKE

*Marguerite Gough, Salida, Colorado*

*Our daughter and her husband operate a cookie factory in Hawaii. After she sent a big supply of macadamia nuts, I came up with this cake that I make for church dinners and ladies lunches.*

  1/2 cup butter *or* margarine, softened
  3/4 cup sugar
    1 egg
  3/4 cup sour cream
  1/2 teaspoon vanilla extract
    1 cup all-purpose flour
  1/4 cup baking cocoa
1-1/2 teaspoons instant coffee granules
  1/2 teaspoon baking powder
  1/2 teaspoon baking soda
  1/4 teaspoon salt
TOPPING:
    1 cup (6 ounces) semisweet chocolate
      chips
  2/3 cup whipping cream
  1/2 cup sugar
    2 tablespoons butter *or* margarine
    2 tablespoons corn syrup
    1 teaspoon vanilla extract
1-1/2 cups coarsely chopped macadamia nuts
      *or* almonds

In a mixing bowl, cream butter and sugar until fluffy. Beat in egg, sour cream and vanilla. Combine flour, cocoa, coffee, baking powder, baking soda and salt; add to creamed mixture and mix well. Pour into a greased 9-in. round baking pan. Bake at 350° for 30 minutes or until cake tests done. Cool for 10 minutes; remove from pan to a wire rack to cool completely. For topping, combine chocolate chips, cream, sugar, butter and corn syrup in a saucepan; bring to a boil, stirring constantly. Reduce heat to medium; cook and stir for 7 minutes. Remove from the heat; stir in vanilla. Cool for 10-15 minutes. Beat with a wooden spoon until slightly thickened, about 4-5 minutes. Stir in nuts. Place cake on a serving plate; pour topping over cake. **Yield:** 8-10 servings.

## DOUBLE BROWNIES

*Rosanne Stevenson, Melfort, Saskatchewan*

**(Pictured at right)**

*Farm chores keep me extra busy–but I always find time to cook and bake. I like to dress up my dinner table with these festive brownies. The rich frosted treats with two layers make a doubly delicious dessert during the holidays or anytime.*

BOTTOM LAYER:
  1/2 cup butter *or* margarine, softened
1-1/2 cups packed brown sugar
    2 eggs
    2 teaspoons vanilla extract
  1/4 teaspoon salt
1-1/2 cups all-purpose flour
  1/2 cup chopped walnuts
MIDDLE LAYER:
  1/2 cup butter *or* margarine, softened
    1 cup sugar
    2 eggs
  1/8 teaspoon salt
  3/4 cup all-purpose flour
  1/4 cup baking cocoa
  1/2 cup chopped walnuts
CARAMEL ICING:
    6 tablespoons butter *or* margarine
  3/4 cup packed brown sugar
    4 to 6 tablespoons milk
2-1/2 cups confectioners' sugar

In a mixing bowl, cream the butter and brown sugar; beat in eggs, vanilla and salt. Stir in flour and nuts. Spread into a greased 13-in. x 9-in. x 2-in. baking pan; set aside. For middle layer, cream butter and sugar; beat in eggs and salt. Stir in flour, cocoa and nuts. Spread over the bottom layer. Bake at 350° for 30-35 minutes. Cool. For icing, melt butter in a saucepan over medium heat. Stir in brown sugar and milk; bring to a boil. Remove from the heat. Cool just until warm; beat in confectioners' sugar until the icing is of spreading consistency. Spread over brownies. **Yield:** 2 dozen.

# Chocolate Party Features Sweet Selections

baked batches of these richly delicious treats as the stars! And don't forget the cups of steaming hot cocoa.

### CHOCOLATE TOFFEE CUPCAKES

**(Pictured at left)**

1-1/2 cups all-purpose flour
1 cup sugar
1/4 cup baking cocoa
1 teaspoon baking soda
1 cup water
1/4 cup vegetable oil
1 tablespoon vinegar
1 teaspoon vanilla extract
1/2 cup English toffee bits (Hershey's SKOR)
FROSTING:
1-1/2 cups confectioners' sugar
1/3 cup baking cocoa
1/3 cup butter *or* margarine, softened
3 tablespoons milk
3/4 teaspoon vanilla extract
3/4 cup English toffee bits, *divided*

In a mixing bowl, combine flour, sugar, cocoa and baking soda. Stir in water, oil, vinegar and vanilla until smooth. Add toffee bits. Fill paper-lined muffin cups two-thirds full. Bake at 350° for 20-25 minutes. Remove to wire racks to cool completely. For frosting, combine confectioners' sugar and cocoa; set aside. In a mixing bowl, beat butter and 1/2 cup cocoa mixture. Add milk, vanilla and remaining cocoa mixture; beat until desired spreading consistency is reached. Stir in 1/2 cup toffee bits. Frost cupcakes. Cover and refrigerate until serving. Top with remaining toffee bits before serving. **Yield:** about 1-1/2 dozen.

WHEN YOU need a host of palate-pleasing foods, turn to these chocolaty confections. The folks at Hershey Foods Corporation, who share these mouth-watering and imaginative recipes, say they're guaranteed to satisfy the sweetest sweet tooth around.

Then enjoy your sweet success with family and friends—plan a Chocolate Party with freshly

### HOMEMADE HOT COCOA

**(Pictured above left)**

1/2 cup sugar
1/4 cup baking cocoa

Dash salt
    1/3 cup hot water
    4 cups milk
    3/4 teaspoon vanilla extract
**Miniature marshmallows, sweetened whipped
    cream *or* cinnamon sticks, optional**

In a saucepan, combine sugar, cocoa and salt. Add water; bring to a boil. Cook and stir for 2 minutes. Stir in milk; heat to serving temperature (do not boil). Remove from the heat; stir in vanilla. Whisk until frothy. If desired, garnish with marshmallows, cream or cinnamon sticks. **Yield:** 5 cups. **For Swiss Mocha Cocoa:** Add 2 to 2-1/2 teaspoons instant coffee with vanilla. **For Canadian Cocoa:** Add 1/2 teaspoon imitation maple flavoring with vanilla. **For Slim-Trim Cocoa:** Omit sugar. Combine cocoa, salt and water. Substitute skim milk. Proceed as above. Stir in vanilla with artificial sweetener equivalent to 1/2 cup sugar.

## WINTER WONDERLAND SNOWMEN BROWNIES

### (Pictured at far left)

3/4 cup baking cocoa
1/2 teaspoon baking soda
2/3 cup butter *or* margarine, melted, *divided*
1/2 cup boiling water
    2 cups sugar
    2 eggs
    1 teaspoon vanilla extract

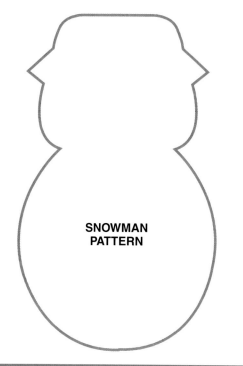

**SNOWMAN
PATTERN**

1-1/2 cups all-purpose flour
    1 package (10 ounces) peanut butter chips
**Confectioners' sugar, optional
Miniature M&M's and semisweet chocolate
    chips, optional**

In a mixing bowl, combine cocoa and baking soda. Beat in 1/3 cup butter. Stir in water until mixture thickens. Stir in sugar, eggs, vanilla and remaining butter. Beat in flour. Stir in peanut butter chips. Line a 13-in. x 9-in. x 2-in. baking pan with foil and grease the foil; spread batter evenly in pan. Bake at 350° for 35-40 minutes or until brownies pull away from sides of pan. Cool completely on a wire rack. Cover and refrigerate until firm. Use snowman pattern (below left) or a cookie cutter to mark brownies; cut with a knife. Dust with confectioners' sugar. Decorate with M&M's and chips if desired. **Yield:** 1 dozen large or 3 dozen small brownies.

## EASY CHOCOLATE MAKING

PLANNING to stir up some chocolate excitement in your kitchen? These tips from the folks at Hershey Foods Corporation will make baking go smoother.

• If chocolate is overheated or water droplets mix with the chocolate, it may become hardened and grainy. To "rescue" it, vigorously beat in 1 teaspoon of shortening for every 2 ounces of chocolate in the recipe.

• To prevent "skin" from forming on top of hot chocolate beverages, beat hot cocoa with a whisk until foamy.

• To grate chocolate, draw the blade of a vegetable parer over the smooth side of a block or square of chocolate.

• Optimum temperature for storing chocolate is between 60° and 75°F. If stored at a higher temperature, white streaks (called "bloom") may appear. To avoid these harmless streaks, wrap any chocolate in foil and then in plastic to protect it from light, moisture and odor. Do *not* refrigerate chocolate.

• Baking chocolate products may be stored up to 1 year in a cool dry place. Baking cocoa will retain its freshness almost indefinitely if stored in its original container at room temperature.

## BLACK 'N' WHITE CHEESECAKE BARS

*Bertille Cooper, St. Inigoes, Maryland*

**(Pictured below)**

*Whenever it's my turn to make dessert for our local fire department auxiliary meeting, I always get requests to bring this delicious recipe.*

- 2 cups (12 ounces) semisweet chocolate chips
- 1/2 cup butter *or* margarine
- 2 cups graham cracker crumbs
- 1 package (8 ounces) cream cheese, softened
- 1 can (14 ounces) sweetened condensed milk
- 1 egg
- 1 teaspoon vanilla extract

In a double boiler or microwave, melt chocolate chips and butter, stirring occasionally. Stir in the graham cracker crumbs. Set aside 1/4 cup for topping. Press the remaining crumbs into an ungreased 13-in. x 9-in. x 2-in. baking pan. In a mixing bowl, beat cream cheese until smooth. Gradually beat in milk, egg and vanilla. Pour over crust. Sprinkle with reserved crumbs. Bake at 325° for 25-30 minutes or until lightly browned. Cool. Refrigerate 3 hours or until completely chilled. Cut into bars. Store in the refrigerator. **Yield:** 4 dozen.

## BUTTERFLY CUPCAKES

*Adeline Piscitelle, Sayreville, New Jersey*

*These cupcakes have been a favorite in our family for years. Now, I make them for my grandchildren.*

- 3/4 cup butter *or* margarine, softened
- 3/4 cup sugar
- 3 eggs
- 1 teaspoon vanilla extract
- 2 cups self-rising flour*
- 1/2 cup milk
- 1 can (15-3/4 ounces) lemon pie filling
- 40 pieces red *and/or* black shoestring licorice (2 inches)

In a mixing bowl, cream butter and sugar; beat in eggs and vanilla. Add flour alternately with milk. Fill greased muffin cups half full. Bake at 350° for 15-20 minutes or until a toothpick inserted near the center comes out clean. Cool in pans 10 minutes before removing to wire racks to cool completely. Slice off the top fourth of each cupcake; cut the slices in half. Spoon 1 tablespoon pie filling onto each cupcake. Place two halves upside down on top of filling for wings. Insert two pieces of licorice for antennae. **Yield:** 20 cupcakes.
**\*Editor's Note:** As a substitute for each cup of self-rising flour, place 1-1/2 teaspoons baking powder and 1/2 teaspoon salt in a measuring cup. Add all-purpose flour to equal 1 cup.

## CHOCOLATE NUT ACORNS

*Penny Clawson, Lititz, Pennsylvania*

*I love to bake these specialty cookies for friends!*

- 1 cup butter *or* margarine, softened
- 3/4 cup packed brown sugar
- 1 teaspoon vanilla extract
- 2-1/2 cups all-purpose flour
- 1/2 teaspoon baking powder
- 1 cup finely chopped nuts, *divided*
- 2 cups (12 ounces) semisweet chocolate chips
- 2 tablespoons shortening

In a mixing bowl, cream butter, brown sugar and vanilla. Combine flour and baking powder; add to creamed mixture and mix well. Stir in 1/4 cup of nuts. Shape rounded teaspoonfuls of dough into 1-1/2-in. x 1-in. ovals. Place 1 in. apart on ungreased baking sheets. Bake at 350° for 15-18 minutes or until light golden brown. Cool on wire racks. In a saucepan over low heat, melt chocolate chips and shortening. Dip half of each cookie into chocolate. Dip chocolate ends into remaining nuts. **Yield:** about 5 dozen.

## ALMOND SPICE COOKIES

*Crystal Landolt, Calgary, Alberta*

*I make these often for my family. They unanimously declare them delicious!*

☑ This tasty dish uses less fat, sugar or salt. Recipe includes Nutritional Analysis and Diabetic Exchanges.

1/2 cup margarine, softened
3/4 cup sugar
Egg substitute equivalent to 1 egg
1/2 teaspoon almond extract
1-1/4 cups all-purpose flour
1/4 teaspoon *each* ground cinnamon, nutmeg and cloves
1/4 teaspoon baking powder
Pinch salt
1/2 cup chopped almonds

In a mixing bowl, cream margarine and sugar; add egg substitute and extract. Combine dry ingredients; add to the creamed mixture. Stir in almonds. Drop by rounded teaspoonfuls onto baking sheets coated with nonstick cooking spray. Bake at 350° for 9-11 minutes or until edges are golden brown. Remove to wire racks to cool. **Yield:** 5 dozen. **Nutritional Analysis:** One serving (2 cookies) equals 85 calories, 62 mg sodium, trace cholesterol, 10 gm carbohydrate, 1 gm protein, 4 gm fat. **Diabetic Exchanges:** 1 fat, 1/2 starch.

## ORANGE BLOSSOM CAKE

*Mrs. E.W. Mueller, Mariposa, California*

**(Pictured above right)**

*Since we planted and maintained a grove of 250 orange trees for almost 20 years, this recipe became a family favorite.*

1/2 cup butter *or* margarine, softened
1 cup sugar
1/2 cup applesauce
2 eggs
1 tablespoon grated orange peel
2-1/2 cups all-purpose flour
1 teaspoon baking powder
1 teaspoon baking soda
1/4 teaspoon salt
1 cup buttermilk
1 cup chopped dates
1 cup chopped nuts
GLAZE:
1 cup sugar
1/2 cup orange juice

In a mixing bowl, cream butter and sugar. Add applesauce, eggs and orange peel; mix well. Combine the flour, baking powder, baking soda and salt. Add to creamed mixture alternately with buttermilk; mix well. Fold in dates and nuts. Pour into a greased 9-in. springform pan. Bake at 350° for 55-60 minutes or until a toothpick inserted near the center comes out clean. Meanwhile, combine glaze ingredients in a saucepan; bring to a boil. Pour over cake. Cool completely in pan. **Yield:** 10-12 servings.

## PECAN COOKIES

*Bonnie Jolly, Bailey, Colorado*

*My family agrees these slightly sweet nutty cookies make a nice breakfast treat.*

☑ This tasty dish uses less fat, sugar or salt. Recipe includes Nutritional Analysis and Diabetic Exchanges.

1-1/2 cups whole wheat flour
1/2 cup all-purpose flour
1 teaspoon baking powder
2 tablespoons quick-cooking oats
1/2 cup margarine
3/4 cup finely chopped pecans
1/2 cup packed brown sugar
1/4 to 1/2 cup skim milk

In a large bowl, combine flours and baking powder; stir in oats. Cut margarine into pieces; cut into flour mixture until well mixed. Add pecans and sugar; mix well. Stir in enough milk with a fork to form a stiff paste. Turn onto a floured surface; knead lightly until smooth. Roll out on a floured surface to 1/4-in. to 1/8-in. thickness. Cut with 1-1/2-in. round cookie cutter. Place on baking sheets coated with nonstick cooking spray. Bake at 375° for 10 minutes or until lightly browned. Cool on wire racks. **Yield:** about 7-1/2 dozen. **Nutritional Analysis:** One serving (2 cookies) equals 60 calories, 36 mg sodium, trace cholesterol, 7 gm carbohydrate, 1 gm protein, 3 gm fat. **Diabetic Exchanges:** 1/2 starch, 1/2 fat.

## EASTER EGG COOKIES

*Barbara Neuweg, West Point, Iowa*

*My mother started baking these cookies with me and my eight brothers and sisters when I was a child, and I carried on the tradition with our four youngsters when they were little.*

> 1 cup butter *or* margarine, softened
> 1/2 cup packed brown sugar
> 1 egg
> 1-1/2 teaspoons vanilla extract
> 3 cups all-purpose flour
> 1 cup quick-cooking oats
> 3/4 teaspoon salt

**GLAZE:**

> 1-1/2 cups confectioners' sugar
> 1/8 teaspoon salt
> 2-1/2 tablespoons half-and-half cream

**Cake decorating gel, optional**

In a mixing bowl, cream butter and brown sugar. Add egg and vanilla; mix well. Combine flour, oats and salt; stir into creamed mixture. Divide dough into three equal portions. Form 12 egg-shaped cookies from each portion. Place on ungreased baking sheets. Bake at 350° for 20-25 minutes or until set. Cool completely. Combine glaze ingredients until smooth; spoon over cookies. Decorate as desired. **Yield:** 3 dozen.

## SOUR CREAM BISCOTTI

*Anna Ciraco, Hawthorne, New York*

**(Pictured above)**

*I got this recipe from my uncle's mother. These crisp cookies are perfect for dunking in milk or coffee.*

> 1 cup butter (no substitutes), softened
> 1 cup sugar
> 2 eggs
> 1/2 cup sour cream
> 1-1/2 teaspoons almond *or* vanilla extract
> 3-1/2 cups all-purpose flour
> 1-1/2 teaspoons baking powder
> 1 teaspoon baking soda

In a mixing bowl, cream butter and sugar. Add the eggs, one at a time, beating well after each addition. Stir in sour cream and extract. Combine dry ingredients; add to creamed mixture. Line two baking sheets with foil; grease the foil. Divide dough into thirds. On a floured surface, shape dough into three 8-in. x 2-1/2-in. x 3/4-in. loaves; place on foil. Bake at 350° for 25 minutes or until golden. Remove from the oven. Lift loaves with foil onto a wire rack; cool for 15 minutes. Place on a cutting board; using a serrated knife, slice diagonally 3/4 in. thick. Place slices, cut side down, on ungreased baking sheets. Bake at 350° for 8-10 minutes or until golden. Turn cookies over; bake 10 minutes longer. Cool on wire racks. Store in an airtight container. **Yield:** about 2-1/2 dozen.

## FESTIVE CRANBERRY CAKE

*Gladys Wilson, Anchorage, Alaska*

*Each fall here in Alaska, an abundant crop of wild cranberries is ripe for cooking. This cake, a favorite in my family, makes good use of the harvest.*

> 3/4 cup butter *or* margarine, softened
> 1 cup sugar
> 2 eggs
> 2-1/4 cups all-purpose flour
> 1 teaspoon baking powder
> 1 teaspoon baking soda
> 1 cup buttermilk
> 1 cup fresh *or* frozen cranberries
> 1 cup chopped dates
> 1 cup chopped pecans

**GLAZE:**

> 1/2 cup orange juice
> 1/4 cup sugar

**Fresh mint and additional cranberries, optional**

In a mixing bowl, cream butter and sugar. Add eggs; beat well. Combine dry ingredients; add to creamed mixture alternately with buttermilk. Stir in cranberries, dates and pecans. Spread in a greased and floured 10-in. tube pan. Bake at

350° for 60-70 minutes or until a toothpick inserted near the center comes out clean. Cool in pan for 10 minutes. Meanwhile, for glaze, heat orange juice and sugar in a small saucepan until sugar dissolves. Invert cake onto a serving plate. With a toothpick, punch holes in cake. Spoon glaze over cake. Cover and refrigerate for at least 8 hours. Garnish with mint and cranberries if desired. **Yield:** 12-16 servings.

## BUTTER PECAN CAKE

*Becky Miller, Tallahassee, Florida*

**(Pictured below)**

*This sweet, delicious cake is one that my family's enjoyed for many years. It's a special treat at Thanksgiving and Christmas.*

**2-2/3 cups chopped pecans**
**1-1/4 cups butter (no substitutes), softened,**
    ***divided***
  **2 cups sugar**
  **4 eggs**
  **3 cups all-purpose flour**
  **2 teaspoons baking powder**
**1/2 teaspoon salt**
  **1 cup milk**
  **2 teaspoons vanilla extract**
**FROSTING:**
  **1 cup butter (no substitutes), softened**
  **8 to 8-1/2 cups confectioners' sugar**
  **1 can (5 ounces) evaporated milk**
  **2 teaspoons vanilla extract**

Place pecans and 1/4 cup of butter in a baking pan. Bake at 350° for 20-25 minutes or until toasted, stirring frequently; set aside. In a mixing bowl, cream sugar and remaining butter. Add eggs, one at a time, beating well after each addition. Combine flour, baking powder and salt; add to the creamed mixture alternately with milk. Stir in vanilla and 1-1/3 cups of toasted pecans. Pour into three greased and floured 9-in. round cake pans. Bake at 350° for 25-30 minutes. Cool for 10 minutes; remove from pans to cool on a wire rack. For frosting, cream butter and sugar in a mixing bowl. Add milk and vanilla; beat until smooth. Stir in remaining toasted pecans. Spread frosting between layers and over top and sides of cake. **Yield:** 12-16 servings.

**FAMILY AND FRIENDS** *will save room for dessert when these fruit and cream pies, ice cream treats, tasty tarts and more are the finale!*

**SWEET SUCCESS.** Clockwise from top left: Rocky Road Freeze (p. 114), Homemade Ice Cream Sandwiches (p. 113), Sunshine Sherbet (p. 113) and Peach Melba Ice Cream Pie (p. 114).

# Pies & Desserts

## HOMEMADE ICE CREAM SANDWICHES

*Kea Fisher, Bridger, Montana*

**(Pictured at left)**

*I inherited my love of cooking from my mother, who sent me this recipe. My family loves it, and so does company I serve it to.*

1 package (18-1/4 ounces) chocolate cake mix
1/4 cup shortening
1/4 cup butter *or* margarine, softened
1 egg
1 tablespoon water
1 teaspoon vanilla extract
1/2 gallon ice cream*

In a mixing bowl, combine cake mix, shortening, butter, egg, water and vanilla; beat until well blended. Divide into four equal parts. Between waxed paper, roll one part into a 10-in. x 6-in. rectangle. Remove one piece of waxed paper and flip dough onto an ungreased baking sheet. Score the dough into eight pieces, each 3 in. x 2-1/2 in. Repeat with remaining dough. Bake at 350° for 8-10 minutes or until puffed. Immediately cut along the scored lines and prick holes in each piece with a fork; cool on baking sheets. Cut ice cream into 16 slices, each 3 in. x 2-1/2 in. x 1 in. Place ice cream between two chocolate cookies; wrap in plastic wrap. Freeze on a baking sheet overnight. Store in an airtight container. **Yield:** 16 servings. **\*Editor's Note:** Purchase a rectangular-shaped package of ice cream in the flavor of your choice for the easiest cutting.

## SUNSHINE SHERBET

*Barbara Looney, Fort Knox, Kentucky*

**(Pictured at left)**

*Together, my mother and I "invented" this recipe. Warm, humid evenings in Georgia, where I grew up, were all the inspiration we needed! It became a favorite part of gatherings with family and friends.*

2 cups sugar
1-1/2 cups water
2 cups milk
2 cups whipping cream
1-1/2 cups orange juice
1 can (12 ounces) evaporated milk
1/3 cup lemon juice
2 teaspoons grated orange peel
8 drops red food coloring, optional
1/2 teaspoon yellow food coloring, optional

In a saucepan over medium heat, bring sugar and water to a boil; boil for 5 minutes. Cool completely. Add remaining ingredients; mix well. Pour into the cylinder of an ice cream freezer; freeze according to manufacturer's directions. Remove from freezer 10 minutes before serving. **Yield:** about 2 quarts.

## APPLE PRALINE CUPS

*Gloria Kirchman, Eden Prairie, Minnesota*

*We have three apple trees in our yard...this recipe puts that delicious fruit to good use! The aroma of this quick-to-fix dessert baking is absolutely wonderful.*

8 flour tortillas (7 or 8 inches), warmed
1/4 cup butter *or* margarine, melted
6 cups sliced peeled tart apples
1 jar (12 ounces) caramel ice cream topping
2 tablespoons all-purpose flour
1/2 teaspoon ground cinnamon
1 carton (8 ounces) frozen whipped topping, thawed
1/2 cup chopped pecans, toasted

Brush both sides of tortillas with butter; press into 10-oz. custard cups. Place on baking sheets. Bake at 375° for 10-12 minutes or until golden. Cool. In a nonstick skillet, saute apples over medium heat for 8 minutes. Stir in the ice cream topping, flour and cinnamon; bring to a boil. Cook and stir over medium heat until mixture is thickened and apples are tender, about 4 minutes. Spoon into tortilla cups. Bake at 375° for 10 minutes. Top with whipped topping and pecans. **Yield:** 8 servings.

# Ice Cream Dishes Out Great Taste

WHENEVER A MEAL calls for an extra-special ending, count on chocolaty Rocky Road Freeze from Sheila Berry, Carrying Place, Ontario.

"Friends like to tease me about my passion for chocolate," Sheila says. "When I serve up this homemade dessert, though, everyone's too busy eating to tease!

"Everyone raves about the rich taste. Still, they hesitate before asking for my recipe. They figure homemade ice cream will be just too complicated.

"So they are pleasantly surprised to learn how easy it is and how few ingredients are needed. In fact, Rocky Road Freeze is ideal for anyone making ice cream for the first time."

To vary the taste, Sheila suggests using walnuts, pecans or cashews on occasion in place of peanuts. For a luscious dessert-on-the-go, put a double dip into a cone. "You can also serve this for fancy occasions," Sheila says. "It looks luxurious in a clear-glass sauce dish."

## ROCKY ROAD FREEZE

**(Pictured on page 112)**

1 can (14 ounces)
  sweetened condensed milk
1/2 cup chocolate syrup
2 cups whipping cream
1 cup miniature
  marshmallows
1/2 cup miniature chocolate
  chips
1/2 cup chopped salted
  peanuts

In a small bowl, combine the milk and chocolate syrup; set aside. In a mixing bowl, beat whipping cream until stiff peaks form. Fold in chocolate mixture, marshmallows, chocolate chips and peanuts. Transfer to a freezer-proof container; cover and freeze for 5 hours or until firm. Remove from freezer 10 minutes before serving. **Yield:** about 1-1/2 quarts.

## PEACH MELBA ICE CREAM PIE

*Judy Vaske, Bancroft, Iowa*

**(Pictured on page 112)**

*On a hot night, this pie makes a refreshing dessert. Like most wonderful recipes, it came from a friend.*

1-1/2 cups flaked coconut
  1/3 cup chopped pecans
    3 tablespoons butter *or* margarine, melted
    1 quart frozen peach yogurt, softened
    1 pint vanilla ice cream, softened
    1 tablespoon cornstarch
    1 tablespoon sugar
    1 package (10 ounces) frozen raspberries in syrup, thawed
    1 cup sliced fresh *or* frozen peaches, thawed

Combine coconut, pecans and butter; press onto the bottom and up the sides of an ungreased 9-in. pie plate. Bake at 350° for 12 minutes or until crust begins to brown around edges. Cool completely. Spoon frozen yogurt into crust; smooth the top. Spread ice cream over yogurt. Cover and freeze for 2 hours or until firm. In a small saucepan, combine cornstarch and sugar; drain raspberry juice into pan. Bring to a boil; cook and stir for 2 minutes. Remove from the heat; add raspberries. Cover and chill. Remove from freezer 10 minutes before serving. Arrange peaches on top of pie; drizzle with a little of the sauce. Pass the remaining sauce. **Yield:** 6-8 servings.

## CANTALOUPE SHERBET

*Rolanda Crawford, Abilene, Texas*

*I make this early in the day, then we sit outside under the evening Texas sky and enjoy it!*

☑ This tasty dish uses less fat, sugar or salt. Recipe includes Nutritional Analysis and Diabetic Exchanges.

1 medium ripe cantaloupe
1 can (14 ounces) fat-free sweetened
  condensed skim milk
2 tablespoons honey

Cut cantaloupe in half; discard seeds. Peel and slice cantaloupe; cut into large pieces. Place in a blender container. Add milk and honey; cover and blend until smooth. Pour into a freezer-proof container. Freeze overnight or until firm. **Yield: 9 servings. Nutritional Analysis:** One 1/2-cup serving equals 158 calories, 52 mg sodium, 3 mg cholesterol, 35 gm carbohydrate, 4 gm protein, trace fat. **Diabetic Exchanges:** 1-1/2 starch, 1 fruit.

## WALNUT TART

*Rovena Wallace, Trafford, Pennsylvania*
*The first time my husband tried this, he said there ought to be a law against anything tasting so good!*

    1/3 cup butter *or* margarine, softened
    1/4 cup sugar
      1 egg yolk
      1 cup all-purpose flour
FILLING:
      2 cups coarsely chopped walnuts
    2/3 cup packed brown sugar
    1/4 cup butter *or* margarine
    1/4 cup dark corn syrup
    1/2 cup whipping cream, *divided*

In a mixing bowl, cream butter and sugar until fluffy. Add egg yolk; mix well. Add flour just until blended (mixture will be crumbly). Press onto the bottom and up the sides of an ungreased 9-in. tart pan with removable bottom. Bake at 375° for 12-14 minutes. Cool in the pan on a wire rack. Sprinkle nuts over crust. In a heavy saucepan, combine sugar, butter, corn syrup and 2 tablespoons of cream. Boil and stir over medium heat for 1 minute. Pour over walnuts. Bake at 375° for 10-12 minutes or until bubbly. Cool. Beat remaining cream until stiff. Serve tart at room temperature with whipped cream. **Yield:** 10-12 servings. **Editor's Note:** An 11-in. x 7-in. x 2-in. baking pan may be used instead of a tart pan.

## MOM'S FRIED APPLES

*Margie Tappe, Prague, Oklahoma*
*Mom made these for me often while I was growing up. The recipe is very dear to me.*

    1/2 cup butter *or* margarine
      6 medium unpeeled tart red apples, sliced
    3/4 cup sugar, *divided*
    3/4 teaspoon ground cinnamon

Melt butter in a large skillet. Add apples and 1/2 cup sugar; stir to mix well. Cover and cook over low heat for 20 minutes or until apples are tender, stirring frequently. Add cinnamon and remaining

sugar. Cook and stir over medium-high heat for 10 minutes. **Yield:** 6-8 servings.

## BONNIE BLUE-BARB PIE

*Andrea Holcomb, Torrington, Connecticut*

**(Pictured below)**

*Rhubarb and blueberries are both native to our area, and this pie combines the flavors beautifully. We are fortunate to have a healthy rhubarb patch in our garden. It keeps us supplied with rhubarb from spring until well into fall.*

    1-1/2 cups fresh *or* frozen rhubarb, cut into
          1/2-inch pieces
    1-1/2 cups fresh *or* frozen blueberries
        1 cup sugar
      1/4 cup all-purpose flour
      1/4 teaspoon salt
Pastry for double-crust pie (9 inches)
        2 tablespoons butter *or* margarine

In a large bowl, combine rhubarb and blueberries. Combine sugar, flour and salt. Sprinkle over the fruit; toss lightly. Line a 9-in. pie plate with pastry; add filling. Dot with butter. Top with a lattice crust. Bake at 450° for 10 minutes. Reduce heat to 350°; bake 35 minutes longer or until golden brown. **Yield:** 8 servings. **Editor's Note:** If using frozen fruit, thaw and drain well.

## SWEET POTATO COBBLER

*Sherry Parker, Jacksonville, Alabama*

**(Pictured below)**

*My grandmother used to make the best sweet potato cobbler, but, like many cooks, she didn't follow a recipe. I tried many cobbler recipes before I discovered this one. It's a favorite for church dinners and is a special treat at home.*

>    2 pounds sweet potatoes, peeled and sliced
>       1/4 inch thick
> 3-1/2 cups water
> 1-1/2 cups sugar
>    3 tablespoons all-purpose flour
>    1/2 teaspoon ground cinnamon
>    1/4 teaspoon ground nutmeg
>    1/4 teaspoon salt
>    3/4 cup butter *or* margarine, cubed

**PASTRY:**

>    2 cups all-purpose flour
>    1/2 teaspoon salt
>    2/3 cup shortening
>    5 to 6 tablespoons cold water
>    2 tablespoons butter *or* margarine, melted
>    4 teaspoons sugar

**Whipped cream, optional**

In a saucepan, cook sweet potatoes in water until crisp-tender, about 10 minutes. Drain, reserving 1-1/2 cups cooking liquid. Layer potatoes in a greased 13-in. x 9-in. x 2-in. baking dish; add reserved liquid. Combine sugar, flour, cinnamon, nutmeg and salt; sprinkle over potatoes. Dot with butter. For pastry, combine flour and salt; cut in shortening until mixture resembles coarse crumbs. Gradually add water, tossing with a fork until a ball forms. On a floured surface, roll pastry into a 13-in. x 9-in. rectangle. Place over filling; cut slits in top. Brush with butter; sprinkle with sugar. Bake at 400° for 30-35 minutes or until top is golden brown. Spoon into dishes; top with whipped cream if desired. **Yield:** 10-12 servings.

## GEORGIA PEACH ICE CREAM

*Marguerite Ethridge, Americus, Georgia*

*My state is known for growing peaches. This delicious recipe has been a family favorite for almost 50 years.*

>    1 quart milk
>    4 eggs
> 2-1/4 cups sugar, *divided*
>    1/2 teaspoon salt
>    2 cans (14 ounces *each*) sweetened
>       condensed milk
> 1-3/4 pounds fresh peaches, peeled and sliced
> Fresh mint, optional

In a heavy saucepan, bring milk to a boil. Meanwhile, beat eggs. Add 1 cup sugar and salt; mix well. Gradually add a small amount of hot milk; return all to the pan. Cook over medium-low heat, stirring constantly, until mixture is thick enough to coat a metal spoon and reaches at least 160°, about 6-8 minutes. Remove from the heat. Set pan in ice and stir the mixture for 5-10 minutes. Gradually stir in condensed milk; mix well. Cover and refrigerate overnight. When ready to freeze, mash peaches with remaining sugar in a small bowl; let stand for 30 minutes. Combine milk mixture and peaches in an ice cream freezer. Freeze according to manufacturer's directions. Garnish with mint if desired. **Yield:** 3-3/4 quarts.

## HONEY PECAN CHEESECAKE

*Tish Frish, Hampden, Maine*

*Birthdays and holidays are great times for cheesecake, and Thanksgiving's ideal for this particular one. In our annual church bake-off, it won first place.*

>    1 cup vanilla wafer crumbs
>    5 tablespoons butter *or* margarine, melted
>    2 tablespoons sugar
>    1/4 cup ground pecans

**FILLING:**

>    3 packages (8 ounces *each*) cream cheese,
>       softened
>    1 cup packed dark brown sugar

Pies & Desserts

3 eggs
2 tablespoons all-purpose flour
1 tablespoon maple flavoring
1 teaspoon vanilla extract
1/2 cup chopped pecans
TOPPING:
1/4 cup honey
1 tablespoon butter *or* margarine
1 tablespoon water
1/2 cup chopped pecans

Combine the first four ingredients; press onto the bottom only of a greased 9-in. springform pan. Refrigerate. In a mixing bowl, beat cream cheese and sugar. Add eggs; beat until smooth. Add flour, maple flavoring and vanilla; mix well. Stir in pecans. Pour into crust. Bake at 350° for 50-55 minutes or until center is nearly set. Turn off the oven; open door and leave cheesecake in oven for 1 hour. Remove from the oven; cool completely. Refrigerate overnight. For topping, combine the honey, butter and water in a small saucepan; cook and stir over medium heat for 2 minutes. Add nuts; cook 2 minutes longer (mixture will be thin). Spoon over cheesecake. Carefully remove sides of pan before serving. Refrigerate leftovers. **Yield:** 12 servings.

## FOUR-NUT BRITTLE

*Kelly-Ann Gibbons*
*Prince George, British Columbia*

*This recipe's one I created myself. I enjoy various kinds of nuts and wanted a candy that has a different crunch in every bite.*

2 cups sugar
1 cup light corn syrup
1/2 cup water
1/2 cup salted peanuts
1/2 cup *each* coarsely chopped almonds,
    pecans and walnuts
1/4 cup butter *or* margarine
2 teaspoons baking soda
1-1/2 teaspoons vanilla extract

Butter the sides of a large heavy saucepan. Add sugar, corn syrup and water; bring to a boil, stirring constantly. Cook and stir over medium-low heat until a candy thermometer reads 238° (soft-ball stage). Stir in nuts and butter. Cook over medium heat to 300° (hard-crack stage). Remove from the heat; vigorously stir in baking soda and vanilla until blended. Quickly pour onto two greased baking sheets, spreading as thinly as possible with a metal spatula. Cool completely; break into pieces. Store in an airtight container with waxed paper between layers. **Yield:** 1-3/4 pounds.

## CRANBERRY APPLE PIE

*Betty Winberg, Nashua, New Hampshire*

**(Pictured above)**

*New England is one of the prime apple- and cranberry-growing regions of the country. This is my all-time favorite cranberry apple pie recipe.*

2 cups sugar
1/4 cup cornstarch
1/4 cup orange juice
1/2 teaspoon ground cinnamon
1/2 teaspoon apple pie spice
1/8 teaspoon ground nutmeg
1/4 teaspoon lemon juice
4 cups sliced peeled tart apples
2 cups fresh *or* frozen cranberries
Pastry for double-crust pie (9 inches)
2 tablespoons butter *or* margarine

In a large bowl, combine the first seven ingredients. Add apples and cranberries; toss gently. Line a 9-in. pie plate with bottom pastry. Add filling; dot with butter. Roll the remaining pastry to fit top of pie. Cut vents in pastry, using a small apple cutter if desired. Place over filling; seal and flute the edges. Bake at 425° for 10 minutes. Reduce heat to 350°; bake 50 minutes longer or until crust is golden brown and filling is bubbly. **Yield:** 6-8 servings.

# Quick & Easy Ice Cream Treats

IF you can't take your sweet time making an ice cream treat, you've come to the right place. Each of these recipes requires only 30 minutes or less to prepare, and only one needs to be frozen before it can be served.

## STRAWBERRY SMOOTHIE

*Emma Birchenough, Lowville, New York*

*My daughters would drink this before their athletic events to build up energy.*

> 1 carton (8 ounces) strawberry yogurt
> 1 cup milk
> 1/2 cup unsweetened frozen strawberries
> 1 tablespoon honey
> 1 pint vanilla ice cream
> 1 medium ripe banana, quartered
> Red food coloring, optional

Place all ingredients in a blender container; cover and process on high until smooth. Pour into glasses. Refrigerate any leftovers. **Yield:** 4-6 servings.

## ORANGE-GLAZED BANANAS

*Rose Randall, Derry, Pennsylvania*

*Since retiring, I have more time to cook, but I still depend on this delicious rapid recipe.*

> 3/4 cup orange juice concentrate
> 3 tablespoons butter *or* margarine
> 3 tablespoons brown sugar
> 2 tablespoons grated orange peel
> 3/4 teaspoon ground ginger
> 4 medium firm bananas, sliced
> Vanilla ice cream

In a saucepan over medium heat, combine the first five ingredients. Cook and stir until the sugar is dissolved. Add bananas and heat through. Serve over ice cream. **Yield:** about 3 cups.

## EASY HOT FUDGE SAUCE

*Nancy Nielson, Cambridge, Ohio*

*For years I had been looking to duplicate hot fudge sauces like those made in restaurants. So I was thrilled to find this recipe.*

> 2 squares (1 ounce *each*) unsweetened chocolate
> 1 can (14 ounces) sweetened condensed milk
> 1/4 to 1/3 cup milk

Place all ingredients in a heavy saucepan; cook and stir over medium heat until chocolate is melted. Serve warm. Store in the refrigerator. **Yield:** 1-1/2 cups.

## DESSERT WAFFLES

*Sheila Watson, Stettler, Alberta*

*Everyone raves about the contrast between the crunchy waffles and creamy ice cream in this dessert.*

> 1/2 cup flaked coconut
> 1/2 cup packed brown sugar
> 1/4 cup butter *or* margarine, softened
> 6 frozen waffles, lightly toasted
> 6 scoops butter pecan ice cream *or* flavor of your choice

In a small bowl, combine the first three ingredients; mix well. Spread over waffles. Broil for 3-4 minutes or until bubbly. Top with ice cream. **Yield:** 6 servings.

## BLUEBERRY MILK SHAKES

*Lynn McAllister, Mount Ulla, North Carolina*

*This "berry" good beverage is especially tasty on a hot summer day.*

1 cup milk
2 tablespoons lemon juice
1 pint vanilla ice cream
1 cup fresh *or* frozen blueberries
1 tablespoon sugar
1 tablespoon grated lemon peel

Place all ingredients in a blender container; cover and process on high until smooth. Pour into glasses. Refrigerate any leftovers. **Yield:** 3-4 servings.

## HOT APPLE SUNDAES

*Delia Gurnow, New Madrid, Missouri*

*After dinner, everyone usually dashes off, but this treat makes them linger around the table.*

1 can (21 ounces) apple pie filling
1/4 cup apple juice
1 tablespoon sugar
1/2 teaspoon ground cinnamon
Vanilla ice cream

In a saucepan, combine the first four ingredients. Cook and stir over medium heat until heated through. Serve over ice cream. **Yield:** 2 cups.

## DIRTY ICE CREAM

*Nora Troyer, Franklin, Kentucky*

*A favorite of my husband's, this easy recipe comes from my sister-in-law.*

2 quarts vanilla ice cream, softened
1 package (16 ounces) cream-filled
   chocolate sandwich cookies, crushed
1 carton (8 ounces) frozen whipped
   topping, thawed
Additional cookies, halved *and/or* crushed,
   optional
Fresh mint, optional

In a large bowl, combine ice cream and cookies. Fold in whipped topping. Pour into an ungreased 13-in. x 9-in. x 2-in. pan. Cover and freeze overnight. Remove from freezer 10 minutes be-

fore serving. Garnish with additional cookies and mint if desired. **Yield:** 16-20 servings.

## CANTALOUPE A LA MODE

*Nancy Walker, Granite City, Illinois*

**(Pictured below)**

*This special dessert is a refreshing finale to a warm-weather meal.*

1/2 cup water
1/2 cup sugar
2 tablespoons lemon juice
1 tablespoon cornstarch
1 teaspoon grated lemon peel
1 cup fresh *or* frozen blueberries
2 small cantaloupe, halved and seeded
4 scoops vanilla ice cream
Fresh mint, optional

In a saucepan, combine the first five ingredients; bring to a boil over medium heat. Boil and stir for 2 minutes. Add blueberries and heat through. Fill cantaloupe with ice cream; top with sauce. Garnish with mint if desired. **Yield:** 4 servings (1 cup sauce).

mon-sugar twice. Roll out remaining dough to fit top of dish and place on top. Using a sharp knife, cut 2-in. slits through all layers at once. For syrup, bring water and sugar to a boil. Cook and stir until sugar is dissolved. Pour over top crust. Bake at 400° for 35-40 minutes or until browned and bubbly. Serve warm with whipped topping or ice cream if desired. Garnish with mint if desired. **Yield:** 12 servings.

---

## STRAWBERRY BROWNIE BOMBE

*Joanne Watts, Kitchener, Ontario*

### (Pictured on page 123)

*A friend and I dreamed up this recipe. We use it to entertain and for special family dinners. For an extra touch, you can dip the strawberries in chocolate.*

   1 package (21-1/2 ounces) fudge brownie mix
1/2 cup chopped walnuts
1/2 cup strawberry preserves
   1 quart strawberry ice cream, softened
   2 cups whipping cream
   3 drops red food coloring, optional
1/4 cup confectioners' sugar
**Pastry bag *or* heavy-duty resealable plastic bag**
**Star pastry tip #8B *or* #20**
**Fresh strawberries and mint, optional**

Prepare brownie mix according to package directions for cake-like brownies. Stir in walnuts. Pour the batter into two greased and waxed paper-lined 8-in. round baking pans. Bake at 350° for 30 minutes or until a toothpick inserted near the center comes out clean. Cool completely in pans. Line a 1-1/2-qt. metal bowl with foil. Cut and fit one brownie layer to evenly line the inside of the bowl (brownie may crack). Spread preserves over brownie layer. Freeze for 15 minutes. Fill brownie-lined bowl with ice cream; smooth top. Cover and freeze for 3 hours or until ice cream is firm. Place remaining brownie layer on a serving plate. Remove bowl from freezer; uncover. Invert onto brownie layer; remove bowl and foil. Return to freezer.* In a mixing bowl, beat cream and food coloring until soft peaks form. Add sugar and beat until stiff peaks form; set aside 1-1/2 cups. Spread remaining whipped cream over top and sides of bombe. Cut a small hole in the corner of a pastry or plastic bag and insert star tip. Fill with reserved whipped cream; pipe border at base of bombe. Holding the bag straight up and down, form stars on top. Garnish with strawberries and mint if desired. **Yield:** 16 servings. **Editor's Note:** Unfrosted bombe may be frozen for up to 3 days.

---

## APPLE DUMPLING DESSERT

*Janet Weaver, Wooster, Ohio*

### (Pictured above)

*This quick-to-fix dessert has a nice bonus: no bites of dry crust without filling since it's all mixed throughout!*

**PASTRY:**
   4 cups all-purpose flour
   2 teaspoons salt
1-1/3 cups shortening
   8 to 9 tablespoons cold water
**FILLING:**
   8 cups chopped peeled tart apples
1/4 cup sugar
3/4 teaspoon ground cinnamon
**SYRUP:**
   2 cups water
   1 cup packed brown sugar
**Whipped topping *or* vanilla ice cream, optional**
**Mint leaves, optional**

In a bowl, combine flour and salt; cut in shortening until the mixture resembles coarse crumbs. Sprinkle with water, 1 tablespoon at a time, and toss with a fork until dough can be formed into a ball. Divide dough into four parts. On a lightly floured surface, roll one part to fit the bottom of an ungreased 13-in. x 9-in. x 2-in. baking dish. Place in dish; top with a third of the apples. Combine sugar and cinnamon; sprinkle a third over apples. Repeat layers of pastry, apples and cinna-

## BERRY GOOD ICE CREAM SAUCE

*Joy Beck, Cincinnati, Ohio*

**(Pictured on page 122)**

*I started cooking as a bride over 40 years ago. I'm thankful to say I improved in time—though I made something once even the dog refused to eat!*

1-3/4 cups sliced fresh *or* frozen rhubarb
2/3 cup pureed fresh *or* frozen strawberries
1/4 cup sugar
1/4 cup orange juice
2 cups sliced fresh *or* frozen strawberries
Vanilla ice cream

In a saucepan, combine the first four ingredients. Cook over medium heat until rhubarb is tender, about 5 minutes. Stir in the sliced strawberries. Store in the refrigerator. Serve over ice cream. **Yield:** 3-1/2 cups.

## CARAMEL FRIED ICE CREAM

*Darlene Markel, Sublimity, Oregon*

**(Pictured on page 122)**

*For birthday parties or outdoor barbecues, this is a hit. At times, I substitute strawberry or Neapolitan for the vanilla ice cream.*

1 quart vanilla ice cream
1/4 cup whipping cream
2 teaspoons vanilla extract
2 cups flaked coconut, finely chopped
2 cups finely crushed cornflakes
1/2 teaspoon ground cinnamon
**CARAMEL SAUCE:**
1 cup sugar
1/2 cup butter *or* margarine
1/2 cup evaporated milk
Oil for deep-fat frying

Using a 1/2-cup ice cream scoop, place eight scoops of ice cream on a baking sheet. Cover and freeze for 2 hours or until firm. In a bowl, combine whipping cream and vanilla. In another bowl, combine coconut, cornflakes and cinnamon. Remove ice cream from freezer; wearing plastic gloves, shape the ice cream into balls. Dip balls into cream mixture, then roll in coconut mixture, making sure to coat entire surface. Place coated balls on a baking sheet. Cover and freeze at least 3 hours or until firm. For caramel sauce, heat sugar in a heavy saucepan over medium heat until partially melted and golden, stirring occasionally. Add butter. Gradually add milk, stirring constantly. Cook and stir for 8 minutes or until sauce is thick and golden; keep warm. Heat oil in an electric skillet or deep-fat fryer to 375°. Fry ice cream balls until golden, about 30 seconds. Drain on paper towels. Serve immediately with caramel sauce. **Yield:** 8 servings.

## FROSTY LEMON PIE

*Judith Wilke, Dousman, Wisconsin*

**(Pictured on page 122 and on cover)**

*This pie is a nice light and refreshing finish to a summertime picnic or patio supper. I like that it can be made ahead.*

3/4 cup sugar
1/3 cup lemon juice
1/4 cup butter *or* margarine
Dash salt
3 eggs, beaten
2 pints vanilla ice cream, softened, *divided*
1 graham cracker crust (9 inches)
Whipped topping, fresh mint and lemon peel, optional

In a saucepan, combine sugar, lemon juice, butter and salt; cook and stir over medium heat until sugar is dissolved and the butter is melted. Add a small amount to eggs; return all to the pan. Cook and stir over medium heat until thickened (do not boil). Refrigerate until completely cooled. Spread half of the ice cream into the crust; freeze for 1 hour or until firm. Cover with half of the lemon mixture; freeze for 1 hour or until firm. Repeat layers. Cover and freeze for several hours or overnight. Remove from the freezer 10 minutes before serving. If desired, garnish with whipped topping, mint and lemon peel. **Yield:** 8 servings.

## OLD-FASHIONED STRAWBERRY SODA

*Ginger Hubbard, Anderson, Missouri*

**(Pictured on page 123)**

*With just a quick pulse of the blender, you will have what I call a "refreshing sipper"—and you'll be asked for more!*

1 cup milk
1/2 cup fresh *or* frozen strawberries
1/2 cup vanilla ice cream, softened
2 tablespoons sugar
2 to 3 drops red food coloring, optional
1 cup ginger ale, chilled

In a blender container, combine the first five ingredients; cover and process until smooth. Pour into two tall glasses. Add ginger ale and serve immediately. **Yield:** 2 servings.

**SUMMERTIME** *in the country offers all sorts of delights—and none of them is more eagerly anticipated than ice cream! It's a dairy-good dessert.*

**ICE CREAM SOCIAL.** Clockwise from upper left: Brownie Ice Cream Cones (p. 124), Peanut Butter Ice Cream (p. 124), Old-Fashioned Strawberry Soda (p. 121), Strawberry Brownie Bombe (p. 120), Chocolate Peanut Ice Cream Dessert (p. 124), Caramel Fried Ice Cream (p. 121), Berry Good Ice Cream Sauce (p. 121) and Frosty Lemon Pie (p. 121).

## CHOCOLATE PEANUT ICE CREAM DESSERT

*Jeanette Neufeld, Boissevain, Manitoba*

**(Pictured on page 123)**

*If you're expecting company or simply want a convenient on-hand dessert, try this. It's easy, but people will think that you slaved for hours to make it.*

    1 cup vanilla wafer crumbs
    1/2 cup finely chopped peanuts
    1/4 cup butter *or* margarine, melted
    2 tablespoons confectioners' sugar
    6 cups chocolate ice cream, softened,
      *divided*
FILLING:
    1 package (3 ounces) cream cheese,
      softened
    1/3 cup crunchy peanut butter
    3/4 cup confectioners' sugar
    1/4 cup milk
    1/2 cup whipping cream, whipped

Line the bottom and sides of a 9-in. x 5-in. x 3-in. loaf pan with heavy-duty aluminum foil. Combine the first four ingredients; press half onto the bottom of the pan. Freeze for 15 minutes. Spread half of the ice cream over crust; freeze for 1 hour or until firm. Meanwhile, for filling, beat cream cheese and peanut butter in a mixing bowl. Add sugar and milk; mix well. Fold in whipped cream. Spread over ice cream; freeze for 1 hour or until firm. Spread with remaining ice cream (pan will be very full). Press remaining crumb mixture on top. Cover and freeze for several hours or overnight. Remove from the freezer 10 minutes before serving. Using foil, remove loaf from pan; discard foil. Cut into slices using a serrated knife. **Yield:** 10-12 servings.

## BROWNIE ICE CREAM CONES

*Marlene Rhodes, Panama City, Florida*

**(Pictured on page 122)**

*Often, I'll find a recipe that sounds interesting, copy it down and put my own twist on it. That's just what I did with these.*

    1 package (4 ounces) German sweet
      chocolate
    1/4 cup butter *or* margarine
    3/4 cup sugar
    2 eggs
    1/2 cup all-purpose flour
    1/2 cup chopped walnuts, optional
    1 teaspoon vanilla extract

    24 cake ice cream cones (about 3 inches
      tall)
    24 scoops ice cream
Colored *or* chocolate sprinkles

In a saucepan over low heat, melt the chocolate and butter, stirring frequently. Cool slightly; pour into a bowl. Add sugar and eggs; mix well. Stir in flour, walnuts if desired and vanilla. Place the ice cream cones in muffin cups; fill half full with batter. Bake at 350° for 20-22 minutes or until brownies are set on top and a toothpick inserted near the center comes out with moist crumbs (do not overbake). Cool completely. Just before serving, top each with a scoop of ice cream and garnish with sprinkles. **Yield:** 2 dozen.

## BLUSHING SNOWBALLS

*Joan Tracht, Huron, Ohio*

*This is an easy-to-make, eye-appealing dessert to serve around the holidays...or anytime of year. Kids of all ages will enjoy it.*

    18 large marshmallows
    3/4 cup sugar
    3/4 cup water
    1/3 cup red-hot candies
    6 small tart apples, peeled, cored and
      halved
    1 teaspoon lemon juice

In a large skillet, combine marshmallows, sugar, water and candies. Cook over medium heat, stirring occasionally, until candies are dissolved. Add apples. Simmer, uncovered, for 20 minutes or until apples are tender, gently turning once. Add lemon juice. Cool. **Yield:** 12 servings.

## PEANUT BUTTER ICE CREAM

*Sigrid Guillot, Thibodaux, Louisiana*

**(Pictured on page 123)**

*It's the big flock of ducks my husband and I used to raise that inspired me to create this recipe. When we found ourselves with a surplus of their eggs, ice cream seemed a good place to put them.*

    1 envelope unflavored gelatin
    1/4 cup cold water
    3 egg yolks
    1-3/4 cups milk
    1 cup sugar
    1/4 teaspoon salt
    3 packages (1.6 ounces *each*) peanut
      butter cups, crumbled

2 cups evaporated milk
1 tablespoon vanilla extract

Combine gelatin and water in a small bowl; stir until softened. Set aside. In a saucepan, beat egg yolks and milk. Stir in sugar and salt. Cook and stir over medium-low heat until mixture is thick enough to coat a metal spoon and reaches 160°, about 12-15 minutes. Remove from the heat. Add peanut butter cups and softened gelatin; stir until melted. Set saucepan in ice and stir the mixture for 5-10 minutes. Stir in evaporated milk and vanilla. Cover and refrigerate overnight. When ready to freeze, pour peanut butter mixture into the cylinder of an ice cream freezer. Freeze according to manufacturer's directions. **Yield:** about 1 quart.

## APPLE STRUDEL CHEESECAKE

*Janice White, Encampment, Wyoming*

*I adapted this recipe from several others. Apples make it less rich and heavy. My family eats it anytime— for breakfast or as a late-night snack—and I serve it for dessert or when company comes for coffee.*

### CRUST:
1 cup all-purpose flour
2/3 cup sugar
1/2 cup cold butter (no substitutes)
1/4 teaspoon vanilla extract
### FILLING:
4 cups sliced peeled tart apples
2 packages (8 ounces *each*) cream cheese, softened
3/4 cup sugar, *divided*
2 eggs
1 teaspoon vanilla extract
1 teaspoon ground cinnamon
1/4 cup chopped walnuts

In a bowl, combine flour and sugar; cut in the butter until crumbly. Stir in vanilla. Press onto the bottom of an ungreased 9-in. springform pan. Bake at 350° for 10 minutes. Cool. Place apples in an ungreased 13-in. x 9-in. x 2-in. baking dish. Cover and bake at 375° for 15 minutes or until tender; drain and cool. Meanwhile, in a large bowl, combine cream cheese, 1/2 cup sugar, eggs and vanilla; mix until light and fluffy. Pour over crust. Toss baked apples with cinnamon and remaining sugar. Arrange apples over cream cheese layer; drizzle with any remaining cinnamon mixture. Sprinkle with nuts. Bake at 375° for 15 minutes. Reduce heat to 350°; bake 45-50 minutes longer or until set. Cool to room temperature. Refrigerate for at least 4 hours. Use a sharp knife to cut. Store in the refrigerator. **Yield:** 12 servings.

## CARAMEL APPLE DUMPLINGS

*Darci VandenHoek, Sherwood, Oregon*

**(Pictured below)**

*The Northwest is known for its wonderful apples. Eating this dessert is a perfect way to warm up on a crisp fall evening.*

### SAUCE:
1-1/2 cups water
1 cup packed brown sugar
2 tablespoons butter *or* margarine
1 teaspoon vanilla extract
1/2 teaspoon salt
### DUMPLINGS:
1-1/4 cups all-purpose flour
1/4 cup sugar
1-1/2 teaspoons baking powder
1/2 cup milk
2 tablespoons butter *or* margarine, melted
1 teaspoon vanilla extract
1 cup diced peeled tart apples
Whipped cream *or* vanilla ice cream, optional

In a large saucepan, combine sauce ingredients; bring to a boil, stirring constantly. For the dumplings, combine flour, sugar and baking powder in a large bowl. Add milk, butter and vanilla; stir just until moistened. Gently fold in apples. Drop by heaping teaspoonfuls into the boiling sauce. Cover and cook over low heat until a knife inserted in the center comes out clean, about 8-10 minutes. Serve warm with whipped cream or ice cream if desired. **Yield:** 6 servings.

## WALNUT APPLESAUCE PIE

*Mrs. F. Verbrugge, Franklin Lakes, New Jersey*

*My mother baked this pie every autumn, and it's become a tradition at our house. My husband always asks for seconds.*

- 1 cup packed dark brown sugar
- 1/3 cup sugar
- 1 tablespoon all-purpose flour
- 1 egg plus 1 egg white
- 1/2 cup unsweetened applesauce
- 2 tablespoons milk
- 1 teaspoon vanilla extract
- 1 cup chopped walnuts
- 1 unbaked pastry shell (9 inches)

Whipped cream, optional

In a mixing bowl, combine sugars and flour. Add egg, egg white, applesauce, milk and vanilla; mix well. Stir in walnuts. Pour into pastry shell. Bake at 375° for 40-45 minutes or until set. Cool completely. Serve with whipped cream if desired. Store in the refrigerator. **Yield:** 6-8 servings.

## PINEAPPLE LIME PIE

*Mrs. Herbert Fischer, Melbourne, Florida*

**(Pictured below)**

*This pie is easy to make and good for any occasion. My husband served in the military for many years and, as we traveled, I served this pie many times.*

- 1 can (14 ounces) sweetened condensed milk

- 1/2 cup lime juice
- 1 can (8 ounces) crushed pineapple, drained
- 2 to 3 drops green food coloring, optional
- 1 pastry shell (9 inches), baked *or* 1 graham cracker crust (9 inches)
- 1 cup whipping cream
- 2 tablespoons sugar

Shaved semisweet chocolate, optional

In a bowl, combine milk, lime juice and pineapple. Stir in food coloring if desired. Spoon into crust. In a small mixing bowl, beat cream until stiff peaks form; beat in the sugar, 1 tablespoon at a time. Spoon over filling. Sprinkle with chocolate if desired. Chill for at least 8 hours. **Yield:** 6-8 servings.

## VERY BERRY MELBA

*Gloria Woudenberg, Atlanta, Michigan*

*I received this recipe from my sister many years ago when we lived in southern Michigan, which has many blueberry farms. We've since moved north and now find our berries growing wild in the woods.*

- 1/2 gallon vanilla ice cream, softened
- 1/4 cup orange juice concentrate
- 1-1/2 to 2 teaspoons ground cinnamon
- 3 cups fresh *or* frozen blueberries
- 2 cups fresh *or* frozen raspberries
- 1 tablespoon lemon juice
- 1/2 cup sugar
- 2 tablespoons cornstarch

In a bowl, combine ice cream, orange juice concentrate and cinnamon. Cover and freeze for 2-3 hours or until firm. Meanwhile, combine berries and lemon juice in a saucepan; cover and cook over low heat for 10 minutes, stirring occasionally. Combine sugar and cornstarch; stir into pan. Bring to a boil over medium heat; boil for 2 minutes, stirring constantly. Remove from the heat. Cool; cover and refrigerate. To serve, spoon ice cream into a bowl or parfait glass; top with the berry sauce. **Yield:** 8-10 servings.

## CARAMEL APPLE CREAM PIE

*Lisa DiNuccio, Boxford, Massachusetts*

*When I first made this pie for my family, the reactions weren't real words—they were more "Ooh!" and "Mmm!" I created it to enter in a local fair, and it ended up winning third prize.*

- 1 pastry shell (9 inches)
- 1/4 cup butter *or* margarine

1/2 cup packed brown sugar
4 medium tart apples, peeled and cut into
    1/2-inch chunks
1-1/2 teaspoons pumpkin pie spice, *divided*
1 to 2 tablespoons all-purpose flour
1/2 cup caramel ice cream topping
1/2 cup chopped pecans
1 package (8 ounces) cream cheese,
    softened
1/4 cup sugar
1 egg
1 tablespoon lemon juice
1 teaspoon vanilla extract
Whipped topping

Bake pastry shell but do not prick. Cool. In a large skillet over medium heat, melt butter and brown sugar. Stir in apples and 1 teaspoon pumpkin pie spice; simmer for 12-15 minutes, stirring frequently, or until tender. Stir in flour; cook and stir for 1 minute. Drizzle caramel topping over pastry shell; sprinkle with pecans. Spoon apple mixture over pecans; set aside. In a mixing bowl, combine cream cheese, sugar, egg, lemon juice and vanilla; beat until smooth. Pour over apples. Bake at 350° for 35-45 minutes or until a knife inserted into the cream cheese layer comes out clean. Cool on a wire rack. Chill thoroughly. To serve, top with dollops of whipped topping; sprinkle with remaining pumpkin pie spice. **Yield:** 8 servings.

### JAYNE'S PEACH-PEAR PIE

*Jayne Littlefield, Ft. Morgan, Colorado*

**(Pictured above right)**

*This pie is my own creation and always draws compliments whenever I make it. I like to serve it cold with vanilla ice cream. I've been collecting recipes since I was a teenager and enjoy changing them to suit my family's tastes.*

1/3 cup packed brown sugar
1/4 cup sugar
3 tablespoons cornstarch
1/2 teaspoon ground cinnamon
1/4 teaspoon ground allspice
2-1/2 cups sliced peeled fresh peaches
2-1/2 cups sliced peeled fresh pears
1 tablespoon lemon juice
1 unbaked pastry shell (9 inches)
WALNUT STREUSEL:
1/2 cup all-purpose flour
1/4 cup sugar
3 tablespoons brown sugar
1/4 teaspoon ground cinnamon
1/4 teaspoon ground nutmeg

1/4 cup cold butter *or* margarine
1/3 cup chopped walnuts

In a bowl, combine sugars, cornstarch, cinnamon and allspice; set aside. Sprinkle peaches and pears with lemon juice. Add to dry ingredients; toss to coat. Pour into pastry shell. For streusel, combine flour, sugars, cinnamon and nutmeg; cut in butter until mixture resembles coarse crumbs. Stir in nuts. Sprinkle over filling. Cover edges with foil. Bake at 375° for 1 hour or until bubbly. Remove foil. **Yield:** 6-8 servings.

### BANANA BOATS

*Brenda Loveless, Garland, Texas*

*This recipe—which was given to me years ago by a good friend—is a favorite with my family when we go camping. It's quick and fun to make!*

4 medium unpeeled ripe bananas
4 teaspoons miniature chocolate chips
4 tablespoons miniature marshmallows

Cut banana peel lengthwise about 1/2 in. deep, leaving 1/2 in. at both ends. Open peel wider to form a pocket. Fill each with 1 teaspoon chocolate chips and 1 tablespoon marshmallows. Crimp and shape four pieces of heavy-duty foil (about 12 in. x 12 in.) around bananas, forming boats. Grill, uncovered, over medium coals for 10-15 minutes or until marshmallows melt and are golden brown. **Yield:** 4 servings.

# Ice Cream Family Fun

● To make a perfectly easy and beautiful dessert, spoon ice cream into individual meringue shells and top with fresh or frozen peach slices and raspberry sauce. —*Violet Stockham*
*Lyons, Kansas*

● Allow ice cream desserts to sit at room temperature for 10 minutes before serving to make cutting easier.
—*Elaine Nivins, Ardrossan, Alberta*

● With their variety of flavors, ice cream muffins are simple and so much fun (our favorite is butter pecan!). Mix 2 cups of self-rising flour and 2 cups of softened ice cream together. Fill greased muffin cups two-thirds full and bake at 400° for 15-20 minutes or until lightly browned. Makes 12 muffins.
—*Pegge Tennant*
*Broken Arrow, Oklahoma*

● Combine 1/2 cup of any chopped fruit with 1 cup milk and 1/2 to 1 cup frozen yogurt for a delicious shake. I often freeze leftover fruit so I can whip this up in a blender anytime I want a sweet shake. —*Kimberly Bennett*
*Ingersoll, Ontario*

● Homemade ice cream will stay soft and creamy if an 8-ounce carton of whipped topping is added to the mixture after the churning process.
—*Dianne Hendricks*
*Vivian, South Dakota*

● For a fun experiment with children, put 1 cup ice cream base into a 1-quart resealable plastic bag and seal. Next, in a 1-gallon resealable plastic bag, place crushed ice and coarse salt. Seal the smaller bag inside the larger bag…then shake, shake, shake! (It's best to do it outside in case you develop a leak.) The mixture will freeze into ice cream right before your kids' eyes. —*Anita Warner*
*Mt. Crawford, Virginia*

● A popular dessert at our house is one part angel food cake chunks blended with two parts softened ice cream. Serve with a topping of your choice.
—*Mary McCreery*
*Boynton Beach, Florida*

● To soften ice cream topping that has been refrigerated, I place the can or jar in hot water until it's pourable. You can also put topping in a microwave-safe dish and heat it in the microwave for just a few seconds.
—*Nancy Newton*
*Greendale, Wisconsin*

● To make an old-fashioned root beer shake, pour 6 ounces of root beer into a blender. Add four scoops of vanilla ice cream; cover and mix until smooth. (By putting the root beer in first, the shake won't foam as much.)
—*Debi Kortum, Gillette, Wyoming*

● Here in Pennsylvania Dutch country, we enjoy crushed pretzels as an ice cream topping. We even have ice cream cones made of pretzels in this area! —*Connie Eddy*
*Macungie, Pennsylvania*

● To give flavored gelatin a different twist, substitute the same amount of any flavor of ice cream for the cold water. Stir until the ice cream melts, then refrigerate as usual. —*Kim Friez*
*Mott, North Dakota*

## TASTY APPLE TART

*Leslie DuPerron, Edmonton, Alberta*

*Since this tart is so pretty, I fix it for fancy gatherings such as ladies get-togethers...but I serve it at informal barbecues as well.*

1-1/2 cups all-purpose flour
1/4 teaspoon salt
1/2 cup cold butter (no substitutes)
6 to 7 tablespoons cold water
4 tablespoons sugar, *divided*
6 medium apples, peeled and sliced
3 tablespoons butter *or* margarine, melted
1/4 cup apricot jam
1 tablespoon water

In a bowl, combine flour and salt; cut in butter until crumbly. Sprinkle with cold water, 1 tablespoon at a time, and toss with a fork until dough can be formed into a ball. On a floured surface, roll dough into a 13-in. circle. Place on an ungreased 12-in. pizza pan; turn edges under. Sprinkle crust with 2 tablespoons sugar. Beginning at the outside, arrange apples in a circular pattern, overlapping each slice. Make a second circle facing the opposite direction. Continue alternating directions until crust is covered. Brush apples with butter; sprinkle with remaining sugar. Bake at 400° for 40-50 minutes or until apples are tender and crust is golden. Combine jam and water; brush over apples. Serve warm. **Yield:** 12-16 servings.

## SOUTHERN PRALINES

*Bernice Eberhart, Fort Payne, Alabama*

*This recipe is truly Southern, and it's been a family favorite for years. I've packed many a Christmas tin with this candy.*

3 cups packed brown sugar
1 cup whipping cream
2 tablespoons corn syrup
1/4 teaspoon salt
1/4 cup butter *or* margarine
2 cups chopped pecans
1-1/4 teaspoons vanilla extract

In a large heavy saucepan over medium heat, bring brown sugar, cream, corn syrup and salt to a boil, stirring constantly. Cook until a candy thermometer reads 234° (soft-ball stage), stirring occasionally. Remove from the heat; add butter (do not stir). Cool until candy thermometer reads 150°, about 35 minutes. Stir in the pecans and vanilla. Stir with a wooden spoon until candy just begins to thicken but is still glossy, about 5-7 minutes. Quickly drop by heaping teaspoon-

fuls onto waxed paper; spread to form 2-in. patties. Store candy in an airtight container. **Yield:** 3-4 dozen.

## COLORADO PEACH COBBLER

*Clara Hinman, Flagler, Colorado*

**(Pictured below)**

*I've served this dessert for family and special guests many times over the years. I've used other fruits that are in season, but we like peaches best.*

1 cup sugar
2 tablespoons all-purpose flour
1/4 teaspoon ground nutmeg
4 cups sliced peeled fresh peaches
TOPPING:
1 cup sugar
1 cup all-purpose flour
1 teaspoon baking powder
1 teaspoon salt
1/3 cup cold butter *or* margarine
1 egg, beaten
Ice cream, optional

In a bowl, combine sugar, flour and nutmeg. Add peaches; stir to coat. Pour into a greased 11-in. x 7-in. x 2-in. baking pan. For topping, combine sugar, flour, baking powder and salt; cut in the butter until the mixture resembles fine crumbs. Stir in egg. Spoon over peaches. Bake at 375° for 35-40 minutes or until filling is bubbly and topping is golden. Serve hot or cold with ice cream if desired. **Yield:** 8-10 servings.

# Meals in Minutes

*Have a home-cooked meal on the table in half an hour with these fast and flavorful dishes.*

## Casserole Chases Away Winter Chills

FILLING BUT FAST—that's a good description of this deliciously hearty three-course menu that you can have on the table in under 30 minutes. It's shared by Rhonda Hogan of Eugene, Oregon, who serves it to family and company alike, as frequently as three times a month.

"Since it takes the pudding a little time to set," she notes, "I usually start it first. Then I make the casserole and beans. By the time dinner's over and coffee is being poured, I'm prepared to ask, 'Does anyone want dessert?'"

Rhonda will often make this meal a day ahead in advance. She informs, "Then all I need to do is heat up the casserole and beans and pull the dessert out of the refrigerator."

### CHILI CASSEROLE

*Sometimes I'll add canned or frozen corn to this hearty casserole to give it more color.*

    1 pound ground beef
1/2 cup chopped onion
    1 can (15-1/2 ounces) kidney beans,
      rinsed and drained
    1 can (15 ounces) tomato sauce
    1 can (14-1/2 ounces) stewed tomatoes
1/4 teaspoon garlic powder
1/4 teaspoon salt
1/4 teaspoon pepper
    2 cups cooked bow tie pasta

In a skillet, brown beef and onion; drain. Stir in beans, tomato sauce, tomatoes, garlic powder, salt and pepper. Cover and simmer for 5 minutes.

Stir in pasta; heat through. **Yield:** 6 servings.

### COMPANY GREEN BEANS

*Top off these green beans with onion rings or toasted bread crumbs for an even fancier side dish.*

1/4 cup chopped onion
    1 tablespoon butter *or* margarine
    4 cups frozen green beans
1/2 cup water
    1 can (16 ounces) whole potatoes, drained
      and quartered
1/4 teaspoon garlic powder
    3 bacon strips, cooked and crumbled

In a skillet, saute onion in butter until tender. Add beans and water; bring to a boil. Reduce heat; cover and simmer for 8-10 minutes or until beans are tender. Add potatoes and heat through. Drain. Sprinkle with garlic powder and bacon. **Yield:** 6 servings.

### CHOCOLATE CREAM CHEESE PIE

*This dessert makes a cool and creamy finish to any meal.*

    1 package (3 ounces) cream cheese,
      softened
    2 tablespoons sugar
1-3/4 cups milk, *divided*
    1 container (4 ounces) frozen whipped
      topping, thawed, *divided*
    1 graham cracker crust (8 *or* 9 inches)
    1 package (3.9 ounces) instant chocolate
      pudding mix
Miniature semisweet chocolate chips, optional

In a small mixing bowl, beat cream cheese, sugar and 1 tablespoon milk until smooth. Gently stir in 1 cup whipped topping. Spread evenly into crust. In a large mixing bowl, beat pudding mix and remaining milk on low speed for 2 minutes. Pour over cream cheese mixture. Chill. Just before serving, garnish with remaining whipped topping and chocolate chips if desired. **Yield:** 6 servings.

# Kettle Creation Cooks Up Quickly

WHETHER for everyday meals or for feeding last-minute dinnertime guests, Jean Atherly of Red Lodge, Montana frequently turns to these three satisfying courses that go from start to finish in under half an hour.

Jean and husband Everett have two young children. "On days when we eat in 'shifts'," Jean notes, "this meal is simple to whip up, serve and serve again later."

You can follow Jean's recipes exactly. But don't feel that you must! "Everett is a former science teacher," she grins. "He describes the kitchen as my laboratory. I love experimenting with recipes and mixing and matching ingredients to come up with original dishes.

"There's room for imagination in this menu, too," she adds. "For instance, you can substitute turkey for the chicken in the soup. And try different greens in the salad—I usually make a fast survey of the fridge before deciding what to use.

"You can make the pudding more of a surprise by also adding whipped topping, chopped nuts or fresh strawberries so that it's like a creamy banana split."

Jean points out that each of the courses in her meal can also be appetizingly called on to be served individually or with other meals.

"Accompanied by bread or rolls, the soup is a light meal in itself," she says. "The salad's something I've served with roasts and other main dishes. And the pudding makes a tasty after-school snack."

### CHICKEN TORTELLINI SOUP

*This recipe puts a different spin on traditional chicken noodle soup. I like to use cheese tortellini instead of plain noodles for a pleasant and filling change of pace. This easy creation has become a family favorite that I can count on often.*

    2 cans (14-1/2 ounces *each*) chicken
      broth
    2 cups water
1-1/2 cups frozen mixed vegetables
    3 boneless skinless chicken breast halves,
      cut into 1-inch cubes

    1 package (8 to 9 ounces) refrigerated
      cheese tortellini
    2 celery ribs, thinly sliced
    1 teaspoon dried basil
 1/2 teaspoon dried oregano
 1/2 teaspoon garlic salt
 1/4 teaspoon pepper
Breadsticks, optional

In a 3-qt. saucepan, combine the first 10 ingredients; bring to a boil. Reduce heat; cover and simmer for 20 minutes. Serve with breadsticks if desired. **Yield:** 8 servings (about 2 quarts).

### TOSSED SALAD WITH VINAIGRETTE

*A crisp salad is the perfect complement to any meal. With its tangy dressing and garden-fresh ingredients, this versatile salad has become a regular on hectic nights—and on those days when I do have time to spare!*

    6 cups mixed greens
    1 large tomato, cut into wedges
    1 small zucchini, sliced
    6 fresh mushrooms, quartered
DRESSING:
    3 tablespoons white wine vinegar
    2 tablespoons vegetable oil
    2 to 3 drops hot pepper sauce
    2 to 2-1/2 teaspoons sugar
 1/4 teaspoon garlic powder
 1/4 teaspoon salt

In a large bowl, toss the greens and vegetables. Combine dressing ingredients in a jar with tight-fitting lid; shake well. Pour over salad and toss. Serve immediately. **Yield:** 8 servings.

### BANANA SURPRISE

*No dinner would be complete without dessert. This one takes little time to prepare—and is a real treat. After just one bite of this chocolaty creation, everyone agrees that bananas have never tasted so good!*

 1/4 cup instant banana *or* chocolate drink
      mix
    4 cups cold milk
    2 packages (3.9 ounces *each*) instant
      chocolate pudding mix*
    4 medium bananas, sliced

In a medium bowl, combine drink mix and milk. Add pudding mix and beat according to package directions. Pour half into eight small bowls; top with banana slices and remaining pudding. **Yield:** 8 servings. **\*Editor's Note:** Vanilla or banana pudding can be substituted for the chocolate pudding.

# Elegant Entree Gives 'Fast Food' New Meaning

FOR Cheryl Mutch of Edmonton, Alberta, "Take-out food and frozen dinners don't hold much appeal—but the time they save in preparation does!"

Time is no minor concern for this cook and her husband. "Neither Rod nor I have 9-to-5 jobs," she notes. "I'm a medical transcriptionist, and he runs various small businesses. Plus, we both do volunteer work for our church and enjoy entertaining family and friends."

Cheryl's found a fast and flavorful answer, however...right at home. This complete meal requires only 30 minutes to get onto the table.

Rather than using the pork called for in the main course recipe, Cheryl sometimes substitutes boneless chicken. No matter how you make it, the results are wonderful.

"If you don't have a taste for tarragon," she says, "try basil. And, for a version lower in fat, replace the sour cream with plain yogurt. Or try going Hawaiian by adding pineapple.

"You can serve this dish over rice or beside green beans as well."

Cheryl's salad can be served several different ways, too. "For a change of pace," she suggests, "replace the pecans with almonds, pistachios or sunflower seeds. Use sweet grapefruit, kiwi, apple slices or grapes in place of the oranges. And orange or plain yogurt with marmalade can be substituted for the peach yogurt.

"If you'd like to turn the salad into a meal in itself, lend it heartiness by mixing in some of your favorite chicken salad or grilled chicken.

"By varying the salad ingredients, we never tire of eating it a few times a week."

Her Strawberry Broil dessert, Cheryl reports, is as tasty with plain yogurt instead of sour cream—and she likes to stir in vanilla extract. In addition to serving it over ice cream, Cheryl uses it as a topping for angel food cake, pancakes and waffles.

### PORK IN MUSTARD SAUCE

*I like to add a little zip to plain pork chops with my mustard sauce. This is a wonderful entree to serve company—it looks fancy but isn't difficult to fix.*

4 boneless pork chops (about 2 pounds)
2 tablespoons butter *or* margarine
Salt and pepper to taste
2 to 3 tablespoons Dijon mustard
1/4 cup chopped onion
1-1/2 teaspoons minced fresh tarragon *or* 1/2 teaspoon dried tarragon
Hot cooked noodles
3/4 cup sour cream
1 teaspoon browning sauce, optional

In a large skillet, brown the pork chops on both sides in butter. Season with salt and pepper. Add mustard, onion and tarragon; cover and simmer for 10-12 minutes or until pork is no longer pink. Remove chops to a platter of cooked noodles and keep warm. To the skillet, add sour cream and browning sauce if desired; heat through (do not boil). Spoon over pork and noodles. **Yield:** 4 servings.

### ORANGE PECAN SALAD

*There are endless ways to make a salad. I like to try something new every time—and I've found that this is one of my family's favorites! It's a light, refreshing salad with a nice, nutty crunch.*

2 oranges, peeled and sectioned *or* 1 can (11 ounces) mandarin oranges, drained
1 small bunch leaf lettuce, torn
1/4 cup pecan halves, toasted
1/2 cup peach yogurt
3 tablespoons mayonnaise

Toss oranges, lettuce and pecans in a large salad bowl; set aside. Combine yogurt and mayonnaise; pour over salad just before serving. **Yield:** 4 servings.

### STRAWBERRY BROIL

*For a naturally sweet addition to your meal, top ice cream with this lovely and delicious dessert. Or serve it warm by itself with a dollop of whipped cream. Either way, it's irresistible!*

2 cups fresh strawberry halves
1/4 cup sour cream
1/4 teaspoon ground cinnamon
1/4 cup packed brown sugar
Vanilla ice cream, optional

Place the strawberries in an ungreased shallow 1-1/2-qt. baking dish. Combine sour cream and cinnamon; spoon over berries. Sprinkle with brown sugar. Broil until bubbly, about 3-4 minutes. Serve over ice cream if desired. **Yield:** 4 servings.

# Satisfying Spread's a Snap To Prepare

DOES this comment by Leah Carrell from Quitman, Texas sound familiar: "Much of the time, we seem to meet ourselves coming and going"?

If so, do what Leah does for her active family of husband Wally and daughter Callie—rely on a "Meal in Minutes" solution. This hearty meal is Leah's favorite quick lifesaver that takes only 30 minutes or less to get on the table.

"I can't decide if I like this meal more because it's easy to prepare or because it's so delicious!" smiles Leah. "Either way, my family is thrilled when it's on the table.

"For a change of pace," Leah advises, "you can substitute pork loin or poultry for the steak in the salad." She adds that, in place of the salsa, a Southwestern-style dressing or a sour cream-chopped avocado-cheese mix also is tasty.

She has several ideas on varying the bread as well. "Sprinkle on onion powder instead of the garlic powder or use a favorite herb seasoning. For a sweeter alternative, leave off the seasonings entirely and spread the fried bread with preserves."

Since she serves the green beans with other meals besides, Leah's found a nice option is sprinkling in Parmesan cheese, crumbling in bacon and putting in a few spoonfuls of Italian dressing.

As for the dessert, "If you'd like a switch from the strawberry filling," Leah notes, "try blackberries, blueberries or even peaches. And, when I serve this cake on a holiday, I've been known to put food coloring in the topping—green works well for Christmas or St. Patrick's Day."

### ZESTY STEAK SALAD

*This hearty salad always satisfies my hungry family.*

**1 pound boneless top sirloin, cut into strips**
**1/3 cup Worcestershire sauce**
**1 medium onion, julienned**
**1 medium green pepper, julienned**
**1 tablespoon butter *or* margarine**
**6 cups shredded lettuce**
**6 to 9 cherry tomatoes, halved**
**Salsa, optional**

In a bowl, combine sirloin and Worcestershire sauce; cover and refrigerate. Meanwhile, in a skillet, saute onion and green pepper in butter for 3-4 minutes. Add sirloin; stir-fry until meat is cooked to desired doneness. Spoon meat and vegetables over lettuce; garnish with tomatoes. Serve with salsa if desired. **Yield:** 4-6 servings.

### FRIED GARLIC TOAST

*I serve this fast toast with many meals and as a snack.*

**1 to 2 tablespoons butter *or* margarine**
**1/4 teaspoon garlic powder**
**6 slices white bread, halved**

Melt butter over low heat in a skillet or griddle. Sprinkle with garlic powder. Fry bread until golden brown on both sides. **Yield:** 4-6 servings.

### SUMMERTIME GREEN BEANS

*This recipe deliciously perks up plain green beans.*

**1-1/2 pounds fresh green beans**
**2 tablespoons dried minced onion**
**2 tablespoons corn syrup**
**2 teaspoons butter *or* margarine**
**1/4 to 1/2 teaspoon salt**

Cut the green beans into 1-1/4-in. pieces; place in a saucepan. Cover with water and bring to a boil. Cover and cook over medium heat until crisp-tender, about 10 minutes. Drain. Add minced onion, corn syrup, butter and salt. Cover and simmer for 5 minutes, stirring occasionally. **Yield:** 4-6 servings.

### ANGEL FOOD DREAM

*No one can resist a slice of this dreamy dessert.*

**1 package (16 ounces) frozen sliced strawberries in syrup**
**1 prepared angel food cake (8 inches)**
**1 carton (8 ounces) frozen whipped topping, thawed, *divided***
**Fresh strawberries and mint, optional**

Drain strawberries, reserving 1/3 cup of syrup. Split cake horizontally into two layers; place bottom layer on a serving plate. Spoon strawberries over bottom layer; spread with 3-1/4 cups whipped topping. Replace top layer. Drizzle with reserved syrup. Garnish with remaining whipped topping, and strawberries and mint if desired. **Yield:** 8-10 servings.

# Teacher's Meal Is Easy As 1, 2, 3!

BY DAY a preschool and kindergarten teacher, Sue Strout has her own version of the golden rule when she's fixing the family dinner in her Cheney, Washington kitchen: "How good a meal tastes doesn't always equal how much time it takes to prepare."

Cooking time's in short supply for Sue, what with husband Chuck's job as a geologist at the local university and the active student days put in by teenage sons Isaak and Emmett. "When we get home from school," she says, "we are all hungry and ready to eat. So the majority of my most-used recipes take under 30 minutes—including those in this perfect-for-autumn meal."

To make dinner preparation faster yet, Sue will often have some of the chili fixings all ready to go when she arrives home by earlier chopping the onions and mixing the soup base, canned beans and other ingredients in a bowl, then refrigerating them.

She sometimes substitutes ground turkey for the ground beef in her chili...or simply increases the beans for a meatless version.

Sue will also preslice the main salad ingredients and marinate them in the refrigerator during the day. "That makes the veggies all the more flavorful by dinnertime," she shares. "And by stirring in sliced chicken, croutons and basil, you can also have a meal in itself."

The dessert can be tossed together in the morning. And garnishing the butterscotch treat with fresh apple wedges and crushed peanuts turns it into an elegant dessert.

## 30-MINUTE CHILI

*On a brisk day, I don't think anything is more appealing than a steaming bowl of this zesty chili. I always make enough so that everyone can have seconds.*

2 pounds ground beef
2 cups chopped onion
2 cans (16 ounces *each*) chili beans, undrained
2 cans (10-3/4 ounces *each*) condensed tomato soup, undiluted
4 teaspoons chili powder
2 teaspoons paprika
1 teaspoon pepper
1 teaspoon salt
1/4 teaspoon garlic powder
Chopped green pepper
Shredded cheddar cheese

In a large saucepan, brown beef and onion; drain. Add the next seven ingredients; bring to a boil. Reduce heat; cover and simmer for 15 minutes or until thick and bubbly. Garnish with green pepper and cheese. **Yield:** 6-8 servings.

## SEASON'S END SALAD

*This quick-to-fix salad is a great way to use the last of your garden's bounty. The vinegar lets the fresh flavor come through.*

3 medium tomatoes, sliced
1 medium onion, sliced
1 medium cucumber, sliced
Salt and pepper to taste
1/2 to 1 teaspoon sugar, optional
3/4 cup cider *or* red wine vinegar
Lettuce leaves, optional

Layer the tomato, onion and cucumber slices in a 1-1/2-qt. dish. Season with salt and pepper. Sprinkle with sugar if desired. Pour vinegar over the vegetables. Cover and refrigerate until ready to serve. Drain; serve on lettuce leaves if desired. **Yield:** 6-8 servings.

## BUTTERSCOTCH APPLE TREAT

*Get ready to dish out second helpings of this sweet treat. It's chock-full of fun ingredients like peanuts, marshmallows, apples and raisins.*

3 cups diced red apples
1 cup miniature marshmallows
1 cup peanuts
1 can (8 ounces) crushed pineapple, drained
1/3 cup raisins, optional
1 carton (8 ounces) frozen whipped topping, thawed
1 package (3.4 ounces) instant butterscotch pudding

In a large bowl, combine apples, marshmallows, peanuts, pineapple and raisins if desired. Combine whipped topping and dry pudding mix; fold into fruit mixture and mix well. Refrigerate until ready to serve. **Yield:** 6-8 servings.

# Reel in Raves With Flavorful Fish Dinner

LIKE her airplane-pilot husband, dinnertime at Gloria Jarrett's Loveland, Ohio country place is often up in the air. So meals that can be made in half an hour or less are a must.

"Anything from poor weather to an extra stop in his flight plan can delay Charles getting home," Gloria notes. "And when he does arrive, I prefer to whip up a fast meal rather than rewarm an overdone one. This quick-to-fix meal is one I can always count on."

Informs Gloria, "Typically, I prepare the pudding first and refrigerate it until we're ready for dessert. Next, I get the vegetable casserole in the oven. Finally, I fix the fish. Charles, who can't abide anything fishy-tasting, actually requests the Mock Lobster!"

Gloria says the fish also goes well with macaroni and cheese or coleslaw. "For a change of taste," she suggests, "you can substitute your favorite seafood sauce for the melted butter and lemon.

"While I usually prepare this fish just for Charles and me, it also makes a nice company dish."

The time-saving vegetable casserole is a tasty accompaniment to fish, rib roast, pork tenderloin or fried chicken. "If you'd like to give it more crunch," she notes, "you could mix in some water chestnuts. Or replace the broccoli and cauliflower with asparagus."

As to the pudding…"For a fancy adaptation," Gloria advises, "turn it into filling for mini tarts or cream puffs. Because he's such a pumpkin pie fan, my husband can't wait for the holidays. To tide him over, I make Pumpkin Pudding all year long."

## MOCK LOBSTER

*When I want a quick fish dinner, this is the mouth-watering recipe I turn to. My husband and I like the flavor so much that I serve it a couple times a month.*

1-1/2 to 2 pounds frozen cod *or* haddock fillets, partially thawed
1-1/2 teaspoons salt
 2 teaspoons seafood seasoning *or* paprika

 3 tablespoons vinegar
Melted butter *or* margarine
Lemon wedges

Cut fillets into 2-in. x 2-in. pieces; place in a skillet. Cover with water. Add salt and seafood seasoning; bring to a boil. Reduce heat; simmer, uncovered, for 10 minutes. Drain. Cover with cold water. Add vinegar and bring to a boil. Reduce heat; simmer, uncovered, for 10 minutes. Drain. Serve with melted butter and lemon. **Yield:** 4-6 servings.

## BROCCOLI CAULIFLOWER CASSEROLE

*Here's a tasty way to dress up plain broccoli and cauliflower. The cheese sauce and french-fried onion topping is irresistible. Even those who don't normally care for these vegetables will finish off big helpings.*

 1 can (10-3/4 ounces) cream of celery *or* chicken soup, undiluted
 1 jar (8 ounces) process cheese spread
 1 package (10 ounces) frozen chopped broccoli
 1 package (10 ounces) frozen chopped cauliflower
 1 can (2.8 ounces) french-fried onions

In a bowl, combine soup and cheese. Add broccoli and cauliflower. Spoon into a greased 2-qt. baking dish. Top with onions. Bake, uncovered, at 350° for 25-30 minutes. **Yield:** 4-6 servings.

## PUMPKIN PUDDING

*Nothing beats this creamy pudding for homemade pumpkin pie flavor. I can make this comforting pudding in the morning or even the night before and pop it in the refrigerator until supper. It's one of my family's favorite desserts.*

1-1/2 cups cold milk
 1 cup whipping cream, *divided*
 1 package (3.4 ounces) instant vanilla pudding mix
 1 teaspoon pumpkin pie spice
 1 cup canned *or* cooked pumpkin
Additional pumpkin pie spice for garnish
Gingersnaps, optional

In a bowl, combine milk, 1/2 cup cream, pudding mix and pie spice; whisk until thickened and smooth, about 2 minutes. Stir in pumpkin. Spoon into dessert dishes. Whip the remaining cream until stiff peaks form; place a dollop on each serving of pudding. Sprinkle with pie spice. Serve with gingersnaps if desired. **Yield:** 4-6 servings.

# Our Most Memorable Meals

*We combined family favorites from individual cooks to come up with complete meals you're sure to remember.*

## Picnic Foods Packed With Flavor

GATHER FAMILY and friends, pack a picnic basket brimming with food and head outdoors!

Mercia Miner of Canfield, Ohio knows Baked Barbecued Beef is a sure picnic-pleaser. "This sandwich was one of the first 'American' dishes I enjoyed in 1949 after arriving in the United States from New Zealand," shares Mercia.

"It's now the most-used recipe in my recipe box! It's easy to prepare and so well liked. I've willingly shared it with my grandchildren and my friends."

From Canterbury, New Brunswick, Susan Furrow provides a new twist with Picnic Potato Squares. "I'm always on the lookout for new and unique recipes," explains Susan. "Firm and cut into squares, they look different than the usual potato salad, and the dill pickle gives them a unique flavor. The squares also travel well and are pretty served on salad greens."

Garlic Deviled Eggs are a perfect finger food. "I created the recipe over 30 years ago, when my new husband requested deviled eggs," remembers Eva Friesen of Carson City, Nevada. "He wouldn't eat celery or pickle relish, so I substituted garlic and onion. He approved.

"My co-workers always request these eggs for our potluck lunches. I'm not sure they know I can cook anything else!" laughs Eva.

Baking Grandma's Blackberry Cake brings back many fond memories for Diana Martin of Moundsville, West Virginia. "I remember going blackberry picking with Mom and Grandma," Diana recalls. "Even at 70 years old, Grandma could pick 3 gallons of berries before I even had my pail half full."

## BAKED BARBECUED BEEF

2-1/2 pounds ground beef
  2 small onions, chopped
  1 large green pepper, chopped
  1 can (10-3/4 ounces) condensed tomato soup, undiluted
  1 cup chili sauce
  1 tablespoon vinegar
  1 teaspoon prepared mustard
  1 teaspoon sugar
1/4 teaspoon salt
1/4 teaspoon pepper
 10 to 12 hamburger buns, split

In a Dutch oven, brown beef and onions; drain. Stir in the next eight ingredients. Bake, uncovered, at 325° for 2 hours, stirring occasionally. Serve on buns. **Yield:** 10-12 servings.

## PICNIC POTATO SQUARES

  2 packages (1/4 ounce *each*) unflavored gelatin
2-1/4 cups milk, *divided*
  1 cup mayonnaise
  1 tablespoon prepared mustard
  2 teaspoons sugar
1/2 teaspoon salt
1/4 teaspoon pepper
2-1/2 cups cubed red potatoes, cooked and cooled
1/2 cup shredded carrot
1/2 cup thinly sliced celery
1/3 cup chopped dill pickle
  2 tablespoons diced onion

Place the gelatin and 1 cup of milk in a saucepan; let stand for 1 minute. Cook and stir over low heat until gelatin is dissolved. Remove from the heat; stir in mayonnaise, mustard, sugar, salt, pepper and remaining milk until smooth. Chill until partially set. Fold in potatoes, carrot, celery, pickle and onion. Pour into an ungreased 8-in. square dish. Chill until firm. Cut into squares. **Yield:** 9 servings.

### GARLIC DEVILED EGGS

6 hard-cooked eggs
1/3 cup mayonnaise
1/2 to 1 teaspoon prepared mustard
2 green onions with tops, chopped
1 garlic clove, minced
1/8 teaspoon salt
Paprika

Slice eggs in half lengthwise; remove yolks and set whites aside. In a small bowl, mash yolks. Add mayonnaise, mustard, onions, garlic and salt. Fill egg whites; sprinkle with paprika. Refrigerate until ready to serve. **Yield:** 1 dozen.

### GRANDMA'S BLACKBERRY CAKE

1 cup fresh blackberries
2 cups all-purpose flour, *divided*

1/2 cup butter *or* margarine, softened
1 cup sugar
2 eggs
1 teaspoon baking soda
1 teaspoon ground cinnamon
1 teaspoon ground nutmeg
1/2 teaspoon salt
1/4 teaspoon ground cloves
1/4 teaspoon ground allspice
3/4 cup buttermilk
Whipped cream, optional

Toss blackberries with 2 tablespoons of flour; set aside. In a mixing bowl, cream butter and sugar. Add eggs; beat well. Combine baking soda, cinnamon, nutmeg, salt, cloves, allspice and remaining flour; add to creamed mixture alternately with buttermilk. Fold in blackberries. Pour into a greased and floured 9-in. square baking pan. Bake at 350° for 45-50 minutes or until the cake tests done. Cool on a wire rack. Serve with whipped cream if desired. **Yield:** 9 servings.

# Sunday Dinner's a Family Affair

WHEN Harriet Cremeen of Hensley, Arkansas was a young girl, Sunday dinners were something special. "I always helped my father prepare the dinner," she says. "He sparked my interest in cooking, and we often made Whistling Marinated Chicken together.

"Papa allowed me to do all the chopping. When I did so, he'd tell me to whistle. Why? Because he knew if I whistled, I wouldn't be eating what I chopped!" Harriet laughs.

Vivian Bailey of Cedar Falls, Iowa comments, "Deluxe Mashed Potatoes is one of my favorite side dishes because it can be made ahead, refrigerated and then popped into the oven just prior to dinnertime.

"When my grandchildren come for dinner, I have to double this recipe. They love it!"

Another crowd-pleasing dish is shared by Debbie Jones of California, Maryland. "I devised Country Corn Casserole when I needed a quick and easy casserole to take to a friend's birthday party," she says.

"I opened a bag of this and a can of that and came up with a dish my family and friends love. Luckily, I wrote it down when I made it. I had a hunch it was going to be a success!"

Dessert will be a success every time, too, when you serve Aunt Lillian's Crumb Cake from Rose Gearheard of Phoenix, Oregon.

Credits Rose, "I was treated to my aunt's cake every weekend when we went to visit. She created this recipe back in the '40's. Knowing my father loved it, she shared the recipe with my mother, who passed it on to me. I serve it as a coffee cake for Sunday brunch or for dessert."

## WHISTLING MARINATED CHICKEN

1/2 cup apple juice
1/4 cup flaked coconut
2 tablespoons lemon juice
1 garlic clove, minced
1 to 2 teaspoons curry powder
1 teaspoon salt
1/4 to 1/2 teaspoon crushed red pepper flakes
4 boneless skinless chicken breast halves
1 tablespoon olive *or* vegetable oil
1-1/4 cups water, *divided*
2 tablespoons cornstarch
1/4 to 1/2 cup minced fresh parsley

In a large resealable plastic bag, combine the first seven ingredients; mix well. Add chicken; seal bag and refrigerate for at least 8 hours. Drain and reserve marinade. In a large skillet over medium heat, brown the chicken in oil. Add the marinade and 1 cup water; bring to a boil. Reduce heat; cover and simmer for 25-30 minutes or until chicken juices run clear. Combine cornstarch and remaining water; stir into pan. Bring to a boil; boil for 2 minutes, stirring constantly. Stir in parsley. **Yield:** 4 servings.

## DELUXE MASHED POTATOES

4 to 5 large potatoes (about 2-1/2 pounds)
1 package (3 ounces) cream cheese, softened
1/2 cup sour cream
1 tablespoon chopped chives
3/4 teaspoon onion salt
1/4 teaspoon pepper
1 tablespoon butter *or* margarine
Paprika, optional

Peel and cube the potatoes; place in a saucepan and cover with water. Cook over medium heat until tender; drain. Mash until smooth (do not add milk or butter). Stir in the cream cheese, sour cream, chives, onion salt and pepper. Spoon into a greased 1-1/2-qt. baking dish. Dot with butter; sprinkle with paprika if desired. Cover and bake at 350° for 35-40 minutes or until heated through. **Yield:** 4-6 servings.

## COUNTRY CORN CASSEROLE

1 package (16 ounces) frozen corn, broccoli and red pepper
1/4 cup water
1/2 cup chopped onion
2 tablespoons butter *or* margarine, *divided*
1 can (10-3/4 ounces) condensed cheddar cheese soup, undiluted
1/4 cup milk
1-1/3 cups crushed saltines

In a saucepan over medium heat, bring vegetables and water to a boil. Reduce heat; cover and simmer for 5-6 minutes or until tender; drain. In a saucepan over medium heat, saute the onion in 1 tablespoon butter until tender. Add soup and

milk; stir until smooth. Add cracker crumbs and cooked vegetables; mix well. Spoon into a greased 8-in. square baking dish. Dot with remaining butter. Bake, uncovered, at 350° for 25-30 minutes or until golden. **Yield:** 6-8 servings.

### AUNT LILLIAN'S CRUMB CAKE

1/2 cup butter *or* margarine, softened
1 cup sugar
2 eggs
1 cup (8 ounces) sour cream
1 teaspoon vanilla extract
1-1/2 cups all-purpose flour
1 teaspoon baking soda
1/4 teaspoon salt

**TOPPING:**
1/2 cup sugar
1/4 cup chopped walnuts
2 tablespoons flaked coconut
2 teaspoons ground cinnamon

In a mixing bowl, cream the butter and sugar. Add eggs, one at a time, beating well after each addition. Add the sour cream and vanilla; mix well. Combine flour, baking soda and salt; add to the creamed mixture and mix well. Spread half into a greased 9-in. square baking pan. Combine topping ingredients; sprinkle half over batter. Carefully spread remaining batter on top; sprinkle with remaining topping. Gently swirl topping through batter with a knife. Bake at 350° for 35-40 minutes or until a toothpick inserted near the center comes out clean. Cool. **Yield:** 9 servings.

# Good Food's Cause for a Celebration

SPECIAL OCCASIONS call for special meals. For your next get-together, turn to these delicious dishes guaranteed to be the hit of the party.

Ham Cups with Cherry Sauce are at the heart of special dinners at Ellen Martin's home in Oxford, New Jersey. "The individual cups are pretty on the plate, especially when topped with the bright cherry sauce," remarks Ellen. "Since we raise pigs, we have a good pork supply."

Jeannine Hopp of Menomonee Falls, Wisconsin is sure to take along a good supply of Macaroni Au Gratin to parties. "I always come home with an empty dish and many requests for the recipe," she says. "It's an easy, tasty dish everyone likes."

For Lenore Wilson of Muskogee, Oklahoma, a family get-together wouldn't be the same without Orange Buttermilk Salad.

"The buttermilk adds a wonderful tang, making it a refreshing accompaniment to any meal," Lenore informs.

To finish off this special occasion, serve Rhubarb Peach Shortcake from Sheila Butler. "I received the recipe from my mother," says this Kansas City, Missouri cook. "It's one of the first desserts I make in the spring when our rhubarb comes in.

"I discovered that rhubarb and peaches really complement each other, and the biscuits make it a hearty dessert."

## HAM CUPS WITH CHERRY SAUCE

    1 egg
1-1/2 cups soft bread crumbs
  1/2 teaspoon ground mustard
    1 pound ground fully cooked ham
  1/2 pound ground pork
  1/4 cup packed brown sugar
    1 teaspoon prepared mustard
CHERRY SAUCE:
    2 tablespoons cornstarch
  1/2 cup sugar
    1 can (16 ounces) pitted red cherries, undrained
Red food coloring, optional

In a bowl, combine egg, bread crumbs and ground mustard. Add ham and pork; mix well. Shape into eight equal portions; pat lightly into 2-3/4-in. muffin cups. Combine brown sugar and prepared mustard; sprinkle over cups. Bake at 350° for 40 minutes or until no longer pink. For sauce, combine cornstarch and sugar in a saucepan. Add cherries; cook and stir over medium-high heat until thickened and bubbly. Cook and stir 2 minutes longer. If desired, stir in 4-5 drops food coloring. Serve over ham cups. **Yield:** 6 servings.

## MACARONI AU GRATIN

    1 package (7 ounces) macaroni
  1/4 cup butter *or* margarine
  1/4 cup all-purpose flour
    2 cups milk
    8 ounces process American cheese, cubed
    1 tablespoon chopped onion
  1/2 teaspoon Worcestershire sauce
  1/2 teaspoon salt
  1/4 teaspoon pepper
  1/4 teaspoon ground mustard
    2 tablespoons seasoned bread crumbs

Cook macaroni according to package directions; drain. Place in a greased 2-qt. baking dish; set aside. In a saucepan, melt butter over medium heat. Stir in flour until well blended. Gradually add milk; bring to a boil. Cook and stir for 2 minutes; reduce heat. Add cheese, onion, Worcestershire sauce, salt, pepper and mustard; stir until cheese melts. Pour over macaroni and mix well. Sprinkle with bread crumbs. Bake, uncovered, at 375° for 30 minutes. **Yield:** 6 servings.

## ORANGE BUTTERMILK SALAD

☑ This tasty dish uses less fat, sugar or salt. Recipe includes Nutritional Analysis and Diabetic Exchanges.

    1 can (20 ounces) crushed pineapple, undrained
    1 package (6 ounces) orange gelatin
    2 cups buttermilk
    1 carton (8 ounces) frozen whipped topping, thawed

In a saucepan, bring pineapple with juice to a boil. Stir in the gelatin until dissolved. Remove from the heat; stir in buttermilk. Cool to room temperature. Fold in whipped topping. Pour into an 11-in. x 7-in. x 2-in. dish or 2-qt. bowl. Chill for at least 4 hours. **Yield:** 10 servings. **Nutritional Analysis:** One serving (prepared with unsweetened pineapple, sugar-free gelatin and light

whipped topping) equals 115 calories, 93 mg sodium, 2 mg cholesterol, 16 gm carbohydrate, 3 gm protein, 3 gm fat. **Diabetic Exchanges:** 1/2 skim milk, 1/2 fruit, 1/2 fat.

### RHUBARB PEACH SHORTCAKE

1/4 cup packed brown sugar
1 tablespoon cornstarch
1 can (16 ounces) sliced peaches, undrained
2 cups chopped fresh *or* frozen rhubarb
1/2 teaspoon vanilla extract
1 tube (5 to 6 ounces) refrigerated buttermilk biscuits
1 tablespoon sugar

In a saucepan, combine brown sugar and cornstarch. Drain peaches, reserving 1/2 cup liquid. Set peaches aside. Stir reserved liquid into brown sugar mixture; bring to a boil. Cook and stir for 2 minutes. Add rhubarb; simmer for 8 minutes. Stir in peaches and vanilla. Pour into an ungreased 8-in. round baking pan. Dip one side of biscuits in sugar; place over hot fruit with sugar side up. Bake, uncovered, at 375° for 20-24 minutes or until biscuits are golden brown. Serve warm. **Yield:** 5 servings.

The Best of Country Cooking 1999

# Old-Time Fare Stands Test Of Time

ONE TASTE and these delicious, traditional dishes will become new family favorites.

"I remember Old-World Pork Roast from my childhood," shares Mary Ann Morgan of Cedartown, Georgia. "My German grandmother made this roast every Sunday—it was our equivalent to everyone else's customary fried chicken dinner."

Lois Gelzer of Oak Bluffs, Massachusetts also shares an old family recipe. "Grandmother often prepared her fresh green beans this way, and we much preferred German-Style Green Beans to plain buttered beans," she says.

"This recipe goes back to before the 1920's and was a favorite dish of our family when I was growing up."

The mouth-watering aroma of Squash Braid is hard to resist. Waddell, Arizona cook Amy Martin claims, "It should be called 'You Can't Have Just One Slice Bread'!

"My friend gave me this recipe when I first started making bread," says Amy. "It's golden on the outside and the inside—beautiful and colorful besides being so delicious.

"I love to bake it in the fall. It blends in with every menu that includes the produce of that season."

And Fay Harrington's Poor Man's Pecan Pie is destined to become a family classic. "My mother-in-law shared the recipe with me several years ago," credits Fay. Now it's become a much-requested dessert in her Seneca, Missouri home.

"It's easy to make, and most of the ingredients are in everybody's cupboard. And it really does taste like pecan pie."

## OLD-WORLD PORK ROAST

    1 teaspoon caraway seeds
    1 teaspoon rubbed sage
1-1/4 teaspoons salt, *divided*
  1/2 teaspoon pepper, *divided*
    1 boneless pork loin roast (3 to 4 pounds), trimmed
  1/2 teaspoon browning sauce, optional

    2 tablespoons cornstarch
**Potato dumplings *or* mashed potatoes, optional**

In a small bowl, combine caraway seeds, sage, 1 teaspoon salt and 1/4 teaspoon pepper; rub over roast. Place roast on a rack in a shallow roasting pan. Bake, uncovered, at 350° for 2 hours or until a meat thermometer reads 160°-170°. Remove roast from pan; keep warm. Pour pan drippings into a large measuring cup; add enough water to equal 2 cups. Pour into a small saucepan; add browning sauce if desired, cornstarch, and remaining salt and pepper. Stir until smooth. Bring to a boil; cook and stir until thickened and bubbly. Slice roast; serve with gravy and dumplings or potatoes if desired. **Yield: 6-8 servings.**

## GERMAN-STYLE GREEN BEANS

1-1/2 pounds fresh green beans, cut into
      1-inch pieces
    6 bacon strips
    1 large onion, chopped
**Salt and pepper to taste**

Place beans in a saucepan and cover with water; bring to a boil. Reduce heat; cover and cook for 15-20 minutes or until tender. Meanwhile, in a skillet, cook bacon until crisp. Remove bacon and set aside. Saute onion in drippings until tender; remove with a slotted spoon. Drain beans; return to pan. Add onion, 1 tablespoon drippings, salt and pepper; heat through. Crumble the bacon; add to the beans and toss. Serve immediately. **Yield: 6 servings.**

## SQUASH BRAID

    1 package (1/4 ounce) active dry yeast
    2 tablespoons warm water (110° to 115°)
    1 cup mashed cooked butternut squash
  1/3 cup warm milk (110° to 115°)
  1/4 cup butter *or* margarine, softened
    1 egg
    3 tablespoons brown sugar
  1/4 teaspoon salt
    3 to 3-1/2 cups all-purpose flour
**GLAZE:**
    1 egg, beaten
    1 tablespoon water

In a small bowl, dissolve yeast in water. In a mixing bowl, combine squash, milk, butter, egg, brown sugar and salt; mix well. Add yeast mixture and 1-1/2 cups flour; mix well. Add enough remaining flour to form a soft dough. Turn onto a floured surface; knead until smooth and elastic,

about 6-8 minutes. Place in a greased bowl, turning once to grease top. Cover and let rise in a warm place until doubled, about 1 hour. Punch dough down. Divide into thirds; roll each third into an 18-in. rope. Place on a greased baking sheet. Braid ropes together; pinch ends. Cover and let rise until nearly doubled, about 30 minutes. Combine glaze ingredients; brush over braid. Bake at 350° for 20-25 minutes or until golden brown. Remove from pan; cool on a wire rack. **Yield:** 1 loaf.

### POOR MAN'S PECAN PIE

3 eggs
1 cup sugar
1 cup old-fashioned oats
3/4 cup dark corn syrup
1/2 cup flaked coconut
2 tablespoons butter *or* margarine, melted
1 teaspoon vanilla extract
1 unbaked pastry shell (9 inches)
Whipped topping and toasted coconut, optional

In a bowl, combine the first seven ingredients; mix well. Pour into the pastry shell. Bake at 375° for 15 minutes; reduce heat to 350°. Bake for 30-35 minutes longer or until a toothpick inserted near the center comes out clean. If necessary, cover edges of crust with foil to prevent overbrowning. Cool on a wire rack. Garnish with whipped topping and toasted coconut if desired. **Yield:** 8-10 servings.

# Spend the Holidays in Good Taste

ENJOY the flavors of the holiday—and cut time in the kitchen—by preparing this tasty and timely dinner.

"Years ago, a neighbor and I collaborated and submitted Turkey Apple Potpie for an apple contest," says Phyllis Atherton of South Burlington, Vermont. "We had such fun experimenting, and I think of her whenever I make this dish."

Explains Erica Ollmann of San Diego, California, "As a graduate student, I'm always looking for fast, nutritious dishes that cost next to nothing to fix and have a minimum of cleanup.

"Wild Rice and Squash Pilaf is fantastic with fish or poultry and especially compatible with turkey. Since it's so colorful, I like to think it makes my turkey dressed for the holidays."

Cranberry Relish Salad, shared by Rosemary Talcott of Worthington, Minnesota, is another quick holiday treat. "So much time and effort went into preparing meals for our large family that it was a real bonus to find a recipe with a shortcut," says Rosemary.

"The dish became part of a special meal our family enjoyed during the holidays. I recall lots of second helpings being requested, but not many leftovers."

And what holiday dinner would be complete without cookies? "We sometimes call Soft Mincemeat Cookies 'Santa's cookies' because they're what we put out for Santa instead of the usual decorated Christmas cutouts," shares Evelyn Wadey of Blackfalds, Alberta.

"These cookies remain a traditional part of my holiday baking. Besides a plate for Santa, they fill gift plates for family and friends. I'm often told they're the first to disappear."

## TURKEY APPLE POTPIE

1/4 cup chopped onion
1 tablespoon butter *or* margarine
2 cans (10-3/4 ounces *each*) condensed
   cream of chicken soup, undiluted
3 cups cubed cooked turkey
1 large tart apple, cubed
1/3 cup raisins
1 teaspoon lemon juice
1/4 teaspoon ground nutmeg
Pastry for single-crust pie (9 inches)

In a saucepan, saute onion in butter until tender. Add the soup, turkey, apple, raisins, lemon juice and nutmeg; mix well. Spoon into an ungreased 11-in. x 7-in. x 2-in. baking dish. On a floured surface, roll pastry to fit top of dish. Cut vents in pastry, using a small apple cookie cutter if desired. Place over filling; flute edges. Bake at 425° for 25-30 minutes or until crust is golden brown and filling is bubbly. **Yield:** 6 servings.

## WILD RICE AND SQUASH PILAF

✓ This tasty dish uses less fat, sugar or salt. Recipe includes Nutritional Analysis and Diabetic Exchanges.

1-1/2 cups sliced fresh mushrooms
1-1/2 cups diced peeled winter squash
2 medium onions, finely chopped
1/2 cup chopped green pepper
2 to 3 garlic cloves, minced
2 tablespoons olive *or* vegetable oil
3 cups cooked wild rice
1/2 cup chicken broth
1 tablespoon soy sauce
1/2 teaspoon dried savory
1/4 cup sliced almonds, toasted, optional

In a large saucepan, saute mushrooms, squash, onions, green pepper and garlic in oil until crisp-tender, about 5-6 minutes. Stir in the rice. Add broth, soy sauce and savory. Cover and simmer for 13-15 minutes or until squash is tender. Toss with almonds if desired. **Yield:** 10 servings. **Nutritional Analysis:** One 1/2-cup serving (prepared with low-sodium chicken broth and light soy sauce and without almonds) equals 116 calories, 60 mg sodium, trace cholesterol, 19 gm carbohydrate, 4 gm protein, 3 gm fat. **Diabetic Exchanges:** 1 starch, 1 vegetable, 1/2 fat.

## CRANBERRY RELISH SALAD

1 package (3 ounces) cherry gelatin
1 package (3 ounces) raspberry gelatin
1/4 cup sugar
1-1/2 cups boiling water
1 can (12 ounces) lemon-lime soda
1 can (8 ounces) crushed pineapple,
   undrained
2 packages (10 ounces *each*) frozen
   cranberry-orange sauce

In a large bowl, dissolve the gelatins and sugar in

boiling water. Add the soda, pineapple and cranberry-orange sauce; chill until partially set. Pour
into individual dishes or an 11-in. x 7-in. x 2-in.
dish. Refrigerate overnight or until firm. **Yield:** 12
servings.

## SOFT MINCEMEAT COOKIES

1/4 cup butter *or* margarine, softened
3/4 cup packed brown sugar
  2 eggs
3/4 cup mincemeat
1-1/2 cups all-purpose flour
1-1/2 teaspoons baking soda
1/2 teaspoon ground cinnamon
1/4 teaspoon ground nutmeg
1/4 teaspoon salt
1-1/2 cups (9 ounces) semisweet chocolate
  chips
1/2 cup chopped walnuts, optional

In a mixing bowl, cream the butter and brown
sugar. Add eggs and mincemeat; mix well. Combine flour, baking soda, cinnamon, nutmeg and
salt; add to the creamed mixture and mix well.
Fold in chocolate chips and walnuts if desired.
Drop by tablespoonfuls 2 in. apart onto greased
baking sheets. Bake at 350° for 10-12 minutes or
until golden brown. Cool on wire racks. **Yield:**
about 4 dozen.

## GARDEN LAYERED SALAD

**(Pictured on page 154)**

12 cups broccoli florets
9 cups cauliflowerets
6 cups sliced fresh mushrooms
3 cups halved sugar snap peas
3 cups sliced radishes
3 cups sliced carrots
3 cups fresh *or* frozen peas
3/4 cup sliced green onions
2-1/4 cups olive *or* vegetable oil
1 cup red wine *or* cider vinegar
6 tablespoons sugar
1/3 cup minced fresh chives
1 tablespoon pepper
1 tablespoon Dijon mustard
1-1/2 teaspoons salt
3 garlic cloves, minced
6 quarts assorted torn greens

In a large bowl, toss the first eight ingredients. Whisk the oil, vinegar, sugar, chives, pepper, mustard, salt and garlic; pour over vegetables and toss. Place 1 qt. of greens in three 4-qt. bowls; top each with 6 cups vegetable mixture. Repeat layers. Cover and refrigerate for at least 6 hours. **Yield:** 50 servings.

## ROSY RHUBARB MOLD

**(Pictured on page 155)**

24 cups chopped rhubarb
6 cups water
3 cups sugar
6 packages (6 ounces *each*) strawberry gelatin
3 cups orange juice
2 tablespoons grated orange peel
6 cups sliced fresh strawberries
Leaf lettuce
Additional strawberries
DRESSING:
3 cups mayonnaise
3 cups whipped topping
6 to 7 tablespoons milk

In a kettle over medium-low heat, cook and stir rhubarb, water and sugar until rhubarb is soft and tender. Remove from the heat; stir in gelatin until dissolved. Stir in orange juice and peel. Chill until partially set, about 2-3 hours. Stir in strawberries. Pour into six 5-cup ring molds coated with nonstick cooking spray. Refrigerate overnight. Unmold onto lettuce-lined platters; garnish with berries. For dressing, combine mayonnaise and whipped topping; add enough milk to thin to desired consistency. Serve in a bowl in center of mold. **Yield:** 50 servings.

## PARTY PINWHEELS

**(Pictured on page 155)**

6 packages (8 ounces *each*) cream cheese, softened, *divided*
2 jars (5-3/4 ounces *each*) stuffed olives, drained and finely chopped
12 flour tortillas (10 inches), *divided*
1 package (6 ounces) thinly sliced cooked turkey
1 cup finely chopped dill pickles
2 tablespoons Dijon mustard
1 package (6 ounces) thinly sliced fully cooked ham
3/4 cup finely chopped celery
1/2 cup hickory-flavored barbecue sauce
1 package (6 ounces) thinly sliced cooked roast beef

In a mixing bowl or food processor, beat two packages of cream cheese until smooth. Add olives and mix well. Spread about 3/4 cup each on four tortillas; top with four slices of turkey. Roll up tightly; wrap in plastic wrap. Beat two packages of cream cheese with pickles and mustard. Spread on four tortillas; top with ham. Roll up and wrap. Beat remaining cream cheese; add celery and barbecue sauce. Spread on remaining tortillas; top with beef. Roll up and wrap. Refrigerate at least 2 hours or freeze. Slice into 1/2-in. pieces (if frozen, thaw for 10 minutes first). **Yield:** about 50 appetizers.

## SALAMI BELLS

**(Pictured on page 155)**

Leaf lettuce *or* kale
1 grapefruit, halved
Fresh parsley sprigs
3 packages (8 ounces *each*) hard *or* cotto salami
Pitted ripe olives *or* pickled onions

Line two serving plates with lettuce. Place a grapefruit half upside down on each plate. Cover grapefruit surface with lettuce and parsley; secure with toothpicks. Fold salami in half. Place an olive or onion in the center, then roll in thirds; secure with a toothpick. Fasten to the grapefruit with a toothpick. **Yield:** 50 appetizers.

*Our Most Memorable Meals*

## GIFT BOX WEDDING CAKE

(Pictured below right and on page 155)

1-1/3 cups poppy seeds, *divided*
    4 packages (18-1/4 ounces *each*)
      white cake mix
    1 package (3.4 ounces) instant lemon
      pudding mix

FROSTING:

1-1/2 cups butter (no substitutes), softened
    15 cups confectioners' sugar
    3/4 cup half-and-half cream
1-1/2 teaspoons vanilla extract
    1/2 teaspoon salt
    2 pastry bags *or* heavy-duty resealable
      plastic bags

Round pastry tips #3 and #5
Pink liquid *or* paste food coloring
    4 covered cardboard bases (10 x 8, 8 x 8,
      7 x 6 and 4 x 4 inches)
Dowel rods (1/4-inch diameter)
Ribbons and silk flowers, optional

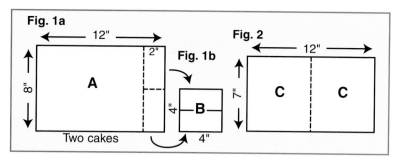

Fig. 1a — 12" — 8" — A — 2" — Two cakes
Fig. 1b — B — 4" — 4"
Fig. 2 — 12" — 7" — C — C

In four bowls, soak 1/3 cup poppy seeds in water required for each cake mix for 1 hour. Mix each cake according to package directions, using poppy seed water. Bake in three greased and floured 13-in. x 9-in. x 2-in. baking pans and two 8-in. square pans; cool. Prepare pudding according to package directions; chill.

For frosting, cream butter and sugar in a mixing bowl on low speed for 1 minute. Add cream, vanilla and salt; mix on medium until light and fluffy, about 3 minutes. (Frosting may need to be made in batches.) Add food coloring to 4-1/2 cups frosting.

Cut a small hole in the corner of two plastic or pastry bags; insert #3 pastry tip in one bag and #5 pastry tip in the other. Place 1/2 cup white frosting in bag with #3 tip and 1/2 cup pink frosting in the other. Cover remaining frosting with a damp cloth until ready to use.

Trim two 13-in. x 9-in. cakes into 12-in. x 8-in. rectangles as in Fig. 1a; level tops. Cut an 8-in. x 2-in. strip off each, leaving two pieces (A). Cut each strip in half, forming four 4-in. x 2-in. pieces. As in Fig. 1b, attach two 4-in. x 2-in. pieces together lengthwise with white frosting to form a 4-in. x 4-in. piece (B); repeat with two remaining pieces and set aside.

Trim remaining 13-in. x 9-in. cake into a 12-in. x 7-in. rectangle as in Fig. 2; level top. Cut cake in half to form two 7-in. x 6-in. pieces (C); set aside.

Level tops of 8-in. square cakes.

Each frosted layer of the cake consists of two cake pieces with a lemon pudding filling in between. Place one piece A on the largest covered board; spread with pudding to within 1/2 in. of edge. Place second piece A on top; set aside. Repeat filling procedure for remaining layers (pieces B, C and 8-in. squares) and place on covered boards.

For bottom layer, frost piece A with 3-1/2 cups white frosting. If desired, attach a ribbon across the corners of piece A (as shown in photo).

For second layer, frost 8-in. cake with 2-1/2 cups pink frosting. With prepared bag of white frosting, pipe a continuous string, curving up, down and around so strings never touch on cake.

For third layer, frost piece C with 2 cups white frosting. With prepared bag of pink frosting, pipe dots 1/2 in. apart over entire cake.

Frost piece B with remaining pink frosting. Add bow on top.

For bottom three layers, cut a dowel into five pieces the height of each layer. Insert dowels 1 to 2 in. apart in center of each cake to support the next layer. Carefully stack layers on a serving platter, working from largest cake to smallest. Decorate with ribbon and silk flowers as desired. Remove dowels before cutting each layer. **Yield:** 50 servings.

**Editor's Note:** Unfrosted cakes can be frozen for up to 6 months wrapped in foil. Frosting can be prepared 2 weeks ahead; store in refrigerator. Rewhip before spreading. Cake can be assembled 8 hours before serving.

# Cooking for Two

*When you need to prepare a meal small in quantity but big on taste, turn to these delectable dishes for two.*

## CRANBERRY CHICKEN

*Angelina Lenhart, Concord, California*

*It's easy to cook chicken to serve any number of people, and now that we are "two", we have chicken often. This dish is tangy and tart...an interesting combination of flavors.*

> 1/2 cup cranberry juice
> 2 tablespoons soy sauce
> 2 tablespoons Worcestershire sauce
> 2 garlic cloves, minced
> 2 bone-in chicken breast halves
> Hot cooked rice, optional

In a resealable plastic bag, combine the first four ingredients. Add chicken and turn to coat. Seal bag and refrigerate 8 hours or overnight. Place chicken and marinade in a small ungreased baking pan. Bake, uncovered, at 350° for 1 hour or until meat juices run clear. Serve over rice if desired. **Yield:** 2 servings.

## CREAM OF BROCCOLI SOUP

*Elsie Quance, Newark, New York*

*When our two sons left home, we had lots of adjustments to make, especially in our menus. This recipe works well for us. It's easy, healthy and tasty!*

> 1 cup water
> 2 chicken bouillon cubes
> 2 cups chopped fresh broccoli
> 2 tablespoons dried minced onion
> 1/4 teaspoon salt
> 1/8 teaspoon pepper
> 1/2 cup milk
> 2 teaspoons butter *or* margarine

In a saucepan, bring water and bouillon to a boil. Add broccoli, onion, salt and pepper. Reduce heat; simmer for 5-7 minutes or until broccoli is tender. Let cool for 10 minutes. Pour into a blender; cover and process until smooth. Return to pan; add milk and heat through. Top each serving with a teaspoon of butter. **Yield:** 2 servings.

## FLUFFY BISCUIT MUFFINS

*Virginia Foster, Paducah, Kentucky*

*These biscuits are simple to make and have a wonderful aroma when baking. This particular recipe is my husband's favorite—and biscuits were a steady diet in the Southern household where he grew up.*

> 1 cup self-rising flour*
> 2 tablespoons mayonnaise (no substitutes)
> 1/2 cup milk

In a bowl, cut flour and mayonnaise together until mixture resembles coarse crumbs. Add milk; stir just until mixed. Spoon into four greased muffin cups. Bake at 425° for 14-16 minutes or until lightly browned. **Yield:** 4 biscuits. ***Editor's Note:** As a substitute for self-rising flour, place 1-1/2 teaspoons of baking powder and 1/2 teaspoon salt in a measuring cup. Add all-purpose flour to equal 1 cup.

## APPLE CRISP FOR TWO

*Patricia Gross, Etna Green, Indiana*

*Delicious with ice cream or whipped topping, this dessert is always a welcome treat at our table. We especially like it served warm. I make this often year-round, but it's even tastier in the fall with newly harvested apples.*

> 2 large tart apples, peeled and sliced
> 1 tablespoon lemon juice
> 2 tablespoons brown sugar
> 2 tablespoons quick-cooking oats
> 2 tablespoons butter *or* margarine, melted
> Dash ground cinnamon
> Whipped cream *or* vanilla ice cream, optional

Place apples in an ungreased 2- or 3-cup baking dish; sprinkle with lemon juice. Combine brown sugar, oats, butter and cinnamon; sprinkle over apples. Cover and bake at 350° for 30 minutes. Uncover and bake 15 minutes longer or until apples are tender. Serve with whipped cream or ice cream if desired. **Yield:** 2 servings.

## CRISPY PARMESAN CHICKEN

*Marian Platt, Sequim, Washington*

*For us, chicken breasts prepared this way is a nice reminder of when abalone was found in markets and menus on the West Coast. These days, abalone is scarce, so my son discovered a way to prepare chicken to resemble our favorite food.*

**2 boneless skinless chicken breast halves**
**1 egg**
**3 tablespoons grated Parmesan cheese**
**3 tablespoons finely crushed saltine *or* butter-flavored cracker crumbs**
**1 tablespoon vegetable oil**

Flatten chicken breasts to 1/4-in. thickness. Beat egg in a shallow bowl. Combine Parmesan cheese and cracker crumbs in another bowl. Dip chicken in egg, then coat with the crumb mixture. Heat oil in a skillet; cook chicken for 2-3 minutes per side or until juices run clear. **Yield:** 2 servings.

## CHILLED VEGETABLE SALAD

*Norma Sliper, Moorhead, Minnesota*

*This delicious dish was served by my sister-in-law years ago for her daughter's graduation party. She shared the recipe with me, and I've made it many times, adjusting it to the number of people I'm serving. Horseradish gives the dressing a little zing.*

**3/4 cup cauliflowerets**
**1/4 cup sliced cucumber, halved**
**1/4 cup chopped seeded tomato**
**1/4 cup cubed American cheese**
**2 tablespoons diced celery**
**2 tablespoons sliced radishes**
**1 tablespoon sliced green onions**
**DRESSING:**
**2 tablespoons mayonnaise**
**1 to 2 tablespoons sugar**
**1 tablespoon prepared horseradish**
**1/4 teaspoon salt**
**1/8 teaspoon pepper**

In a medium bowl, toss the first seven ingredients. Combine dressing ingredients in a small bowl; mix well. Pour over salad. Cover and chill for at least 1 hour. **Yield:** 2 servings.

## BROILED RED POTATOES

*Mary Favatella Becker, Mohnton, Pennsylvania*
*My husband is a typical "meat and potatoes" man.*

*Tired of the usual mashed or baked potato treatment, I began to experiment in the kitchen, and this recipe is the deliciously different result. Potatoes prepared this way go well with an omelet for breakfast or a steak for dinner. It's a wonderful, simple recipe.*

☑ This tasty dish uses less fat, sugar or salt. Recipe includes Nutritional Analysis and Diabetic Exchanges.

**2 unpeeled medium red potatoes**
**1 tablespoon butter *or* margarine**
**1 teaspoon Worcestershire sauce**
**1/2 teaspoon salt, optional**
**1/8 teaspoon pepper**

Cut potatoes into 1/4-in. slices; place in a microwave-safe bowl. Combine butter, Worcestershire sauce, salt if desired and pepper; pour over potatoes. Cover and cook on high for 1-2 minutes or until butter melts. Place potatoes in a single layer on a greased baking sheet. Broil for 5-6 minutes on each side or until browned. **Yield:** 2 servings. **Editor's Note:** This recipe was tested using a 700-watt microwave. **Nutritional Analysis:** One serving (prepared with margarine and without salt) equals 151 calories, 83 mg sodium, 0 cholesterol, 23 gm carbohydrate, 2 gm protein, 6 gm fat. **Diabetic Exchanges:** 1-1/2 starch, 1 fat.

## CRACKLE COOKIES

*Ruth Cain, Hartselle, Alabama*

*This cookie recipe comes close to the wonderful taste of chocolate that Mama was able to produce in her cakes and cookies. Because of the "crackles" in these cookies, my granddaughter tells me I've made a mistake when I bake them. "But they taste so good," she adds.*

**1/2 cup sugar**
**1 egg**
**2 tablespoons vegetable oil**
**1 square (1 ounce) unsweetened chocolate, melted and cooled**
**1/2 teaspoon vanilla extract**
**1/2 cup all-purpose flour**
**1/2 to 3/4 teaspoon baking powder**
**1/8 teaspoon salt**
**Confectioners' sugar**

In a mixing bowl, combine sugar, egg, oil, chocolate and vanilla; mix well. Combine flour, baking powder and salt; gradually add to creamed mixture and mix well. Chill dough for at least 2 hours. With sugared hands, shape dough into 1-in. balls. Roll in confectioners' sugar. Place 2 in. apart on greased baking sheets. Bake at 350° for 10-12 minutes or until set. Remove to a wire rack to cool. **Yield:** about 1-1/2 dozen.

## CABBAGE ROLLS

*Lucille Proctor, Panguitch, Utah*

*Since our three daughters are now away from home, I cook just for the two of us. These cabbage rolls make a hearty and tasty meal when accompanied by salad and bread.*

4 large cabbage leaves
1/4 pound ground beef
1/4 pound bulk pork sausage
1/4 cup chopped onion
1/2 cup cooked rice
1 teaspoon Worcestershire sauce
1/2 teaspoon Dijon mustard
1 egg
1 cup tomato juice
2 tablespoons brown sugar, optional

In a large saucepan, cook the cabbage leaves in boiling water for 5 minutes; drain and set aside. In a medium skillet, brown beef, sausage and onion; drain. Stir in rice, Worcestershire sauce, mustard and egg; mix well. Spoon about 1/3 cup onto each cabbage leaf. Fold in sides and roll up leaf; place with seam side down in a greased 11-in. x 7-in. x 2-in. baking dish. Pour juice over rolls; sprinkle with brown sugar if desired. Cover and bake at 350° for 50 minutes. Uncover and bake 10 minutes longer. **Yield:** 2 servings.

## ZUCCHINI PASTA CASSEROLE

*Nettie Gornick, Butler, Pennsylvania*

*My husband plants a large vegetable garden every year. This tasty dish is the result of an especially bountiful zucchini harvest.*

☑ This tasty dish uses less fat, sugar or salt. Recipe includes Nutritional Analysis and Diabetic Exchanges.

1 cup diced zucchini
1/2 cup diced green pepper
1/2 cup diced sweet red pepper
1/4 cup diced onion
2 tablespoons vegetable oil
1/4 cup seasoned bread crumbs
1/4 teaspoon salt
1/8 teaspoon pepper
1 cup cooked tricolor spiral pasta
Grated Parmesan cheese, optional

In a small skillet, saute vegetables in oil until tender, about 7 minutes. Stir in the bread crumbs, salt and pepper; cook for 2-3 minutes. Remove from the heat; stir in pasta. Pour into a greased 1-qt. baking dish. Sprinkle with Parmesan cheese if desired. Bake, uncovered, at 375° for 10 minutes or until heated through. **Yield:** 2 servings. **Nutri-**

tional Analysis: One serving (prepared without Parmesan cheese) equals 305 calories, 668 mg sodium, trace cholesterol, 37 gm carbohydrate, 7 gm protein, 15 gm fat. **Diabetic Exchanges:** 3 fat, 2 starch, 1 vegetable.

## FRUIT SALAD DESSERT

*Muriel Fay, Walton, Kentucky*

*This was one of my favorite desserts when I was growing up. It's just as good today.*

1 egg
1/4 cup sugar
1 tablespoon lemon juice
2 teaspoons butter or margarine
1 can (8 ounces) pineapple chunks, drained
1/2 cup green grapes
1/2 cup fresh orange pieces
1/2 cup colored miniature marshmallows
1/2 cup whipping cream
1 tablespoon confectioners' sugar

In a small saucepan, combine egg, sugar, lemon juice and butter; cook and stir over low heat for 5-7 minutes or until thickened. Cool. Meanwhile, combine pineapple, grapes, oranges and marshmallows in a small bowl; set aside. In a small mixing bowl, beat cream and confectioners' sugar until soft peaks form. Fold into fruit mixture. Add cooled dressing. Chill for at least 1 hour. **Yield:** 2 servings.

## QUICK CORN SALAD

*Mildred Sherrer, Bay City, Texas*

**(Not pictured)**

*I double or triple this recipe for potlucks or when we have dinner guests. In either case, someone's always sure to ask for the recipe.*

1/4 cup mayonnaise
2 tablespoons lemon juice
3/4 teaspoon ground mustard
1/4 teaspoon sugar
1 cup frozen corn, thawed
2 green onions, thinly sliced
1 tablespoon chopped green pepper
Salt and pepper to taste
Leaf lettuce, optional

In a small bowl, combine mayonnaise, lemon juice, mustard and sugar; mix well. Stir in corn, onions, green pepper, salt and pepper. Cover and refrigerate for 4 hours or overnight. Serve on lettuce if desired. **Yield:** 2 servings.

## Spaghetti and Meatballs For Two

*David Stierheim, Pittsburgh, Pennsylvania*

*When I was a teenager, I cooked dinner every night for our family of four—Mom, Dad, Grandmother, who lived next door, and myself. Through the years, I have modified and changed this recipe for two people to better fit our needs. That's one of the great things about this dish. It's easy to do just that!*

    1 egg
    3 tablespoons seasoned bread crumbs
    2 tablespoons chopped onion
    1 tablespoon grated Parmesan cheese
  1/8 teaspoon pepper
  1/4 pound ground beef
  1/4 pound bulk Italian sausage
    1 jar (14 ounces) spaghetti sauce *or* 1-1/2
      cups homemade spaghetti sauce
Hot cooked spaghetti
**Additional Parmesan cheese, optional**

In a bowl, combine the first five ingredients; mix well. Add the beef and sausage; mix well. Shape into 2-in. meatballs; brown in a skillet over medium heat. Drain. Stir in the spaghetti sauce. Simmer, uncovered, for 20-30 minutes or until the meatballs are no longer pink. Serve over spaghetti; sprinkle with Parmesan cheese if desired. **Yield:** 2 servings.

## Garden Vegetable Salad

*Rosalie Wright, San Jose, California*

*I got this recipe from my grandma, who made this light garden salad quite often. I especially like to serve it in spring and summer, when we can use fresh vegetables from our own garden. The tangy Italian dressing is true to tradition. Crisp and refreshing, this salad complements any meal.*

  1/3 cup sliced zucchini
  1/3 cup sliced fresh mushrooms
    1 small tomato, sliced
  1/3 cup sliced green pepper
  1/3 cup sliced celery
  1/3 cup sliced green onions with tops
  1/2 teaspoon chopped fresh basil
**DRESSING:**
  1/4 cup olive *or* vegetable oil
    2 tablespoons red wine vinegar
  1/4 teaspoon dried oregano
  1/8 teaspoon garlic powder
  1/8 teaspoon salt
  1/8 teaspoon pepper

Combine the first seven ingredients in a salad bowl. In a small bowl, whisk together dressing ingredients. Pour over salad and toss to coat. **Yield:** 2 servings.

## Walnut Pudding

*Peggy Foster, La Plata, Missouri*

*This recipe brings back many warm memories of the important people in my life. My grandmother always made this pudding for holiday gatherings…my mother served it to us often as we were growing up…and now I make it as a special treat for my family.*

  1/2 cup sugar
  1/4 cup all-purpose flour
  1/2 teaspoon baking soda
    2 cups warm milk (120°)
  1/2 cup chopped walnuts
**Whipped cream and additional walnuts,
  optional**

In a 10-in. heavy skillet, combine sugar, flour and baking soda; cook and stir over medium heat until light brown. Reduce heat to low; gradually stir in milk. Cook and stir until thickened and bubbly. Stir in nuts. Pour into two serving dishes. Chill. Garnish with whipped cream and walnuts if desired. **Yield:** 2 servings.

## Cheesy Baked Onions

*Louise Elliott, Gallipolis, Ohio*

**(Not pictured)**

*I found this recipe in the newspaper many years ago. It has been a family favorite ever since. Since it goes well with any meat, it's a good dish to double or triple for family gatherings or potluck suppers. Someone will always ask, "Who brought the onions?"*

    1 medium onion
    1 tablespoon butter *or* margarine
    1 tablespoon all-purpose flour
  1/4 teaspoon salt
  1/2 cup milk
  1/3 cup shredded cheddar cheese

Slice onion and separate into rings; place in a greased 1-qt. baking dish and set aside. In a small saucepan over low heat, melt the butter. Stir in flour and salt until smooth. Gradually add milk; bring to a boil over medium heat. Cook and stir for 2 minutes. Remove from the heat; stir in cheese until melted. Pour over onions. Bake, uncovered, at 350° for 45-50 minutes or until onions are tender and cheese is browned. **Yield:** 2 servings.

## ITALIAN BEEF SANDWICHES

*Margery Bryan, Royal City, Washington*

*My husband and I are retired ranchers—so beef is a frequent favorite main dish at our house. Everyone enjoys these hearty, tasty sandwiches that can be made for two—or any size group.*

☑ This tasty dish uses less fat, sugar or salt. Recipe includes Nutritional Analysis and Diabetic Exchanges.

    3 garlic cloves, *divided*
    2 cups beef broth
1/2 teaspoon dried oregano, *divided*
    1 small onion, sliced
    1 small green pepper, cut into strips
    1 tablespoon vegetable oil
    2 beef tip *or* sandwich steaks (1/4 inch thick)
    2 Italian rolls, split

Cut one garlic clove in half; place in a saucepan. Add broth and 1/4 teaspoon oregano; cook over medium-low heat for 10 minutes. Discard garlic clove. Remove broth from the heat and set aside. Mince remaining garlic; place in a skillet. Add the onion, green pepper, oil and remaining oregano; cook and stir over medium heat until crisp-tender. Remove vegetables and keep warm. Add meat to the skillet; cook over medium heat until browned on both sides. Add reserved broth; simmer for 10-12 minutes or until meat is tender. To serve, brush cut sides of rolls with some of the broth; top with meat and vegetables. **Yield:** 2 servings. **Nutritional Analysis:** One serving (prepared with low-sodium broth) equals 331 calories, 341 mg sodium, 58 mg cholesterol, 32 gm carbohydrate, 27 gm protein, 10 gm fat. **Diabetic Exchanges:** 3 lean meat, 2 starch, 1 vegetable.

## CRISP MARINATED CUKES

*Kathy Wallace, Madison, Tennessee*

*This recipe is a favorite of mine not only because it's delicious, but because it was given to me by a very dear friend. I take this dish to many different gatherings and often get requests for the recipe. It's a wonderful side dish, compatible with any meal.*

1/2 cup sugar
1/4 cup vinegar
1/2 teaspoon salt
1/4 teaspoon celery seed
    2 cups sliced cucumbers
1/4 cup sliced onions

In a bowl, combine the first four ingredients; mix well. Stir in the cucumbers and onions. Cover and refrigerate for several hours or overnight. **Yield:**

2 servings. **Editor's Note:** This salad may be frozen for up to 2 months.

## OLD-FASHIONED POTATO SALAD

*Mary Elizabeth Martucci, South Bend, Indiana*

*The secret to the fine taste of this salad results from adding the warm potatoes to the mayonnaise mixture. Friends and family often prefer a second helping of this potato salad instead of dessert!*

    3 medium red potatoes, peeled and cubed (about 2 cups)
1/2 cup mayonnaise
    2 teaspoons sweet pickle relish
1/8 teaspoon salt
1/8 teaspoon pepper
    2 tablespoons chopped carrots
    2 tablespoons chopped celery
    2 tablespoons chopped red onion
    2 hard-cooked eggs, chopped
1/8 teaspoon paprika

Cook potatoes in boiling salted water for 10-15 minutes or until tender. Meanwhile, in a bowl, combine mayonnaise, relish, salt and pepper; add carrots, celery, onion and eggs. Drain the potatoes; gently stir into mayonnaise mixture. Sprinkle with paprika. Cover and refrigerate until ready to serve. **Yield:** 2 servings.

## STRAWBERRY BISCUIT SHORTCAKE

*Elaine Gagnon, Pawtucket, Rhode Island*

*It seems Mom was always making biscuits. She served them plain for breakfast and dinner, especially when we had stew or baked beans. My favorite was when she served them like this—topped with fresh strawberries and whipped cream!*

1/2 cup all-purpose flour
1/4 cup sugar
3/4 teaspoon baking powder
1/8 teaspoon salt
    1 tablespoon shortening
    4 tablespoons milk, *divided*
**Fresh strawberries and whipped cream**

In a bowl, combine flour, sugar, baking powder and salt; cut in shortening until mixture resembles coarse crumbs. Stir in 3 tablespoons of milk until a thick batter forms. Drop four mounds of batter onto a greased baking sheet. Brush with remaining milk. Bake at 375° for 14-16 minutes or until golden brown. Layer biscuits with berries and whipped cream in small bowls or on dessert plates. **Yield:** 2 servings.

## REUBEN BURGERS

*Betty Ruenholl, Syracuse, Nebraska*

A reuben sandwich was always my first choice when eating out—until I found this recipe in a local newspaper. After that, my family could eat reubens anytime. Our daughters used to make these when they were in charge of preparing a meal. I usually had all the ingredients on hand, so it didn't take long to get everything on the table.

1/4 cup sauerkraut
1/4 teaspoon caraway seeds
1/2 pound ground pork
2 slices Swiss cheese
2 hamburger buns, split and toasted

In a small saucepan, heat sauerkraut and caraway seeds; keep warm. Shape pork into two patties; broil or grill until meat is no longer pink. Top each patty with a slice of cheese; continue cooking until cheese melts. Drain sauerkraut. Place patties on buns; top with sauerkraut. **Yield:** 2 servings.

## POTATO PANCAKES FOR TWO

*Ede Righetti, Hayward, California*

Years ago, my grandson requested a special dish to be included in his class cookbook, and this is the recipe I gave him. It was his favorite whenever he ate at our house, so he was delighted. I often still serve it as a side dish—it's a good complement to any entree.

2 medium potatoes
1 egg
2 tablespoons all-purpose flour
1/2 teaspoon salt
1/4 teaspoon garlic salt
Vegetable oil

Peel the potatoes; shred and rinse in cold water. Drain thoroughly; place in a bowl. Add egg, flour, salt and garlic salt; mix well. In a skillet over medium heat, heat 1/4 in. of oil. Pour batter by 1/4 cupfuls into hot oil. Fry for 5-6 minutes on each side or until potatoes are tender and pancakes are golden brown. Drain on paper towels. **Yield:** 2 servings.

## CHILLY DILLY CARROTS

*Lizzie Sartin, Brookhaven, Mississippi*

We've always taken advantage of the fresh produce we're fortunate to have almost year-round. I prepare carrots often, since they're so nutritious and versatile. This dish is one of my favorites. It can be prepared a few days ahead of time, so it's easy when you're planning to serve it for a special meal.

☑ This tasty dish uses less fat, sugar or salt. Recipe includes Nutritional Analysis and Diabetic Exchanges.

1/2 pound carrots, sliced
2 tablespoons Italian salad dressing
2 tablespoons ranch salad dressing
2 tablespoons chopped onion
1-1/2 teaspoons minced fresh dill *or* 1/2 teaspoon dill weed
1-1/2 teaspoons minced fresh parsley *or* 1/2 teaspoon dried parsley flakes
1 teaspoon sugar
1/8 teaspoon salt
Dash pepper

Place carrots in a small saucepan and cover with water; cook until crisp-tender. Drain and place in a small bowl. Combine remaining ingredients; pour over carrots. Cover and refrigerate for 6 hours or overnight, stirring occasionally. **Yield:** 2 servings. **Nutritional Analysis:** One 3/4-cup serving (prepared with fat-free salad dressings) equals 91 calories, 474 mg sodium, 0 cholesterol, 21 gm carbohydrate, 2 gm protein, trace fat. **Diabetic Exchanges:** 2 vegetable, 1 starch.

## MOIST CHOCOLATE CAKE

*Beulah Sak, Fairport, New York*

This cake is so moist it doesn't need frosting. I simply sprinkle powdered sugar over the top. It's my favorite dessert to have on hand in the freezer, but the pieces always disappear too quickly!

1-1/2 cups all-purpose flour
1 cup sugar
3 tablespoons baking cocoa
1 teaspoon baking soda
1/2 teaspoon salt
6 tablespoons vegetable oil
1 tablespoon vinegar
1 teaspoon vanilla extract
1 cup cold water
Confectioners' sugar

In a mixing bowl, combine dry ingredients. Using a spoon, make three wells in the dry ingredients. Pour oil into one, vinegar into another and vanilla into the third. Slowly pour water over all. Mix on low speed until thoroughly combined (batter will be thin). Pour into a greased and floured 8-in. square baking pan. Bake at 375° for 30-35 minutes or until a toothpick inserted near the center comes out clean. Cool. Dust with confectioners' sugar. **Yield:** 6-8 servings. **Editor's Note:** Pieces of cake can be wrapped individually and frozen for a quick dessert.

## BARBECUED BEEF RIBS FOR TWO

*Margery Bryan, Royal City, Washington*

*I've shared this recipe with many friends who also cook for two. We all agree—small recipes are hard to find! This dish remains one of my favorites since it takes little effort to prepare and is so tasty. Plus, if you are serving a larger group, it is easy to double.*

    2 pounds beef back ribs
1/2 cup ketchup
    2 tablespoons finely chopped onion
    2 garlic cloves, minced
    2 tablespoons vinegar
    1 tablespoon brown sugar
1/2 teaspoon chili powder
1/2 teaspoon Worcestershire sauce
1/8 teaspoon garlic powder
**Dash hot pepper sauce**

Cut ribs into serving-size pieces; place in a large kettle and cover with water. Simmer, uncovered, for 50-60 minutes or until tender. Meanwhile, combine ketchup, onion, garlic cloves, vinegar, brown sugar, chili powder, Worcestershire sauce, garlic powder and hot pepper sauce in a small saucepan. Simmer, uncovered, for 10 minutes. Drain ribs; place in a greased shallow 2-qt. baking dish. Cover with sauce. Bake, uncovered, at 350° for 50-60 minutes or until ribs are glazed and heated through. **Yield:** 2 servings.

## TOMATO DELIGHT

*Cora Miller, Lewiston, Michigan*

*I don't remember where this recipe came from, but I have made it quite often over the years. This is the first recipe I reach for when fresh tomatoes are in season. It goes great with a sandwich or makes a bright addition to a main course. The tomatoes look so pretty and taste so good!*

    1 medium tomato
1/8 teaspoon garlic salt
    1 to 2 tablespoons mayonnaise
    4 bacon strips, cooked and crumbled
1/2 cup shredded mozzarella cheese
3/4 teaspoon dried oregano

Slice tomato into 1/2-in.-thick slices; drain on a paper towel for 5-10 minutes. Place tomato slices on a greased broiler pan. Sprinkle with garlic salt. Spread each tomato slice with mayonnaise. Top with crumbled bacon, mozzarella cheese and oregano. Broil 3 in. from the heat for 2-3 minutes or until cheese is melted. **Yield:** 2 servings.

## STUFFED CUCUMBERS

*Mrs. Howard Phipps, Hernando, Mississippi*

*For a change of pace, I like to serve these stuffed cucumbers in place of a lettuce salad. They're really refreshing, and a touch of French dressing makes them a colorful addition to any meal.*

    1 medium cucumber
1/2 teaspoon salt
    1 package (3 ounces) cream cheese, softened
1/4 cup chopped green pepper
    2 tablespoons chopped onion
1/2 teaspoon Worcestershire sauce
1/8 teaspoon pepper
**Dash paprika**
**French salad dressing, optional**

Cut cucumber in half lengthwise. Scoop out seeds and pulp, leaving a 1/4-in. shell. Place seeds and pulp in a colander. Sprinkle with salt; drain for 30 minutes. Meanwhile, combine the cream cheese, green pepper, onion, Worcestershire sauce and pepper; mix well. Stir in 2-3 tablespoons of the drained pulp. Spoon into cucumber shells; sprinkle with paprika. Refrigerate until ready to serve. Serve with French dressing if desired. **Yield:** 2 servings.

## WALNUT BROWNIES

*Lorraine Silver, Chicopee, Massachusetts*

*I learned to make these brownies in 1957 in home economics class. They were the first goodies I'd ever baked by myself. Now, over 40 years later, I still make a batch occasionally.*

1/4 cup shortening
    3 tablespoons baking cocoa
    1 egg
1/2 cup sugar
1/4 teaspoon vanilla extract
1/2 cup all-purpose flour
1/4 teaspoon baking powder
1/8 teaspoon salt
1/4 cup chopped walnuts

In a small mixing bowl, cream shortening and baking cocoa; beat in egg, sugar and vanilla. Combine the dry ingredients; gradually add to the creamed mixture. Beat on low speed until thoroughly combined. Stir in chopped walnuts. Pour into a greased 8-in. x 4-in. x 2-in. loaf pan. Bake at 350° for 15-20 minutes or until a toothpick inserted near the center comes out clean. **Yield:** 8 brownies. **Editor's Note:** This recipe may be doubled and baked in an 8-in. square pan for 20-25 minutes.

## HAM AND BROCCOLI ROLL-UPS

*Eleanor Carroll, Ellicott City, Maryland*

*I started gathering recipes with smaller amounts when our two children went away to school. This is one my daughter sent that I make often. The sauce is what makes this ham and broccoli dish so special.*

> 2 teaspoons butter *or* margarine
> 2 teaspoons all-purpose flour
> 1/8 teaspoon salt
> 1 teaspoon prepared mustard
> 1/2 teaspoon prepared horseradish
> 1/4 teaspoon Worcestershire sauce
> 1/4 teaspoon minced onion
> 1/2 cup pineapple juice
> 1/4 cup milk
> 1 egg yolk
> 4 slices fully cooked ham (1/8 inch thick)
> 4 slices Swiss cheese
> 1 package (10 ounces) frozen broccoli
>    spears, cooked and drained

Melt butter in a small saucepan; stir in flour. Blend in salt, mustard, horseradish, Worcestershire sauce and onion. Combine pineapple juice, milk and egg yolk; mix well. Gradually stir into butter mixture. Bring to a gentle boil; cook until thickened. Remove from the heat and set aside. Top each piece of ham with a slice of cheese and two to three broccoli spears. Spoon 1 tablespoon sauce over broccoli. Roll up, securing with toothpicks if necessary. Place, seam side down, in a greased shallow baking dish. Top with remaining sauce. Cover and bake at 350° for 15-20 minutes or until heated through. Remove toothpicks if used. **Yield:** 2 servings.

## HEARTY STUFFED POTATOES

*Margaret Allen, Abingdon, Virginia*

*I came up with this recipe because I wanted to add flavor to plain baked potatoes. I combined several ideas and ended up with this stuffing. These potatoes are so hearty, they can be a meal by themselves!*

> 2 large baking potatoes
> 1/4 pound smoked Polish sausage, cut into
>    1/4-inch slices
> 1 tart green apple, chopped
> 3 garlic cloves, minced
> 1 can (8 ounces) sauerkraut, rinsed and
>    drained
> 1/2 teaspoon caraway seed
> 1/2 cup sour cream

Bake the potatoes at 400° for 1 hour or until tender. In a medium skillet, brown sausage for 2-3 minutes. Add apple and garlic; cook over low heat for 3-4 minutes or until apple is tender. Add sauerkraut and caraway; cook 4-5 minutes longer or until heated through. Stir in sour cream. To serve, cut an "X" in the top of each potato. Fluff pulp with a fork; spoon sausage mixture over potatoes. **Yield:** 2 servings.

## CORN MEDLEY

*Donna Brockett, Kingfisher, Oklahoma*

*I clipped this recipe many years ago, and it remains one of our favorites. This colorful blend is a great side dish for any entree and a complement to other vegetables as well.*

> 2 bacon strips
> 1 cup whole kernel corn
> 2 tablespoons finely chopped onion
> 1/2 cup chopped fresh tomato
> 1/4 teaspoon dried basil
> Salt and pepper to taste

In a medium skillet, cook bacon until crisp. Remove to paper towel to drain; reserve 1 tablespoon of drippings. Add corn and onion to skillet; cook and stir over medium-low heat until onion is tender. Add tomato and basil. Reduce heat to low; cover and cook for 5-7 minutes or until vegetables are tender, stirring occasionally. Crumble bacon; add to the vegetables. Season with salt and pepper. **Yield:** 2 servings.

## COCONUT PARFAITS

*Merval Harvey, Glennie, Michigan*

*Every time I serve this simple but elegant dessert to guests, I have to give them the recipe, too. I found this recipe in the early '50s and since then, it has earned a place in my tried-and-true file.*

> 6 tablespoons water
> 3 tablespoons sugar
> 1/2 cup flaked coconut
> 1-1/2 teaspoons vanilla extract
> 1/2 cup whipping cream
> 1 tablespoon sliced almonds, toasted
> 1 tablespoon flaked coconut, toasted

In a saucepan over medium heat, bring water and sugar to a boil; boil for 5 minutes. Remove from the heat; cool for 10 minutes. Stir in coconut and vanilla. Cool to room temperature. Whip cream until soft peaks form; fold into coconut mixture. Pour into dishes. Freeze 1 hour or overnight. Just before serving, sprinkle with almonds and coconut. **Yield:** 2 servings.

## HONEY DIJON PORK

*Audrey Thibodeau, Mesa, Arizona*

*I'm very fond of honey-mustard salad dressing, so I attempted to duplicate that taste when I created this pork recipe. My husband thinks it's delicious. It's quick and easy to prepare. Sometimes I'll put a sweet potato in the oven to bake at the same time, then I'll have a complete meal for two.*

    2 boneless pork loin chops (1/2 inch
      thick)
    1/4 teaspoon salt
    Dash pepper
    1 tablespoon all-purpose flour
    1/2 cup orange juice, *divided*
    1/2 cup honey
    1 tablespoon Dijon mustard
    1/4 teaspoon dried basil
    2 medium carrots, cut into 1-inch pieces
    1 small onion, cut into eighths
    1/2 small green pepper, cut into squares
    1/2 small sweet red pepper, cut into squares

Sprinkle pork chops with salt and pepper; place in a heavy ovenproof skillet. In a small bowl, whisk flour and 2 tablespoons orange juice until smooth; whisk in honey, mustard, basil and remaining orange juice. Pour over chops. Place carrots and onion around chops. Cover and bake at 350° for 30 minutes. Add peppers; cover and bake 20 minutes longer or until vegetables are tender and pork is no longer pink. **Yield:** 2 servings.

## SCALLOPED POTATOES

*Leah Brandenburg, Charleston, West Virginia*

*I found this recipe in an old magazine. Later, I discovered that adding garlic gave these potatoes a unique flavor. My greatest compliment came from a neighbor who's a retired chef—he said this was the most delicious potato dish he'd ever tasted!*

    2 tablespoons all-purpose flour
    1-1/4 cups milk
    1 garlic clove, minced
    1 teaspoon butter *or* margarine
    1/4 teaspoon salt
    1/2 cup shredded cheddar cheese
    4 thin onion slices
    2 medium potatoes, peeled and thinly
      sliced

In a saucepan, stir flour and milk until smooth. Add garlic, butter and salt; bring to a boil. Cook and stir for 2 minutes. Remove from the heat; stir in cheese until melted. In a greased 1-qt. baking dish, layer onion and potato slices; pour

sauce over all. Cover and bake at 350° for 20 minutes; uncover and bake 20 minutes longer or until the potatoes are tender. **Yield:** 2 servings.

## BROCCOLI APPLE SALAD

*Vera Schmidt, Celina, Ohio*

*My husband and I agree—this salad is one of our favorites. The yogurt gives it a unique flavor, and the nuts add extra crunch. I don't remember where I discovered this recipe, but it's nutritious, tasty and adds color to any meal.*

☑ This tasty dish uses less fat, sugar or salt. Recipe includes Nutritional Analysis and Diabetic Exchanges.

    2 cups broccoli florets
    1 large red apple, chopped
    1/2 cup vanilla yogurt
    1/4 cup chopped walnuts, optional
    1/4 cup raisins
    1 tablespoon chopped onion

In a medium bowl, combine all the ingredients. Cover and refrigerate until ready to serve. **Yield:** 2 servings. **Nutritional Analysis:** One 1-1/4-cup serving (prepared with nonfat yogurt and without walnuts) equals 187 calories, 56 mg sodium, 1 mg cholesterol, 44 gm carbohydrate, 5 gm protein, 1 gm fat. **Diabetic Exchanges:** 2 vegetable, 2 fruit.

## CRUMB CAKE

*Kathy Lucas, Mechanicsburg, Pennsylvania*

*My favorite time to visit my grandmother was when she'd just taken her crumb cake out of the oven. A warm piece of this cake with a cold glass of milk was the best treat.*

    1/2 cup shortening
    1 cup sugar
    2 cups all-purpose flour
    1 teaspoon baking soda
    1/2 teaspoon salt
    1 cup buttermilk
    Confectioners' sugar

In a mixing bowl, cream shortening and sugar. Combine dry ingredients; add to creamed mixture alternately with buttermilk. Pour into a greased 9-in. round baking pan. Bake at 375° for 35 minutes or until a toothpick inserted near the center comes out clean. Cool for 10 minutes; remove from pan to a wire rack to cool completely. Before serving, dust with confectioners' sugar. **Yield:** 8 servings. **Editor's Note:** Pieces of cake can be wrapped individually and frozen for a quick dessert.

## Southern Breakfast Skillet

*James Newton, Minocqua, Wisconsin*

*When I was a child, my mother served this skillet creation as a special family meal.*

1/4 pound sliced bacon, diced
1/4 cup chopped onion
1 can (15-1/2 ounces) hominy, drained
4 eggs, beaten
1/8 teaspoon pepper

In a skillet, cook bacon until almost crisp; drain. Add onion; continue cooking until bacon is crisp and onion is tender. Stir in hominy, eggs and pepper. Cook and stir until the eggs are completely set. **Yield:** 2 servings.

## Vanilla French Toast

*Joe and Bobbi Schott, Castroville, Texas*

*Vanilla is the secret ingredient in this scrumptious French toast.*

2 eggs
1/2 cup milk
1 tablespoon sugar
1 teaspoon vanilla extract
Pinch salt
6 slices day-old bread
Maple syrup *or* cinnamon-sugar

In a bowl, beat eggs; add milk, sugar, vanilla and salt. Soak bread for 30 seconds on each side. Cook on a greased hot griddle until golden brown on both sides and cooked through. Serve with syrup or cinnamon-sugar. **Yield:** 2 servings.

## Fluffy Pancakes

*Eugene Presley, Council, Virginia*

**(Not pictured)**

*I found this recipe among our old family favorites and adapted it to make a small amount.*

1 cup all-purpose flour
1 tablespoon sugar
2 teaspoons baking powder
1/2 teaspoon salt
3/4 cup milk
1 egg
1/4 cup shortening, melted

In a bowl, combine flour, sugar, baking powder and salt. Combine milk, egg and shortening; stir into dry ingredients and mix well. Pour batter by 1/4 cupfuls onto a lightly greased hot griddle; turn when bubbles form on top of pancakes. Cook until second side is golden brown. **Yield:** 2 servings (8 pancakes).

## Banana Milk Drink

*Jeanne Brown, Buffalo, New York*

*I recall running home from school, hoping to find this delicious drink ready for me.*

1 large ripe banana
1 cup milk
1-1/2 to 2 teaspoons sugar
1/2 teaspoon vanilla extract
**Dash ground cinnamon, optional**

Place the first four ingredients in a blender; cover and process until smooth. Pour into glasses; sprinkle with cinnamon if desired. Serve immediately. **Yield:** 2 servings.

## Sweet-and-Sour Ham

*Diane Widmer, Blue Island, Illinois*

**(Not pictured)**

*This recipe has always been my standby for when I have leftover ham.*

☑ This tasty dish uses less fat, sugar or salt. Recipe includes Nutritional Analysis and Diabetic Exchanges.

1 can (8 ounces) unsweetened pineapple chunks, undrained
1/4 cup ketchup
2 teaspoons light soy sauce
2 teaspoons sugar
2 cups cubed fully cooked ham
2/3 cup cubed green *or* sweet red pepper
1 tablespoon cornstarch
2 tablespoons cold water
**Hot cooked rice, optional**

Drain pineapple, reserving 1/3 cup of juice; set pineapple aside. Combine reserved juice, ketchup, soy sauce and sugar. Add ham and green pepper. If desired, cover and refrigerate for 30 minutes to marinate. In a skillet, cook and stir ham mixture over medium heat for 5-7 minutes or until green pepper is tender. Dissolve cornstarch in water; stir into skillet. Bring to a boil over medium heat; boil for 2 minutes, stirring constantly. Reduce heat. Stir in pineapple; heat through. Serve over rice if desired. **Yield:** 2 servings. **Nutritional Analysis:** One serving (prepared with low-fat ham and without rice) equals 320 calories, 2,534 mg sodium, 66 mg cholesterol, 36 gm carbohydrate, 27 gm protein, 7 gm fat. **Diabetic Exchanges:** 3 lean meat, 2 fruit, 1 vegetable.

## MUSHROOM CUBE STEAKS

*Marie Ritchie, Apple Valley, California*

*When my husband retired, we traveled the country for 10 years in our house trailer. It was wonderful meeting people from all over. We tried foods we never ate before and exchanged recipes. This hearty, tasty main dish from a traveling friend has become one of our favorites.*

- 1 tablespoon all-purpose flour
- 1/4 teaspoon salt
- Dash pepper
- 2 cube steaks (1/4 to 1/3 pound *each*)
- 2 tablespoons butter *or* margarine, *divided*
- 1 teaspoon Dijon mustard
- 1 teaspoon Worcestershire sauce, *divided*
- 1/2 pound fresh mushrooms, sliced
- 1 tablespoon chopped onion
- 2 tablespoons minced fresh parsley

In a shallow bowl or resealable plastic bag, combine flour, salt and pepper. Add steaks; dredge or toss to coat. In a skillet over medium heat, brown steaks in 1 tablespoon of butter. Remove the steaks; spread each with 1/2 teaspoon mustard. Pour 1/4 teaspoon Worcestershire sauce over each; keep warm. In the same skillet, saute the mushrooms and onion in remaining butter until tender. Add parsley and remaining Worcestershire sauce. Return steaks to skillet; cover and simmer for 5-7 minutes or until meat is tender. **Yield:** 2 servings.

## BAKED POTATO SOUP

*Linda Mumm, Davenport, Iowa*

*Not only is this soup delicious, but it's easy to prepare and makes a small amount perfect for my husband and me. It tastes like "restaurant" soup but is lower in fat.*

- 2 medium potatoes, baked  and cooled
- 1 can (14-1/2 ounces) chicken broth
- 2 tablespoons sour cream
- 1/8 teaspoon pepper
- 1/4 cup shredded cheddar cheese
- 1 tablespoon cooked crumbled bacon *or* bacon bits
- 1 green onion, sliced

Peel potatoes and cut into 1/2-in. cubes; place half in a blender. Add broth; cover and process until smooth. Pour into a saucepan. Stir in sour cream, pepper and remaining potatoes. Cook over low heat until heated through (do not boil). Garnish with the cheese, bacon and onion. **Yield:** 2 servings.

## CHEESY CARROT CASSEROLE

*Diane Hixon, Niceville, Florida*

*Since all our children are grown, I like to make simple dishes for my husband and me. I usually have cheese, carrots and rice on hand, so this is a very handy side dish to whip up at any time. The cashews add crunch and great flavor.*

- 1 cup cooked rice
- 1/2 cup shredded carrots
- 1/2 cup shredded process American cheese
- 1 egg
- 2 tablespoons finely chopped salted cashews
- 1 teaspoon dried parsley flakes

In a bowl, combine rice, carrots, cheese and egg; mix well. Spoon into a greased 2-cup baking dish. Combine the cashews and parsley; sprinkle on top. Bake, uncovered, at 350° for 20-25 minutes or until lightly browned. **Yield:** 2 servings. **Editor's Note:** Two 8-oz. baking dishes may be used for this recipe; bake for 15-20 minutes.

## HOLIDAY MERINGUE DESSERT

*Catherine Morrison, Newport, Pennsylvania*

*This recipe was featured in one of Grandma's favorite cookbooks from the '50s. It's become our traditional dessert for Christmas dinner and seems appropriate for the season since the meringue shells look like mounds of snow. Whatever the topping, it's very festive.*

- 1 egg white
- 1/8 teaspoon cream of tartar
- 1/8 teaspoon almond extract
- Dash salt
- 1/3 cup sugar
- 2 scoops chocolate ice cream
- Chocolate sauce
- 2 tablespoons flaked coconut, toasted
- Maraschino cherries

Place egg white in a mixing bowl and let stand at room temperature for 30 minutes. Beat until foamy. Add cream of tartar, extract and salt; beat until soft peaks form. Gradually add sugar, 1 tablespoon at a time, beating on high until very stiff peaks form. Cover a baking sheet with foil or parchment paper. Spoon the egg mixture into two mounds on paper. Using the back of a spoon, build up the edges slightly. Bake at 300° for 35 minutes. Turn oven off; let shells dry in the oven for at least 1 hour with the door closed. To serve, fill shells with ice cream; top with chocolate sauce, coconut and cherries. **Yield:** 2 servings.

# Index

▀▄▀▄▀▄▀▄▀▄▀▄▀▄

# D

Maple Baked Onions, 54
Vidalia Casserole, 67

## ORANGE
Morning Orange Drink, 10
Nutmeg Orange Sauce, 39
Orange Blossom Cake, 109
Orange Buttermilk Salad, 148
Orange-Glazed Bananas, 118
Orange Pecan Salad, 135
Sunshine Sherbet, 113
Sweet Potato Orange Cups, 64

▪▪▪▪▪▪▪▪▪▪▪▪▪
# P

## PASTA & NOODLES
Asparagus Spaghetti Pie, 30
Bow Tie Garden Pasta, 64
Chicken Tortellini Soup, 133
Fresh Tomato Pasta Toss, 35
Lasagna Florentine, 83
Macaroni Au Gratin, 148
Macaroni Salad, 54
Pasta Salad with Poppy Seed Dressing, 66
Southwestern Lasagna, 50
Spaghetti and Meatballs for Two, 165
Spiral Pasta Salad, 68
Turkey Pasta Primavera, 44
Zucchini Pasta Casserole, 163

## PEACHES
Colorado Peach Cobbler, 129
Georgia Peach Ice Cream, 116
Jayne's Peach-Pear Pie, 127
Peach Melba Ice Cream Pie, 114
Rhubarb Peach Shortcake, 149

## PEPPERS
Chicken Fajitas, 22
Honey Pork and Peppers, 45
Jalapeno Pepper Appetizers, 7
Three-Pepper Salad, 63

## PIES
Bonnie Blue-Barb Pie, 115
Caramel Apple Cream Pie, 126
Chocolate Cream Cheese Pie, 131
Cranberry Apple Pie, 117
Frosty Lemon Pie, 121
Jayne's Peach-Pear Pie, 127
Peach Melba Ice Cream Pie, 114
Pineapple Lime Pie, 126
Poor Man's Pecan Pie, 151
Walnut Applesauce Pie, 126

## PINEAPPLE
Breakfast Skewers, 73
Pineapple Lime Pie, 126

Pineapple Zucchini Bread, 92
Sweet-and-Sour Ham, 177
Sweet-and-Sour Ribs, 47
Sweet-and-Sour Skewered Shrimp, 40

## PORK (also see Bacon; Ham; Sausage)
Barbecued Spareribs, 19
Cranberry-Glazed Pork Roast, 43
Creamy Pork Tenderloin, 41
Honey Dijon Pork, 175
Honey-Garlic Pork Ribs, 41
Honey Pork and Peppers, 45
Marinated Pork Strips, 38
Mexican Pork Stew, 26
Old-World Pork Roast, 150
Pork and Apple Skewers, 30
Pork Burgers Deluxe, 48
Pork Chops O'Brien, 28
Pork Chops with Mushroom Gravy, 24
Pork Chow Mein, 19
Pork in Mustard Sauce, 135
Pork Roast with Apple Topping, 42
Pork with Tangy Mustard Sauce, 20
Reuben Burgers, 169
Rice-Stuffed Roast, 28
Shredded Pork Sandwiches, 51
Spicy Pork Roast, 40
Spicy Pork Stir-Fry, 50
Sweet-and-Sour Ribs, 47
Zucchini Pork Dinner, 22

## POTATOES & SWEET POTATOES
Almond Potato Puff, 59
Baked Potato Soup, 179
Breakfast Pizza, 81
Breakfast Pockets, 74
Broiled Red Potatoes, 161
Company Green Beans, 131
Deluxe Mashed Potatoes, 144
Farmer's Casserole, 74
German Farmer's Breakfast, 77
Ham 'n' Potatoes Au Gratin, 36
Hearty Stuffed Potatoes, 173
Old-Fashioned Potato Salad, 167
Old-Fashioned Potatoes Anna, 59
Picnic Potato Squares, 142
Pimiento Potato Salad, 69
Pork Chops O'Brien, 28
Potato-Crust Pizza, 27
Potato Pancakes for Two, 169
Potato-Topped Chili Loaf, 31
Potatoes Supreme, 53
Red Scalloped Potatoes, 68
Scalloped Potatoes, 175
Shrimp Potato Salad, 70
Sweet Potato Cobbler, 116
Sweet Potato Orange Cups, 64
Warm Beef Salad in Potato Baskets, 62

## PUMPKIN
Cranberry Pumpkin Bread, 91
Pumpkin Pudding, 141

▪▪▪▪▪▪▪▪▪▪▪▪▪
# R

## RHUBARB
Berry Good Ice Cream Sauce, 121
Bonnie Blue-Barb Pie, 115
Refreshing Rhubarb Salad, 62
Rhubarb Muffins, 88
Rhubarb Peach Shortcake, 149
Rosy Rhubarb Mold, 156

## RICE & WILD RICE
Breakfast in a Cup, 76
Chicken Wild Rice Dish, 154
Rice-Stuffed Roast, 28
Robbie's Red Rice, 60
Wild Rice and Squash Pilaf, 152

## ROLLS
Cinnamon Rolls, 90
Cranberry Sweet Rolls, 94
Honey Whole Wheat Rolls, 93
Oatmeal Yeast Rolls, 154

▪▪▪▪▪▪▪▪▪▪▪▪▪
# S

## SALADS
Apple Luncheon Salad, 66
Asparagus Tomato Salad, 54
Blushing Apples, 69
Bow Tie Garden Pasta, 64
Broccoli Apple Salad, 175
California Harvest Salad, 56
Chilled Vegetable Salad, 161
Colorful Antipasto, 58
Cranberry Relish Salad, 152
Creamy Apple Salad, 71
Create-Your-Own Egg Salad, 82
Crisp Marinated Cukes, 167
Crowd-Pleasing Chicken Salad, 64
Fresh Cucumber Salad, 53
Garden Layered Salad, 156
Garden Vegetable Salad, 165
Honey Apple Salad, 58
Macaroni Salad, 54
Marinated Fresh Vegetables, 67
Old-Fashioned Potato Salad, 167
Orange Buttermilk Salad, 148
Orange Pecan Salad, 135
Pasta Salad with Poppy Seed Dressing, 66
Pimiento Potato Salad, 69
Quick Corn Salad, 163
Refreshing Rhubarb Salad, 62
Rosy Rhubarb Mold, 156
Season's End Salad, 139
Sesame Asparagus Salad, 60
Shrimp Potato Salad, 70
Spiral Pasta Salad, 68
Sunshine Salad, 77
Tex-Mex Green Bean Salad, 56
↷